VARIETIES OF AUSTERITY

Heather Whiteside, Stephen McBride
and Bryan M. Evans

BRISTOL
UNIVERSITY
PRESS

First published in Great Britain in 2021 by

Bristol University Press
University of Bristol
1-9 Old Park Hill
Bristol
BS2 8BB
UK
+44 (0)117 954 5940
bup-info@bristol.ac.uk

Details of international sales and distribution partners are available at bristoluniversitypress.co.uk

British Library Cataloguing in Publication Data
A catalogue record for this book is available from the British Library

ISBN 978-1-5292-1224-2 hardcover
ISBN 978-1-5292-1226-6 ePub
ISBN 978-1-5292-1225-9 ePdf

Cover design: Clifford Hayes
Front cover image: 'Scissors cutting white paper' © Freepik

Bristol University Press uses environmentally responsible print partners.

Printed in Great Britain by CPI Group (UK) Ltd, Croydon, CR0 4YY

FSC
www.fsc.org
MIX
Paper from responsible sources
FSC® C013604

Contents

List of Figures and Tables

Figures

Tables

About the Authors

Heather Whiteside is Associate Professor of Political Science at the University of Waterloo and Fellow at the Balsillie School of International Affairs, Canada. Her research centres on the political economy of privatization, financialization and fiscal austerity. Her books include *Purchase for Profit: Public-Private Partnerships and Canada's Public Health Care System* (2015), *Canadian Political Economy* (2020) and *Capitalist Political Economy: Thinkers and Theories* (2020). She has published in journals such as *Cambridge Journal of Regions, Economy and Society*, *Economic Geography*, *Environment and Planning A*, *Review of International Political Economy* and *Urban Studies*.

Stephen McBride is Professor of Political Science and Canada Research Chair in Public Policy and Globalization at McMaster University. Recent publications include: *Working? Employment Policy in Canada* (2017); *Austerity: 12 Myths Exposed* (2019) (co-edited with Dieter Plehwe, Moritz Neujeffski and Bryan Evans); *Austerity: The Lived Experience* (2017) and *The Austerity State* (2017) (both co-edited with Bryan Evans), as well as journal articles in *Global Policy*, *Transfer: European Review of Labour and Research* and *Studies in Political Economy*.

Bryan Evans is Professor, Department of Politics and Public Administration, Ryerson University, Toronto. Prior to his appointment at Ryerson he worked as a policy researcher, adviser and manager at the Ontario Legislative Assembly and the Ontario Public Service. His research centres on co-governance, policy work and processes, policy analysis in non-government organizations, state restructuring and recomposition, and the contemporary left in the neoliberal era. He is Director of the Centre for Policy Innovation and Public Engagement. Recent publications include: *The Austerity State* (2017) and *Austerity: The Lived Experience* (2017) (both co-edited with Stephen McBride); *The Public Sector in an Age of Austerity: Perspectives from Canada's Provinces and Territories* (2018) (co-authored with Carlo Fanelli); *Divided Province: Ontario Politics in the Age of Neoliberalism* (2018) (co-edited with Greg Albo); *Austerity: 12 Myths Exposed* (2019) (co-edited with Dieter Plehwe, Moritz Neujeffski and Stephen McBride).

Acknowledgements

The authors gratefully acknowledge funding from the Social Sciences and Humanities Research Council of Canada (SSHRC) through an Insight Grant (number 435-2016-0638) on varieties of austerity. We would like to thank the research assistants who worked on various aspects of the project and made valuable contributions over the years: Nour Afara, Juan Arasanz, Sylvie Babadjide, Skylar Brooks, Siu Mee Cheng, Matt Corbeil, Lily Eskin, Mohammad Ferdosi, Rasmus Hovedskov Hansen, John Hayes, Sorin Mitrea, Colette Nyirakamana, Justin Rain, Sune Sandbeck, Joy Schnittker, and James Watson. Our research was also enriched by insights from not-for-attribution interviews in all four of our case countries. We would like to thank the government and legislative officials, representatives of trade unions and business associations, academic experts and think-tank personnel who generously gave their time and expertise.

1

Introduction: Varieties of Austerity

Industry-wide bargaining to be suspended, €50 billion to be raised through privatization, social security to be cut by more than €4 billion over four years, nominal public sector wages to be slashed by 20 per cent, and on it went. Such was the list, so named were the targets. It was 2011, the Eurozone was in chaos, the global economy was in tatters, and the stimulus era proved fleeting. Austerity was widely *en vogue* and it was being visited in dramatic fashion on Greece: the Troika bailout demanded it, capitalist interests needed it, and the government and its people were put on notice (BBC, 2011). Greece is an exceptional case, but it is far from an isolated one.

The global financial crisis of 2008, the ensuing and prolonged economic crisis, and policies of austerity implemented from 2010 have imposed major costs on most Western societies. These include direct economic costs such as lower GDP, slower economic growth, higher unemployment and lost output, various forms of underemployment, much of it in precarious and poorly paid jobs, and increased household debt obligations that drag down disposable income. Other, perhaps less direct, effects can be categorized as social and human costs. Phenomena such as inequality (a legacy of the entire neoliberal period: see Piketty, 2014; Atkinson, 2015) increased in the post-crisis years (Schneider et al, 2017), and higher unemployment and insecurity were exacerbated by austerity measures such as cuts in social and health care spending, and labour market restructuring. Inequality and unemployment are linked to various social problems involving mental health, drug use and addiction, lower life expectancy, increased obesity, low education achievement and aspirations, more violence and less social mobility (Wilkinson and Pickett, 2009, chapters 4–12). The human and social costs are significant; and often compounded by divisions of gender, race, migration status and age (on the gendered effects of the global financial crisis, see Hozic and True, 2016, part I). For youth in Ireland and Spain, for example, the damage to their employment and economic prospects was so severe that talk of a 'lost generation' became commonplace.

With some exceptions, the initial panic-induced response to the 2008 crisis was not one of austerity. Rather, as the prospect of a complete financial and economic meltdown loomed, most states and international organizations resorted to economic stimulus on a scale not previously witnessed in the neoliberal years. Stimulus was short-lived. Once signs of economic stabilization appeared, most states, such as those in the G20, declared austerity (in the sense of deficit and debt reduction) to be a policy priority. Some countries experienced successive rounds of austerity. Picking up on the Greek example once more, numerous austerity packages, each one consisting of some combination of public sector freezes and cuts to budgets, services, programmes and employment were implemented after 2010.

The COVID-19 crisis of 2020, a crisis of public health caused by the global spread of a life-threatening virus, revealed the consequences of years of austerity. Austerity did not cause this crisis but it was responsible for a lack of public capacity to deal with it effectively. National and international responses to the pandemic and the economic shocks caused by job losses, lock-downs, and the collapse of some economic sectors like tourism and hospitality show significant departures from orthodox public finance in the age of austerity. Countries in North America and Europe have allowed unprecedented monetary stimulus through central bank interventions, and fiscal rules limiting deficits and public debt have been ignored, at least temporarily. Fiscal austerity has therefore been abandoned for now, but a lively debate is beginning about whether fiscal orthodoxy and its correlates – a diminished public sector and flexibilization of labour markets – will be reintroduced once the crisis is over, or whether this exogenous crisis provides an opportunity to fundamentally change the direction of neoliberal capitalism and to build a different type of society.

In our concluding chapter we offer some comments on how austerity and the COVID-19 health crisis intersect, and survey some debates on consequences and ways forward.

Austerity was applied to varying degrees and in unique ways within national contexts over the decade of 2008–18. Austerity measures in the UK were comparatively severe, with the British government being described as '[leading] the way in voluntary deficit reduction' (Giles and Bounds, 2012), with all but a few departmental budgets cut by 25 per cent. In Puerto Rico, government insolvency in 2017, the product of decades-long complex structural, economic and political problems (see

Whiteside, 2018), went hand-in-hand with punitive austerity measures aimed at stabilizing the island's affairs: pension spending reduced by 10 per cent, Christmas bonuses cut, health care spending slashed by at least USD$300[1] million, employee furloughs, fewer government agencies, employee redundancies, and temporary workers severed. And, indeed, across the US, the post-2008 period meant deep austerity and associated hardships for many jurisdictions (some examples can be seen in Peck and Whiteside, 2016; Hinkley, 2017).

Worldwide, opposition to austerity ranged from marches, demonstrations and protests, to general strikes and political party organizing around anti-austerity platforms (see Chapter 7). Sometimes nationally determined, at other times imposed by supranational organizations or otherwise more empowered levels of government, austerity raised alarm among social movements around the world for its deleterious repercussions and the troublesome relationship between cause (crisis) and effect (burden). 'Against a backdrop of violent protests against the latest tough austerity measures,' writes Konzelmann (2019: 109), 'the second Troika bailout, ratified in February 2012 [...] worth €130 billion ([USD]$173 billion), included €48 billion for recapitalizing the four largest Greek banks.'

There was nothing novel about the turn to austerity after 2008. Neoliberalism had always involved fiscal constraints for the state, at least as far as its capacity to engage in any socially progressive measures was concerned (Konzelmann, 2019; Shefner and Blad, 2020). Books quickly emerged demonstrating the lengthy history of austerity as a familiar idea towards which elites quickly gravitate in times of trouble. Blyth (2013: 98–9) argued that elite concerns about the state were part of liberalism from its inception (a point later picked up by Konzelmann, 2019, as well). The state was as necessary for the development and protection of the capitalist system in its early days as it remains today. As we shall see in Chapter 2, that can involve lavishing resources on capital even in the midst of austerity for others, yet the state also represents a potential threat to the freedom of capital. By imposing limits on state actions, fiscal austerity cuts into the dynamic relationship between capital and the state by curtailing state actions through spending constraints in the name of balanced budgets and by imposing limits on its capacity to raise debt to finance its activities. Moreover, according to Blyth (2013: 115) the general narrative of austerity speaks to 'parsimony, frugality, morality, and a pathological fear of the consequences of government debt [that] lie deep within early liberalisms' fossil record from its very inception.' Without nuance, this may be an overstatement. Financial interests have been willing to lend the state money, in effect owning the public debt, and to be the recipients of the state's largesse. But the state's capacity and willingness to prioritize servicing its creditors has always been a concern (Streek, 2014: 76–8).

Elite suspicion of the state, twinned with long-standing state support for capitalism, extends our definition of austerity to three closely linked dimensions. First, there is the well-known emphasis on fiscal balance and consolidation, balanced budgets and limits on public debt (see Chapters 2 and 3). The second component consists of restructuring the public sector to make it both a replica and servant of the private sector (see Chapter 4). Third, is restructuring labour to render its organizations weaker and the labour market more flexible, with predictable results in representational capacity, individual insecurity and downward pressures on wages (see Chapters 5 and 6).

It has been argued (Blyth, 2013; McBride, 2014; Whiteside, 2016a; Shefner and Blad, 2020) that the emergence of austerity as a default strategy to respond to economic crises is less the result of immediate cost-benefit calculations than it is about a longer-term tendency to protect the advantages of capitalist elites. Power and position are supported when austerity is able to contain the threat of interventionism through the dull compulsion of fiscal constraints, and the threat of class struggle when the already weak bargaining power of labour is further limited through the normalization of highly flexible labour markets; privatization and individualization triumph over solidarity as a social value (see McBride, 2014), and resistance is reduced to maintaining a pre-crisis status quo by an often fragmented working class. 'Fiscal consolidation' often defines austerity as getting state budgets back into balance within a reasonable period and reducing public debt as a percentage of GDP (OECD, 2012); the fact that austerity policies may not actually produce these results is less important than their impact in terms of diminished wages, insecurity, reduced living standards and expectations (Albo, 2012).

Balanced budgets and reduced debt-to-GDP ratios could be theoretically achieved by tax increases, earning income off state assets, stimulating growth through currency devaluation, or reducing the debt through inflationary policies. But in the *austerian* world most of these are undesirable, indicating that resort to austerity is less a technical issue than an ideological preference aimed at constraining the state or redirecting the burden of post-crisis adjustment. Thus, contrary to the technical presentation of the case for austerity, it is highly ideological. Spending reductions, supplemented in some cases by selective tax increases like regressive consumption taxes, broadening tax coverage and closing certain tax loopholes, are the favoured instruments. At the centre of the rationale for fiscal austerity is the claim that public debt results from state profligacy to which spending curbs provide the answer. This completely evades the question of responsibility for the crisis (see Blyth, 2013: 5–6). Suzanne Konzelmann (2019) explained that state, private and household budgets are interrelated – state debt can be a shock absorber if accommodating, otherwise the pain of crises will need to be shouldered more directly by household and private sectors. Ian Gough (2011: 53–8) furthermore identified the drivers of increased public debt as the costs of governments' financial interventions to avert collapse of the banking and financial sector, the costs of fiscal stimulus in the 2008–10 period to prevent depression and mass unemployment, and the impact of automatic stabilizers such as unemployment insurance and increased social spending resulting from the effects of recessions, together with the impact of slower, or negative growth on tax revenues. All these drivers of increased public (sovereign) debt are related to the crisis resulting from the implementation of the dominant neoliberal paradigm. Such fiscal measures are generally presented in combination with 'structural reforms' to further flexibilize the labour market and other measures to make the economy more competitive.

States following austerity policies have performed poorly in terms of the claims made on behalf of those policies (Blyth, 2013). Public spending cuts are not expansionary but rather increase unemployment. This places yet more fiscal pressure on government programmes. All the European countries under Troika (the International Monetary Fund, European Commission and European Central Bank) supervision and severe austerity policies experienced deterioration in employment levels and debt ratios as a result of imposed austerity policies.

Such poor empirical results lend credence to theoretical critiques that would predict precisely such a result (Konzelmann, 2019; Shefner and Blad, 2020). In the context of the 2008 crisis, for example, 'austerian' analysis was entirely a-historical; it ignored the deeper roots of the crisis, and really rested on a triumph of discourse that consisted of shifting the blame for the crisis from the reckless behaviour of an under-regulated private sector to public or sovereign debt, for which the public authorities are responsible (Peck, 2014). Its persistence in public policies has meant dodging or denying evidence that fiscal consolidation is at least partially responsible for poor growth/recession and social malaise since 2010 (Wolf, 2013).

Failure and continuity

Given this record, intellectual arguments for austerity policies have been challenged. Promoters of austerity emphasize that imposing strict limits on government debt and deficits is necessary. Expenditure reductions are favoured over tax increases, which would be another logical way of restoring balance. That, however, would contravene the neoliberal goal of slimming the state. With fiscal affairs back under control, the argument runs, investor confidence is restored, investment follows and prosperity returns. This narrative of the crisis attributes blame to public sector excess, and focuses on fiscal consolidation and other measures to correct it. This admittedly oversimplified account of the crisis and the solutions to it, nevertheless contains the core justification for the austerity policies pursued since 2010.

More specific claims are that once the public debt-to-GDP ratio passes a threshold of 90 per cent, growth declines rapidly (Reinhart and Rogoff, 2010a, 2010b). A second holds that fiscal contraction can nevertheless lead to economic expansion through improved expectations and confidence (see Alesina and Ardagna, 1998; Alesina et al, 2015). The corollary is that budgets should be controlled such that debt does not rise to dangerous levels, and that the fiscal discipline needed to ensure this is not harmful to economic growth. Though widely cited, the Reinhart and Rogoff thesis was effectively demolished when Herndon et al probed the numbers they had used and concluded that

> when properly calculated, the average real GDP growth rate for countries carrying a public-debt-to-GDP ratio of over 90 per cent is actually 2.2 per cent, not −0.1 per cent as published in Reinhart and Rogoff. That is, average GDP growth at public debt/GDP ratios over 90 per cent is not dramatically different than when debt/GDP ratios are lower. (Herndon et al, 2013: 1)

Similarly, the case for 'expansionary fiscal contraction' has been effectively debunked (Guajardo et al, 2011; Blyth, 2013; Lee, 2017; Russell, 2017). Paul Krugman (2013) issued the damning, if rather journalistic conclusion that, 'Alesina and Ardagna [one of Alesina's co-authors] have been more thoroughly refuted by both academic criticism and real-world experience than any other popular doctrine I can think of.' Likewise, by 2013, financial journalist Jim Tankersley could offer an unequivocal verdict: 'no advanced economy has proved Alesina correct in the wake of the Great Recession' (quoted in Mason and Jayadev, 2019).

Both heterodox economists (Stanford, 2008; Quiggin, 2010) and, increasingly, mainstream ones (Stiglitz, 2011, 2012; Krugman, 2013) are critical of orthodox claims about austerity. Even IMF staff have conceded that the implementation of austerity policies has been poor: too much austerity, too fast, and miscalculation of the multiplier effect of spending cuts (Blanchard, 2012; Blanchard and Leigh, 2013).

Although it might be expected that the deep crisis of neoliberalism, and the failure of policy to address it, would produce political and policy change, this has not materialized. Crises create opportunities to effect paradigm change but they do not guarantee it (see Farnsworth and Irving, 2011; Utting et al, 2012). Surveying the literature on policy change yields the not overly helpful insight that crises may lead to critical junctures when the existing policy system is challenged by an *exogenous* shock; that is, a challenge posed by events, natural or political, that lie outside the boundaries of the system itself. Examples might include natural disasters, health pandemics, or the economic effects of security-related events such as the oil price increases in the 1970s. Much of the standard public policy literature on policy change has settled on an orthodoxy that understands policy change as an historical and evolutionary process, punctuated by exogenous shocks, conflict and competition, which generate possibilities for paradigmatic change. Stiglitz (2011: 169) noted that orthodox economics similarly must resort to external explanations for crises – according to the model and its assumptions there is no room for such dislocations to develop.

Theories of policy change have tended to interpret policy change as incrementally evolving and navigating structural, ideational and institutional path dependencies, constraints and opportunities. The orthodoxy, rooted in works such as that by Hall (1993), identifies exogenous shocks, or focusing events, or policy windows (Kingdon, 1984), as generating the conditions, including greater scope for agency (Katznelson, 2003), under which more dramatic and paradigmatic policy and institutional transformations can occur. Less seems to have been written on the link between *endogenous* shocks and policy change and this literature tends to emphasize a gradual or incremental version of change rather than the more fundamental type. In the case of the 2008 crisis, it is much more plausible to portray the implosion of the sub-prime mortgage market as an endogenous shock. That is, the crisis was produced by the internal contradictions of the dominant paradigm and policies and practices based on it. Of course, whether exogenous or endogenous factors are responsible, different narratives that contest the nature and severity of the crisis and its implications will be related to the power of the actors presenting them.

Jessop (2012: 24–6) makes a useful distinction between a crisis that is *in* the system and one that is *of* the system. If the former, then the solution can be depicted as lying within the boundaries of existing arrangements and policy which can be adjusted. This will be linked to the question of who is to pay for the clean-up the crisis has necessitated. If the latter, a crisis *of* the system, to the extent that it can be interpreted as being produced by contradictions of the dominant accumulation strategy, and of the dominant paradigm being exhausted and untenable, then the opportunity for more fundamental change exists. The battle about which narrative prevails is vital and is only secondarily a scientific issue. The power of the various interests behind the interpretations is the key element determining structural change or the lack thereof.

Ideas and interpretations do matter in their own right. The rhetorical conversion of the 2008 crisis from one of the (private) financial sector, underpinned by poor regulation and predatory behaviour, into a sovereign debt crisis, for which public authorities are responsible, and to which public sector austerity is the solution, is revealing. To the extent that this interpretation has taken hold, whatever its empirical foundation, it becomes a material factor in addressing the crisis.

Although these approaches concede that change, sometimes radical, can occur, they are better at explaining continuity, and, at a superficial level, might seem well suited to an explanation of why neoliberalism and austerity persisted despite their theoretical and practical problems. Only in the context of a major and unpredictable, or unpredicted, exogenous shock do the range of possible choices open up and new directions become possible. Even so, the odds remain stacked in favour of continuity. Blyth (2001) suggests ideational practices. Ideas function in three ways to contextualize shock: as institutional blueprints, as weapons, and as cognitive locks. The third, cognitive locks, focuses on constraints around the range of policy options that agents perceive are at their disposal. Cognitive lock-in suggests that policy change does not inevitably follow from crisis and shock because policy makers operate with strong cognitive attachments to existing policy preferences and ideas. Thus, in the context of shock, policy makers debate and define the parameters of potential responses within cognitive, rather than structural, boundaries (Blyth, 2001; Starke et al, 2013: 182–4).

Essentially psychological explanations like these are unsatisfactory in that they leave out the elephant in the room – power and interests. They do not sufficiently address systemic political economy and the instrumental and structural power wielded by those who forged the neoliberal era and who continue to benefit from it. Utting et al (2012: 4) argued that established elites have 'shown remarkable capacity to shape the post-crisis recovery process' through instrumental power (being directly involved in decision making) and discursive power (the ability to frame how the crisis and responses to it are understood – see Chapter 3). They go on to argue that structural changes in the economy – global production chains that focus on export-led growth, trade and investment liberalization and privatization (all central aspects of the neoliberal paradigm) – have weakened governments, and governments' perceptions of what choices are available to them. Yet as we noted above, an important element of the elite account of the crisis, and of governments' complicity in it, is the political construction of the powerless state (Weiss, 1997). Perhaps ironically, there has been considerable activity to render this image of a powerless state an accurate one, by quasi-constitutional measures to limit the ability of government to engage in expansionary policies, and to bind them to the three components of austerity as we have defined them (McBride and Whiteside, 2011; McBride and Mitrea, 2017).

It is misleading to depict austerity's tools as technocratic imperatives for resolving debt and budgetary disequilibrium. The associated structural reforms of the public sector and of labour markets, which have an impact on both employees' livelihoods and the welfare of society in general, show that there is clearly much more at stake than a narrow interpretation of austerity will allow. Given our disappointment, outlined above, with standard explanations of change and continuity in mainstream policy studies, this book argues that the austerity period must be understood through a political economy lens.

Political economy of austerity

We have noted that austerity, defined as fiscal consolidation, public sector reforms and the flexibilization of labour markets, presents a common thread among capitalist states in the neoliberal era. At times of crisis, such as that of 2008, austerity receives particular prominence. This common thread is expressed by neoliberal theory or ideology, driven by the accumulation needs of capital, with special emphasis on financial capital in this period, and by capitalist actors in the political process, and is reflected in the beliefs and actions of state elites. Austerity is reinforced by their equivalents at the international level, and by institutions and practices at all levels.

Thus, neoliberal austerity is a class-based, institutionalized capital accumulation strategy, implemented by political and economic elite actors and organizations, and articulated in terms of neoliberal ideas about how the economy, society and polity should be organized and conducted. Austerity has been a central component of this decades-long amalgam of ideology, strategy and programme. It is commonly agreed that neoliberalism displaced its Keynesian predecessor between the mid-1970s and the mid-1990s, depending partly on the analyst (which indicators or markers were deemed most significant) and partly on place – not all countries proceeded at the same pace or from the same starting point. It is not our purpose to revisit the neoliberal transition in any detail. Rather, we simply note that the new neoliberal approach organized capital's response to a crisis of the 1970s. The nature of that crisis is much debated but again need not detain us here. It led to an upward redistribution of economic advantage eventually encapsulated an almost unprecedented level of inequality. Neoliberalism reflected a redistribution and intensification of capitalist class power in society and was associated with a period of internationalization (globalization) that replaced the (rather weak) national economic planning that was a feature of the Keynesian era.

Much of the literature about neoliberalism and globalization posits a diminution of the state, seen as losing power to markets and capital, domestically and internationally, and unable to exert control over national political economies or territories. Thus, the long period of Westphalian nation-state prominence internationally, and the shorter period of domestic Keynesian market modification by the state, were both said to have been eclipsed (see Steger, 2017). In our view this is quite misleading. States continue to matter, and it is quite realistic to expect different varieties of neoliberalism, even though that is clearly the dominant paradigm, and different varieties of austerity within it, even if that is the internationally prescribed response to economic crisis. With that being said, the state's focus has certainly changed. What was necessary and generally achieved after the 1970s was not the removal or obsolescence of the state, but rather a change of direction or focus. This was central in the transition to neoliberalism and has remained so in governing that system ever since (examples can be seen in Mitchell and Fazi, 2017).

The state's role and its implications for the politics of austerity can be understood in several ways. We can begin by pointing out that the term 'state' has two general meanings and both need to be incorporated into a theoretical account of how austerity was applied in the post-crisis context. First, *state* can refer to countries – territorial units recognized by other states as players of equal legal status in the international system. The attribute of equal legal status is called *sovereignty*, although the concept is more complex than common usage of that term would indicate, and the extent to which states possess sovereignty is a matter of controversy (see Krasner, 1999). Second, *state* is often used in the sense of *government*, but more properly as a system of power that incorporates the complex of governing institutions that rule over sovereign territorial units, along with the interactions between these institutions and the social forces present or, if externally based, active in these territories. At a minimum, these state institutions include the executive, parliament and judiciary together with the bureaucratic and coercive apparatuses of military and police, at national and subnational levels. Social forces include those based on class, minority nationalities and, potentially, other groupings like those based on income, gender and age.

In the 1990s, the state, in both senses of the word, was widely seen as being in retreat in the face of an expanded role for markets. Roger Burbach and William I. Robinson, (1999: 30) declared that, 'the whole set of nation-state institutions is becoming superseded by transnational institutions'. States supposedly lost sovereignty, policy-making capacity, and their status as a focal point of identity. Others argued that states had implemented a series of deregulatory actions that had liberated capital from national constraints; this, in turn, made any reassertion of national power problematic (Scharpf, 1991). If accurate, one would expect states to follow a common trajectory and to exhibit significant convergence in their approaches to similar problems – often adduced as evidence of powerful structural pressures to conform to the necessities of the new global economy. Suzanne Berger (1996: 1) aptly summarized the convergence thesis as follows: remaining national variations are attributable to historical legacies, politics or special interests that hinder the unfolding of 'competition, imitation, diffusion of best practice, trade and capital mobility,' which together 'naturally operate to produce convergence across nations in the structures of production and in the relations among economy, society and the state.' In this volume, we do find a common trajectory (amidst some variety) in the area of austerity. However, we are not inclined a priori to attribute this to state compliance with internationally determined imperatives. Rather we consider that states retain considerable autonomy that accounts for both variety and commonality in this area.

The extent to which national states retained autonomy in the face of international pressures and economic crises remains an open question. We align our analysis with Marxist international political economy, but acknowledge some insights from realist international relations theory. Citing realist scholars like John Mearsheimer and Kenneth Waltz, Barrow and Keck (2017: 184–5) argue that international organizations 'reflect the distribution of state power in the system' and states are capable of discarding them if they become unfit for purpose. However, not all states are created equal, contrary to the legal fiction of sovereignty. Rather, asymmetries of power enhance the capacities of some while constraining those of others. The powerful have 'enlarged their control over the international system' (Barrow and Keck, 2017: 185). For Leo Panitch and Sam Gindin (2013) the US state and US capital have been the chief drivers of the globalization or internationalization of the economic system. Yet they note that as new international institutions were created to coordinate the system, national states, embedded as they were in the international economy, retained jurisdiction over 'social relations and institutions of class, property, currency, contract, and markets' (Panitch and Gindin, 2013: 8). Some elements of this assessment may have been modified by the subsequent emergence of new regional blocs and international agreements, but it remains broadly true that the organization and reproduction of those relations is rooted at the national level. This is why, as Panitch and Gindin (2013) note, the conflicts produced by the 2008 crisis and its aftermath run *within* capitalist states rather than *between* them. Given the costs inflicted on some sectors of society during the period of austerity, and the protection afforded to other sectors, much of the conflict occurring within capitalist states is class conflict, whether overt or muted. Our own schema, to be outlined later in the chapter, similarly runs primarily within states. That schema identifies varieties of austerity based on the concepts of institutionalization, insulation and insinuation. It seeks to capture the dynamic interactions between measures enacted under the general theme of austerity. Given this domestic focus, while we expect to find resistance to austerity within the states we have selected for our study, we do not expect to find the states themselves resisting internationally coordinated austerity measures. There may be variety there too – but it is likely to be of adaptation rather than resistance or opposition.

Next, it will be useful to comment on the theorization of the state in its second sense: as a system of power. Our analysis is located within Marxian state theory for its close concern with the relationship between class and politics in the capitalist system.

Clyde Barrow (1993: 146) noted that Marxian theories of the state diverge on their answers to two questions: '(1) How does the state realize the interests of the capitalist class? (2) Why does the state serve the interests of the capitalist class?'. The answer to the first leads to a focus on the content of public policies, and the shifting degree to which they address the accumulation, legitimation and coercion needs of capital (see O'Connor, 1973; Panitch, 1977).[2] In understanding how the state serves, or sometimes fails to serve, the interests of capital, attention is focused on the degree to which capitalist interests prevail over other social formations, notably those connected to the working class. The reconstruction of the public sector, detailed in Chapter 4, reflects the triumph of particular class-based forces within the state apparatus, as does the account of labour restructuring in Chapter 5. The state, and the public administrative units that compose it, is not technical and neutral machinery but rather is the means through which a system of power relations is maintained.

However, it bears repeating that 'the state is not simply a tool of capital, it is an arena of struggle' (Clarke, 1991: 195). As Poulantzas (1978) suggested, the state is not above the class struggle fray. The struggles of subaltern classes, 'traverse the state from top to bottom [...] these very struggles always have 'long range' effects within the state' (Poulantzas, 1978: 141). Defeat of the working class on the shop floor, at the ballot box, within social democracy and beyond, left little more than a strategy to protect what remained. In short, it was merely 'to acquiesce to wage moderation, more flexible working conditions or privatized social services in exchange for maintaining employment' (Bieling and Lux, 2014: 154). The demobilization of the working class is the general legacy, though varying across our cases, which explains the inability of labour to resist the imposition of austerity after 2010 (see Chapter 7).

Structural explanations are the other side of the coin: the capitalist system has certain needs (accumulation, legitimation, coercion) and the state is an integral part of systemic support made especially visible during times of crises. The 2008 crisis is the focus of this book; however, it is but one in a series of endemic capitalist crises. States are regularly called on to help restore the conditions for profitable accumulation (see Harvey, 2003 for more on how capital responds through spatio-temporal fixes). The underlying roles of the state retain the same flavour even if manifesting in contingent and contextually different ways.

Throughout the recent crisis (2008 and beyond) the role of the capitalist state has maintained the familiar accumulation and legitimation activities described earlier, but these have recently taken new forms to match the needs of a system embroiled in crises. This included unprecedented attempts to rescue leading capitalist sectors in the form of bailouts, quasi nationalization and other asset guarantees, and temporary stimulus packages aimed at promoting job creation and investment. Stimulus packages generally were designed to be temporary and shallow; bailouts have not been tailored to maximize taxpayer investments and instead have served mainly to socialize private debt, and little reregulation of global financial markets has occurred. In the sphere of global financial governance, the policy reaction has been focused on encouraging better surveillance, reporting, and transparency of financial markets, rather than introducing capital controls or the creation of novel regulatory institutions. Furthermore, deep disequilibrium remains between surplus and deficit trading countries, and in the EU in particular this has exacerbated sovereign debt crises and fuelled austerity measures (Lapavitsas, 2019).

Varieties of austerity

Having emphasized thus far the common thread of austerity measures, we now turn to explore the issue of how much variety there has been within this common framework. To assist with this we made a selection of national cases – Canada, Denmark, Ireland and Spain, a choice based partly on the desire to include neither hegemons (like the US or Germany), nor abject peripheries whose situation made any exercise of autonomous state power unlikely (as seen in Greece). These countries are also differently situated within the main typologies of comparative public policy and political economy that categorize countries by type of welfare state and variety of capitalism. If national varieties of austerity were to become apparent, such a schema would enable us to judge the resilience of existing institutional configurations and, at the same time, the degree to which these types might be eroded by common pressures toward austerity in the post-2008 period. On the other hand, if variations in austerity manifest themselves within each type, then we need an alternative framework to capture these dimensions, such as the one we develop later in the chapter.

The comparative political economy of welfare states and types of economy has yielded two major classification systems. The most famous welfare state typology (Esping-Andersen, 1990) identified three types – liberal, social democratic and conservative/corporatist[3] – and advanced explanations for their development and characteristics (Korpi, 1983; Danforth, 2014; Manow, 2015). The varieties of capitalism schema (Hall and Soskice, 2001) identified two main models: liberal market economies and coordinated market economies (Iversen and Soskice, 2015). Both typologies have been extended to fit non-conforming systems – for example, southern European or Mediterranean systems – and frequently countries are identified as 'hybrids' exhibiting some combination of characteristics.

In our study, Canada provides the clearest example of a liberal welfare state. Social benefits are typically modest and recipients often stigmatized. The effect of such a regime is to reinforce the primacy of the market. The social democratic welfare state was traditionally infused with the ethos of universalism and promoted high levels of equally available benefits. Denmark is the example in this study. Spain is an example of the Mediterranean or southern European type, characterized as developing later than the welfare systems of northern Europe, and of showing signs of uneven development: dualism or segmentation in labour markets with good benefits in some areas (pensions for core workers) and gaps for others; a considerable role for private actors even in areas of universal coverage like health; and clientelism in the administration of locally provided benefits (Ferrera, 1996). Ireland is a hybrid: it mostly conforms to the liberal model but with aspects of corporatism through social partnership institutions and the lingering influence of Catholic social doctrines. These ideal-types varied widely in their structure and policies both in time and place, and the adoption of one or the other model was generally explained by the nature of coalitions between different social classes and the balance of power in the state and civil society (Ferragina and Seeleib-Kaiser, 2011). Thus, unlike the varieties of capitalism literature that largely ignores issues of power (Coates, 2005), the welfare state typology partly rests on power resources in society.

The welfare state and varieties of capitalism literatures do not '"speak to" each other as explicitly as they could' (Clift, 2014: 268) but welfare state types do tend to overlap with the varieties of capitalism classification scheme (see Hall and Soskice, 2001). Liberal market economies (LMEs) leave *coordination* to market-based mechanisms and competitive market arrangements both between firms and within the labour market. For our study, Canada provides the purest case. Firms in LMEs are heavily dependent on their valuation in equity markets and are evaluated on their share prices and current profitability. This promotes certain types of behaviour on their part including the pursuit of flexible employment practices to cut costs. Since this flexibility makes hiring and firing easier depending on the business cycle, individuals are encouraged to invest in general skills, rather than firm-specific skills (Hall and Soskice, 2001: 30). Further, social policy in LMEs is usually considered to undesirably interfere with markets by either enforcing regulatory regimes on them, or raising labour costs by tightening labour markets (Hall and Soskice, 2001: 50). As a result, market-based solutions are generally preferred to state intervention, unless state intervention provides institutional infrastructure for enhancing advanced sector firms' comparative advantage (Iversen and Soskice, 2015). Thus, while Hall and Soskice do not equate their types with any particular type of social model, LMEs are virtually always accompanied by liberal welfare states that emphasize low levels of benefits to maintain fluid labour markets.

Coordinated market economies (CMEs), of which Denmark provides our example, typically have higher union density, and tend to set wages through industry-level bargaining, due to the overall level of coordination (as opposed to competition) in the economy. CMEs are more likely to pursue production strategies that depend on integrating a highly skilled labour force, which entails high levels of private sector commitment through longer employment tenures, industry-negotiated wages and protective labour organizations (Iversen and Soskice, 2015). Corporate governance and a firm's ability to secure capital investments are furthermore based less on stock prices or current profitability, and revolve more on diffuse knowledge networks and firm reputation. CMEs tend to have either conservative or social democratic welfare states.

Mediterranean economies (MEs), such as Spain, are characterized by larger agrarian sectors and recent histories of significant government intervention, leading to specific kinds of capacities for non-market coordination in corporate finance, but with more liberal arrangements otherwise (Lallement, 2011: 637; Azmanova, 2012; Gambarotto and Solari, 2015). MEs have relatively weaker education and training systems than CMEs and differ from LMEs insofar as banks play a more significant role in corporate financing (Lallement, 2011). MEs also experience difficulty designing and executing industrial strategy for high value-added products, which leads to larger low-wage sectors (as employers focus on reducing labour costs) and poorer integration of youth into labour markets (Azmanova, 2012; Gambarotto and Solari, 2015). These characteristics are likely to be associated with the sort of Mediterranean welfare system outlined above. Ireland once again features as a hybrid – predominantly liberal with an admixture of corporatist coordination through its social partnership arrangements (Hastings et al, 2007).

The connections between economic and social policy fit into what Hall and Soskice term 'institutional complementarities' (2001: 17) given that political economies are associated with social policies that augment the comparative advantages provided by the economic system, and vice versa. Once these institutional complementarities are established, the system may become resistant to change. Institutional complementarities are a part of the cohesive connection between social and economic policy. However, this notion has come under fire from multiple critics who claim that this typology assumes resilience of welfare regimes (and varieties of capitalism) and that the typologies give too much weight to national factors in comparison to international ones (Fast, 2016). For many states, the reality may be convergence or at least erosion of differences under common pressures of globalization and neoliberalism. Schelkle (2012) points out that many reforms over the last two decades have gone against the logic of supposed complementarities. Examples include the creation of temporary and casualized employment even in the CMEs. This raises the possibility of convergence between LMEs, CMEs and their corresponding welfare state regimes due to processes of globalization and neoliberalism. The institutional configurations that comprise different varieties of welfare state and capitalist economies thus provide but one potential source of variations in austerity, and their influence is duly noted in some of the chapters that follow.

Our selected cases provide the opportunity to evaluate important issues such as whether pre-crisis policy stance or early crisis performance conditioned whether states would be subject to international pressure or coercion, and also the extent to which imposed or partially imposed templates (Ireland, Spain) produced a different policy mix from states retaining greater autonomy (Canada, Denmark). Our cases equally enable a deeper understanding of policy variation amid domestic social and political coalitions, party incumbency, the structure of interest representation, and the influence of particular interests such as finance. However, our research led us to the conclusion that rather than *between* state variations, those *within* states, categorized as dynamics of institutionalization, insulation and insinuation (see later in the chapter), provided a more robust entry into analyzing varieties of austerity. Before exploring those arguments, however, we first present ten important graphs demonstrating the variable impact of the crisis and austerity on our national cases, hinting at political complexity and the limits of a purely economic view of austerity, again urging a political economy analysis sensitive to both.

Of particular relevance, especially for Chapter 2, government debt statistics indicate fluctuating rates of indebtedness among these four countries (Figure 1), with Denmark's debt as quite a bit lower than the other three. Generally, however, with the exception of Ireland (owing to its unprecedented blanket guarantee of toxic banking sector assets), it is notable that debt across this decade is fairly constant for general governments (consolidated accounts of all national and local governments in a country). Spain's debt does rise; however, its peak is Canada's consistent normal. Canada's federal government debt is much lower than the general government figure would suggest. From 2014–16, Canada's federal government enjoyed the lowest ratio of net debt to GDP in the G7, at around 27 per cent (IMF, 2016). Thus, when relying on debt

Figure 1: General government debt (% of GDP)

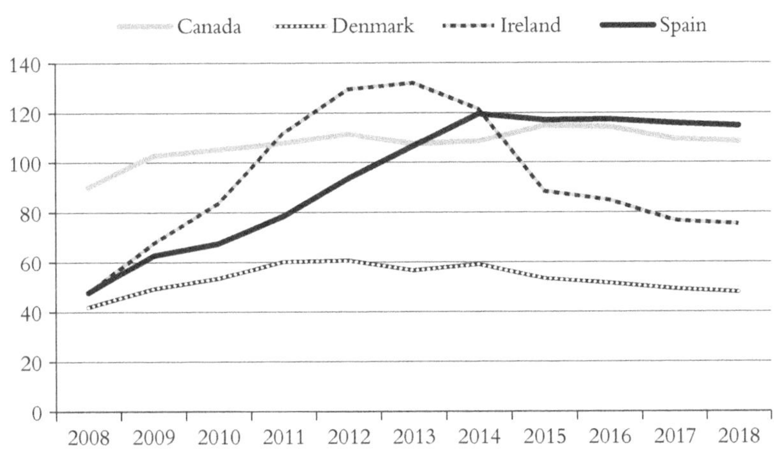

Source: OECD (2020a)

statistics to make authoritative claims, it is important to consider what is happening with economic growth, various levels of government, whether it is net or gross debt, the magnitude of foreign ownership, and myriad other qualifiers and considerations like whether household debt is rising when government debt is falling. Government debt alone is an insufficient justification or indicator of austerity.

Government deficits as a percentage of GDP are more straightforward (Figure 2). Aside from the issue that these are again consolidated government deficits, this graph illustrates the dramatic impact of a cyclical budget deficit wrought through economic crisis. Harmonization around *zero* (or budget balance) by 2018 equally indicates the unwavering commitment to fiscal austerity principles, with Chapter 3 delving into how this was framed through speeches and justified politically.

Short-term interest rates (Figure 3) show the exhaustion of traditional monetarist monetary policy early on in the 2008 crisis, with rock bottom rates by 2009. For the Eurozone countries of Ireland and Spain, the European Central Bank's (ECB) one-size-fits-all strategy of inflation targeting frustrated national differences in areas like unemployment and growth. While inflation myopia has drawn much criticism, aside from unwinding quantitative easing, inflation remained the focus of the ECB into 2018 (Constâncio, 2018).

For government bonds, long-term interest rates illustrate the risk premium put on Irish and Spanish government debt around 2011–12

Figure 2: Government deficit (% of GDP)

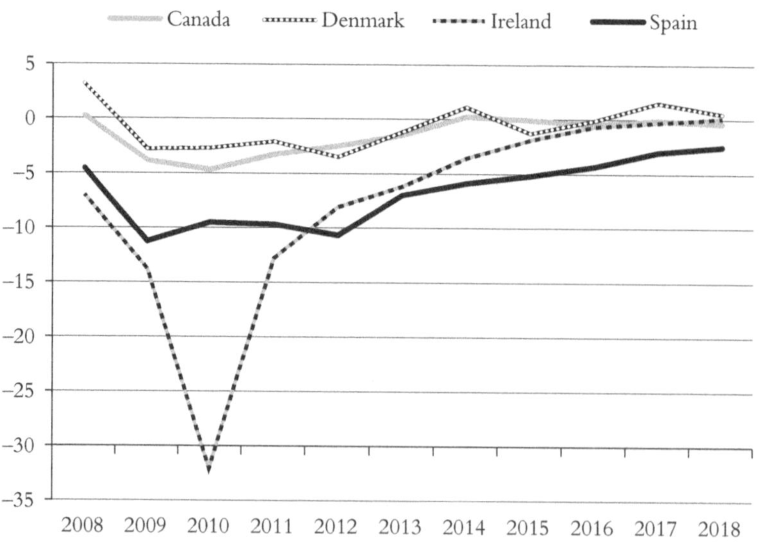

Source: OECD (2020b)

Figure 3: Short-term interest rates

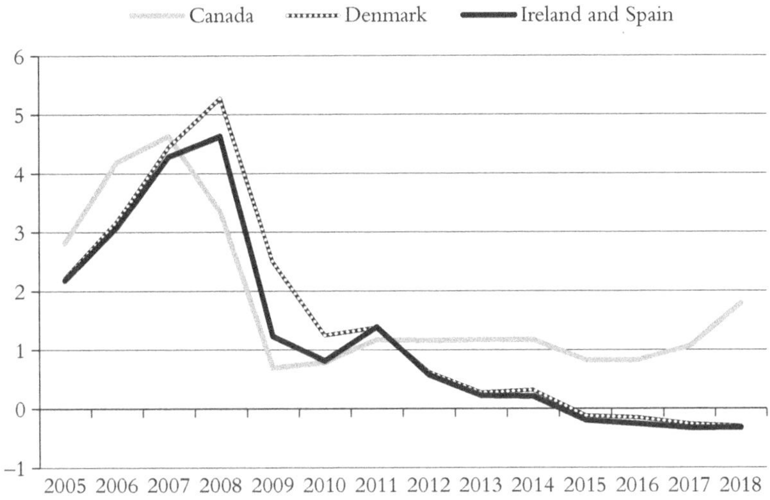

Source: OECD (2020c)

(Figure 4). Bailouts and austerity, examined in Chapter 2, having satisfied markets, helped ensure convergence after 2015, and in fact rates were lower by 2018 than they had been even in 2005.

Chapter 4 analyzes the implications of austerity within the public sector. Note that aggregate statistics indicate public sector employment

Figure 4: Long-term interest rates

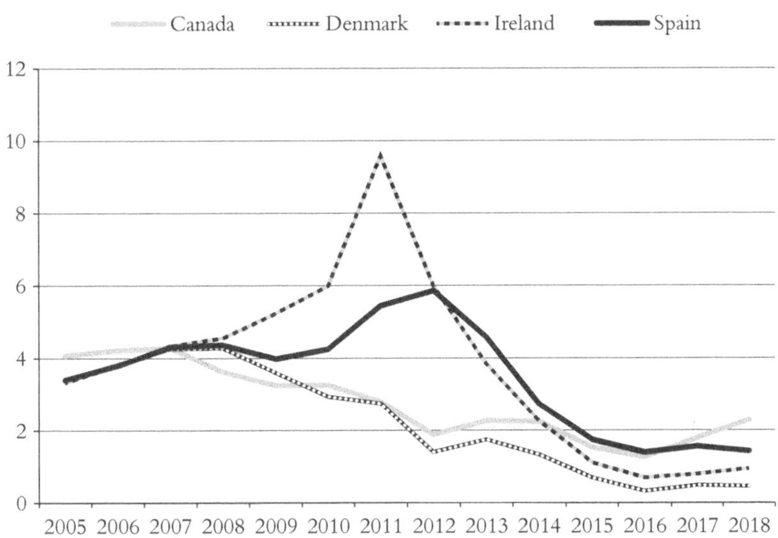

Source: OECD (2020c)

numbers are flat across the crisis, stimulus and austerity period (Figure 5), prompting the need for a qualitative understanding of the conditions of public sector activities, changes in the types of activities and the incidence of partnerships with for-profit sectors, and related concerns such as dynamics of political power, centralization, downloading, and what is happening with the total labour force denominator.

Chapter 5 attends to the flexibilization of labour under various austerity regimes. Labour market data (Figures 6–9) show employment and unemployment rates fairly constant for Canada and Denmark, with Ireland and Spain experiencing particularly painful conditions in 2012–13. The differences were minor in the case of Canada, somewhat more significant for Denmark, and most noticeable for Ireland and Spain. At the peak of the crisis (years vary by country), there was a deep impact in the latter two countries. The post-crisis upward trend in the long-term unemployment rate, apart from Ireland in the combined part-time and temporary employment rate, also reveals ongoing labour market problems.

Controlling the cost of labour through internal devaluation is an important part of austerity, particularly in Ireland (Figure 10). However, in every single case there was a significant decline in the increase in unit labour costs (and sometimes negative growth) after 2007–09.

What these statistics cannot always uncover is that, ultimately, austerity is only partially demonstrated through basic economic indicators; the qualitative story of redistribution, restructuring, offloading, downloading, blame, displacement, social relations, adjustment and institutionalization within the state, from capital to labour, and from the wealthy to the

Figure 5: Public sector employment (% of total labour force)

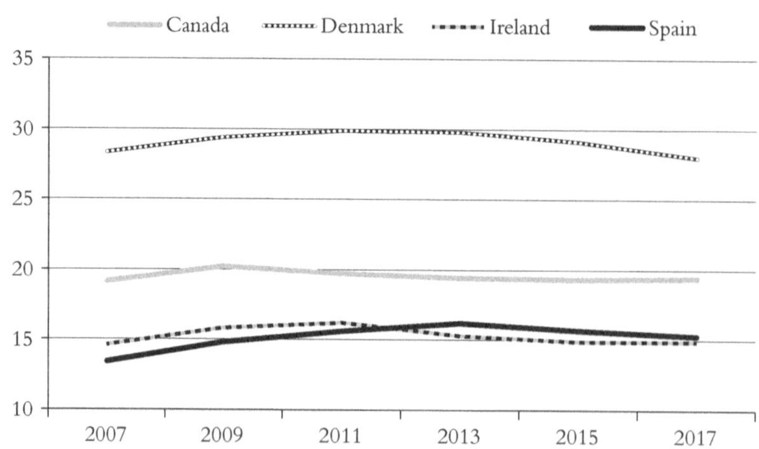

Source: OECD (2019a: 84–5)

Figure 6: Employment rate (%)

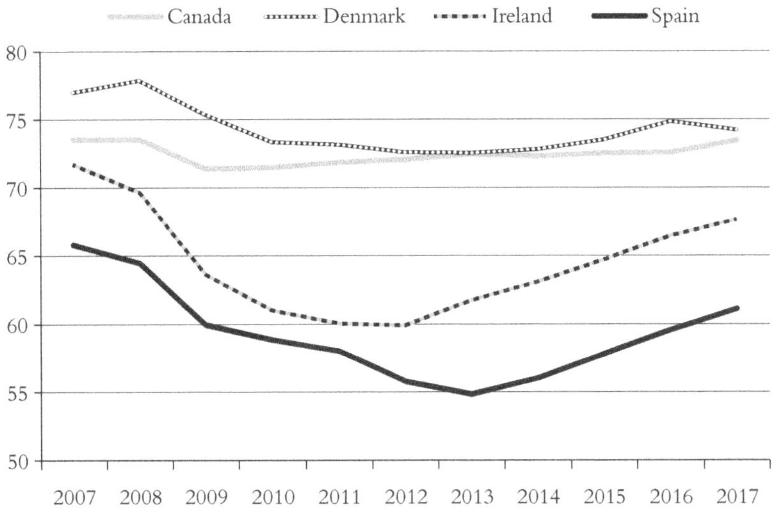

Source: OECD (2018a)

Figure 7: Unemployment rate (%)

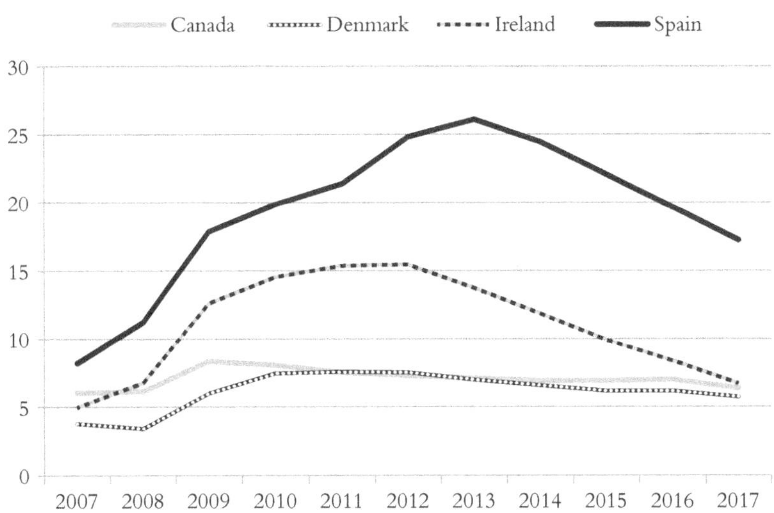

Source: OECD (2018b)

Figure 8: Long-term unemployment rate (%)

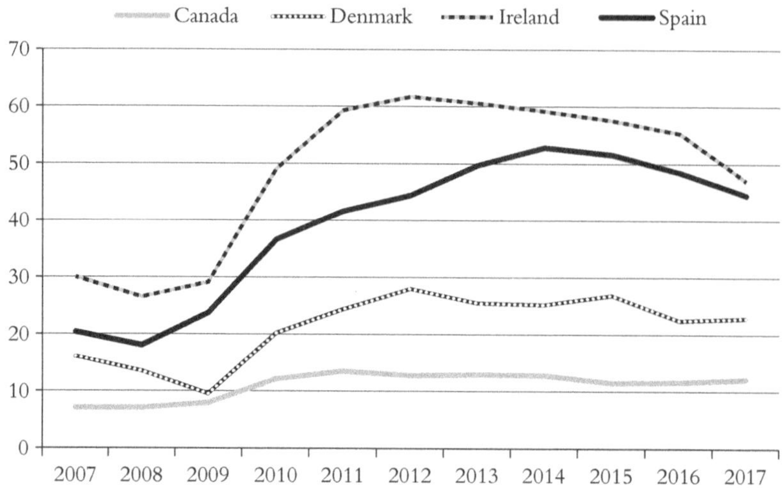

Source: OECD (2018c)

Figure 9: Combined part-time and temporary employment rate (%)

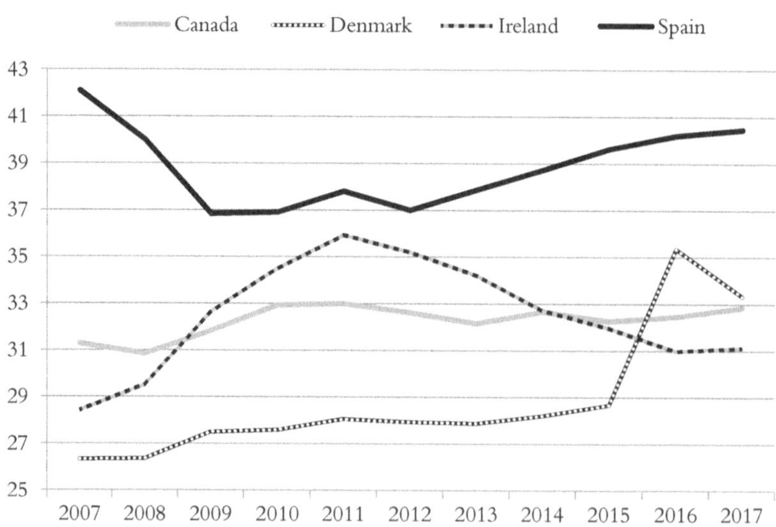

Source: OECD (2018d)

Figure 10: Unit labour costs (2007 to 2018)

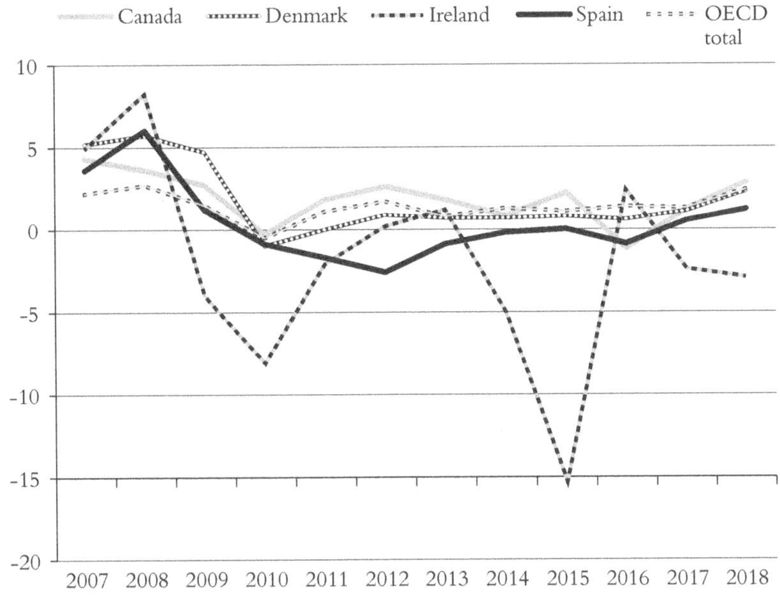

Source: OECD (2019b)

already-precarious, are of equal (if not greater) significance. The political economy of austerity thus extends far beyond mere budget balancing and staff or employment counting. The economics of austerity may be fairly straightforward (Konzelmann, 2019) but its political economy is much more complex, and demands a shift in focus from the (not only) quantitative to the (equally important) qualitative.

Throughout this book, we address the multifaceted dimensions of austerity by focusing on bailouts and related spending measures (Chapter 2), how austerity budgets were framed and justified politically (Chapter 3), the long arc of public sector restructuring and transformation (Chapter 4), labour market flexibilization (Chapter 5), increasing precarity (Chapter 6), and the complexities and contradictions involved in resistance (Chapter 7).

Notable varieties of austerity emerge in relation to *dynamics* and *degrees* of institutionalization (entrenchment), insulation (protection), and insinuation (blame) that span or cross-cut the various dimensions of austerity captured in the book's chapters, the core themes of each chapter, and the varieties of capitalism/welfare state into which these states are often separately placed by orthodox comparative political economy.

Table 1 can be read in several ways. First, as a whole it represents the wide spectrum that is the political economy of austerity. Far more than mere economic measures, processes across national jurisdictions reveal varying degrees of intensive and extensive reforms, reallocations and redistributions.

The table should also be understood as, to a large extent, capturing the individual thematic chapters that make up the book when it is read horizontally for how the '3Is' – that is, institutionalization, insulation and insinuation – manifest as, say, varieties of austerity in the public sector, or labour market, or in public sector budgeting. The table is not intended to fully represent national varieties of austerity given the problematic nature of nationally bounded appraisals where trends may be crosscutting, overlapping, and even contradictory in nature. The chapters that make up the book provide some measure of national analysis but they too strive for the thematic (more details are provided on individual chapter treatment below).

When Table 1 is read vertically, each attribute of a particular 3I is revealed.

Institutionalization Along with the more concrete sense of agencies and organizations, institutionalization encapsulates the processes of creating an air of permanency for austerity-related approaches and customs. Institutionalization is expressed by means of: the agencies and arrangements that provide private sector debt relief (banking and automobile industries) and the socialization of toxic assets by the state (Ireland's National Asset Management Agency; the Canada Mortgage and Housing Corporation; Denmark's Financial Stability Corporation; Spain's SAREB – Sociedad de Gestión de Activos Procedentes de la Reestructuración Bancaria); the agencies and actors empowered to make crucial decisions about fiscal allocation (Spain's Commission to Reform the Public Administration, Ireland's Department of Public Expenditure and Reform); the scope of changes in public spending and decision making through public-private partnerships (PPPs), bureaucratic reforms (New Public Management (NPM)), downloading responsibility and centralization; the bolstering or bypassing of social dialogue (or similar) procedures for labour market bargaining; the measures and methods for attending to poverty and precarity, and addressing the needs of low-income and high-debt households; and the extent to which routes for dissent exist in formal or informal channels (whether unions, protests, political campaigns, or the like).

Insulation captures dynamics or degrees of economic and political protection. A counterpart to the restraint and removal that is often associated with austerity as less, by insulating particular segments of

Table 1: Varieties of austerity – dynamics or degrees

	Institutionalization	Insulation	Insinuation
Debt and finance	Exceptionalism: mobilizing new or existing government or public-private agencies for private sector debt relief and the socialization of toxic assets by the state	Bailouts and guarantees: size of contribution, 'haircuts', terms and conditions	Return on bailout
Public money	Decision-making agencies: empowering particular agencies or departments and actors to make crucial decisions about who gets what, when and how (fiscal allocation)	Degree of autonomy from centralized or supranational decree; budgetary ring fencing	Target of debt/deficit: responsibility and repayment
Public sector restructuring	Scope of changes in public spending and decision making: public-private partnerships, devolution, downloading and centralization	Nature of the contribution of public services and the public sector; nature of budget imbalance; contribution to income support	PPPs and value for money; NPM and efficiency, effectiveness
Labour market flexibility	Bypassed or bolstered institutional starting points (pre-crisis): statutory or voluntarist collective bargaining systems, social dialogue procedures (or similar)	Extending, affirming, or rescinding: legal rights, protections, automatic stabilizers, addressing 'rigidities', impinging on trade union strength	Controlling unit labour costs: internal devaluation, supply-side low-wage competition
Precarity	Voice and organizing predicaments for those who are poor, in precarious, low-wage jobs, and have high debt	Impact of crisis and austerity measures on particular sectors, occupations, households, individuals	Causalities of austerity: poor, precarious and vulnerable people
Resistance	Routes for dissent: unions, protests, political campaigns (formal to informal, legal to illegal)	Roots of austerity: one-offs, systemic	Triggers and victims: political parties and political system

society (class-based or otherwise), redistribution and reforms complexify the austerity period. Particular groups are insulated, or not, from harsh austerity measures through fiscal mechanisms such as: ring fencing particular areas of the public sector budget (PPP infrastructure) or protecting certain public sector staff (departments of finance); offsetting the impact of austerity through remnant Keynesian-style automatic stabilizers (unemployment insurance and other income supports); relative pressures imposed by international markets (interest and exchange rates, currency pegs and trading partners) and organizations (OECD, EU, Troika); the extent to which capital is held to account for its role in fiscal-financial crises ('haircuts' on bondholders; the degree of support for banking, from insurance and underwriting to asset nationalization); the magnitude of crisis, the size and proximity of economic impact, the sectors and segments affected by recession (construction, exports, precarious jobs), the nature of budget imbalance (cyclical, structural, bubbles), and the contribution of the public sector to offsetting crisis-related income loss (from financiers to fishers). Resistance to privilege and protection varies based on whether the roots of austerity are perceived to be more systemic in nature (capitalism, financialization, privatization), or related to one-off aspects of austerity reforms (water pricing, service suspension, closures).

Insinuation Given that austerity is about more than less, and is indeed a process of multi-faceted transformation where clear winners and losers emerge, we see insinuation – that is, the dynamics or degrees of burden and blame shifting – as crucial in and of itself, and as a part of institutionalization and insulation. Internal devaluation of the labour market is clearly an economic process of wage and rights suppression; it is also about targeting blame, suggesting that both structural and cyclical economic problems are rooted in (unreasonably) high labour costs in particular sectors (not banking and finance but typically export market related jobs or lower-wage occupations). The chief casualties of austerity are thus those living precarious lives and in poverty – either those made such by austerity, or made worse-off through austerity: youth, immigrants, women and indebted households. Here too, there are degrees: sometimes the various forms of disadvantage are collective (sectoral, occupational), sometimes individualized (personal debt, housing poverty). Official programmes of austerity are, however, seldom – if ever – about blame for those who are affluent, for the public and private decision makers who led society down a perilous path of crisis and breakdown (bankers, departments of finance, economists, consultants, credit rating agencies), and other beneficiaries like public-private partnerships. In some cases, arbitraging nationalized assets further lets banking off the hook when states earn money from bailouts (Denmark). And yet, we can also see, sometimes with a time lag, varying impacts on established political parties and the formal political system, as outlined in Chapter 7.

With these varieties of austerity in mind, the chapters elaborate the following themes.

Chapter 2, 'Spending in an Austere Era', provides an economic background for fiscal adjustments and drivers of spending in an austere time. The analysis includes assessment of factors such as domestic economic imbalances, financial and housing bubbles, and exposure to international economic downturn. It also delineates national and cross-national banking sector dynamics as identified in measures like stimulus and guarantees (credit underwriting, insurance support, and the like); bailouts (asset taking, nationalization); write-offs and taxpayer-borne risks; partnerships and privatization; and international pressures (from supranational institutions and investors). These varied responses involved mobilizing, creating or reconfiguring public sector institutions, insulating the banking sector from a crisis of its own making, and blaming the state for debt and deficits that will be used to insinuate public sector culpability.

Chapter 3, 'Selling Restraint', examines the main aspects of austerity budgeting in each country and delves into the budget discourse offered at the height of austerity (roughly, 2008 to 2013). Substantively it examines themes such as: fiscal narratives and budget framing; characterizing the nation; justifying crisis management via austerity; priorities of crisis era governance; rationalizing reforms beyond cuts; and European citizenship. Given that budgets focus the relationship between government and economy, their design and discourse implicates existing institutions, empowers (new or recently established) agencies, insulates or exposes particular segments of society, and insinuates degrees of blame and responsibility for both the good and bad times.

Chapter 4, 'Transforming the Public Sector', historicizes post-2008 reforms by summarizing the New Public Management (NPM) ideals and forms of public sector restructuring that first began to emerge in the 1980s, followed by national snapshots of state restructuring up to 2008 and the relevant austerity packages implicating the public sector (employment and programmes) after 2008. While each country has its own story to tell, several varieties of austerity in relation to public sector restructuring after the global financial crisis are discernible, with common features centred on changes in public sector employment, increased centralization of political decision making, and the privatization of state-owned enterprises and/or programme delivery. Austerity-era transformations within the public sector involved new institutions forcing restructuring, exposing many public sector workers but insulating a few areas (primarily those responsible for economic decision making and associated with privatization), along with the insinuation of public sector flaws inherent to NPM ideology. Some of the negative effects of these strategies became glaringly apparent during the COVID-19 pandemic and are noted in the concluding chapter.

Chapter 5, 'Class Struggle from Above', looks at how a focus on controlling unit labour costs, insinuated to be the reason for loss of competitiveness, are characterized by state actions to increase employers' flexibility and reduce workers' protections or means of insulation within the labour market. Institutionally, measures to weaken collective bargaining, impose outcomes on bargaining, and reduce or bypass the influence of social dialogue institutions complete the picture.

Chapter 6, 'Insecurity and Poverty', notes the disconnect between the treatment of those responsible for the crisis who, as we saw in Chapter 2, were largely insulated from its effects, and those, the focus of this chapter, who were the victims of it and whose degree of already-meagre insulation from market turbulence was much reduced. This is evidenced through changes in household poverty and insecurity (personal debt), labour market precarity (workers' rights, youth), housing insecurity, food insecurity and diminished voice (advocacy). Vulnerable populations and communities were to be much more affected by the COVID-19 pandemic than other groups.

Chapter 7, 'Limits and Possibilities of Resistance', looks at reactions to austerity by labour, social movements and political parties, and, in some cases, the impact of these contradictory interactions on the political system itself through the rise of populist parties.

In conclusion, in Chapter 8, 'Beyond Austerity', we summarize the book's findings and arguments, and go beyond the legacy of post-2008 austerity to address more recent events. This includes a preliminary assessment of the intersections between the austerity agenda and the experience of the COVID-19 pandemic and its associated economic crisis. The chapter also looks at possible alternatives and ways ahead.

2

Spending in an Austere Era

When the 2008 crisis hit, all four countries (Canada, Denmark, Ireland and Spain) were in relatively good shape fiscally. Within a few short years the public sector and its finances were not only implicated in, but also targeted as causing, a crisis of profligate spending. While the bulk of this book focuses on cutbacks, retrenchment and restructuring, in this chapter we expose the significant commitments to capital made in the name of austerity. Thus, the austerity era should not be confused with one where public sector spending is simply curtailed; instead state support for capital is often extended in new and familiar ways. In short, there is a lot of spending to account for in times of austerity.

In this chapter we: 1) provide an economic background for, and brief overview of, fiscal adjustments and drivers of spending in an austere time – these being related most closely to a) domestic economic imbalances, b) financial and housing bubbles, and c) exposure to international economic downturn; and 2) summarize the massive bank bailouts and aid to the financial sector that each country offered capital in the wake of the 2008 crisis (often institutionalized through public sector agencies). We begin with national snapshots of each country's fiscal–financial condition when the 2008 crisis first hit, weaving in, where appropriate, an historical overview. Next, we provide a thematic description of the nation-specific bailouts and banking sector guarantees (insulations): a) stimulus and guarantees (credit underwriting, insurance support and the like), b) bailouts (asset taking, nationalization), c) write-offs and taxpayer-borne risks, d) partnerships and privatization, and e) international pressures (from supranational institutions and investors).

We also note monetary policy exhaustion through rock-bottom interest rates (see Figures 3 and 4 in Chapter 1), exchange rate concerns (Canada, Denmark), and Eurozone monetary stability initiatives (Ireland, Spain). These themes are interrelated and overlap with national peculiarities and identifiably cross-cutting varieties. The chapter concludes with a comparison and analysis of similarities and differences, discussing the range of government and institutional responses and providing explanations for the crisis-driven political economy of debt and finance (shifting the dynamics of insinuation away from banking through institutionalization and insulation). While the data and graphs provided in Chapter 1 focus on general government debt and related issues, this chapter mainly focuses on national government accounts.

National snapshots

Three aspects of economic concern create a backdrop for understanding the political economy of debt and finance in the early moments of the 2008 crisis: domestic economic imbalances; financial and housing bubbles; and exposure to international economic downturn. In some countries, all three are evident; in others, only one or two. Whether taken together or separately, they suggest a complex story of long-run capitalist volatility, of domestic and international structural conditions, of ideological change, and of oscillations between spending and restraint, not a simple story of profligate state spending cured through austerity.

Canada

The election of a Conservative government in 1984 signalled the end of the Keynesian welfare state in Canada; however, even by the late 1980s some welfare state institutions were proving resilient (Banting, 1987), and the prevailing view indicated incremental change by erosion rather than outright dismantling (Banting, 1987: 213). A deep recession of the early 1990s and ensuing budget deficits would upend this incremental dynamic, crystallized in the 1995 federal Liberal budget that marked a fundamental shift in the role of the federal state in Canada. The erosion of social programmes ended and their demolition began (Kroeger, 1996). The primacy of deficit reduction over maintenance of the social safety net became absolutely clear. Declining federal transfers to provinces and a fundamental redesign of the unemployment benefit and other social assistance systems also encouraged/enabled subnational provincial government redesigns and budget cutting. Likewise, the 1989 Canada–US Free Trade Agreement and 1994 North American Free Trade Agreement signalled a more disciplined continental integration, and Canada's eager participation in the establishment of the World Trade Organization in 1995 cast the die for the country's reliance on international markets and trade. By the early 2000s, Canada's exchange rate and national income were twined with oil exports and other primary commodities, neoliberal structural shifts having decimated the productive and manufacturing sectors. The 1990s and 2000s nurtured a rich but internationally vulnerable economy (see Carroll et al, 2018; Stanford, 2018).

Going into 2008, the Canadian federal government enjoyed a small but comfortable budget surplus in 2007. With the global financial crisis soon leading to the Great Recession, and the Canadian economy being long since oriented toward international (particularly US) markets, national growth slowed in 2008. Federal government revenues fell accordingly, and expenditures on automatic stabilizers (covering items such as employment insurance) rose, leading to a cyclical budget deficit by 2009. Despite worsening economic conditions, the federal Conservative government initially denied the existence of a recession in Canada and ignored calls from opposition parties to take a more activist macroeconomic approach. It was only in late 2008/early 2009, after G20 leaders collectively committed to extraordinary efforts of fiscal stimulus, that Canada acknowledged its need for substantial countercyclical spending.

The federal 2009 budget unveiled an economic action plan (EAP) to stimulate growth and support markets with tens of billions of dollars in new spending and tax cuts over two years. The first year of the EAP coincided with the toughest year of the crisis. The Canadian economy slumped and unemployment rose; the deficit had worsened by 2010. Stimulus spending continued, and with two years of modest growth, the budget deficit shrank. Barely out of the woods, in 2011, a few short years after the worst global economic crisis since the 1930s Great Depression, the Conservative government shifted back to a balanced budget orientation. Austerity would come to overtake 'extraordinary stimulus' around the world, too. Neoliberalism promised to solve its own crisis, excessive public sector spending being framed for economic fragility and substantial debt accumulation in harder-hit regions. Given the relatively light effects of crisis in Canada, and the relatively timid stimulus measures, the deficit was eliminated quite quickly and in surplus by 2014–15. Contra the (now debunked) predictions of the neoclassical 'expansionary fiscal consolidation thesis,' the Canadian economy did not respond with unbridled positivity to government spending cuts. After two years of growth (2010 and 2011), national income had slowed by 2012; growth picked up slightly in 2013 and 2014 but contracted once more in 2015 in response to a sharp decline in global oil prices. This was a 'double-dip' recession in action.

Looking more closely at revenues and expenditures, a clearer picture of Canadian fiscal policy emerges (see CBC, 2015). Revenues and expenditures as a percentage of GDP both rose from 2005–06 to 2015–16, the former by 27 per cent, the latter by 42 per cent. The discrepancy between the two can be explained in a few ways. First, and most obviously, the global financial crisis, recession, and fiscal policy response led to a surge in spending set amid simultaneous decline in tax-derived income for government (revenues shrank for two consecutive years from 2008–09 to 2009–10). Second, and fairly significant for understanding the implicit neoliberalism at play even during a time of Keynesian revival in the form of stimulus spending, the Conservative government introduced a number of tax cuts to boost consumer and corporate spending over the crisis period, which reduced the overall size of the public sector in the Canadian economy. Total revenues grew in absolute nominal terms while declining as a percentage of GDP given that state resources relative to the overall size of the economy had shrunk.

Taxes as a proportion of GDP also declined over the ten-year period of 2005/06 to 2015/16. During this time, the Conservative government gradually lowered the federal corporate tax rate, from 34 to 26.5 per cent, and revenue from corporate income taxes declined relative to both personal income tax and total revenues. The decision to cut the national Goods and Services Tax and the corporate tax rate has, for Stoney and Krawchenko (2013: 38, emphasis in original), 'been instrumental in the *narrative of austerity*' given that federal revenues as a percentage of GDP have dropped from 18 to 15 per cent from 2000–01 to 2010–11, whereas expenses rose in 2009–11 due largely to the crisis and its effect on automatic stabilizers.

We must also qualify the overall growth of expenditures during the crisis period. Spending in nominal terms and relative to revenues did increase over 2005–15 but the types of expenditure growth during the stimulus period (2005–10) and the austerity period (2010–15) differed. As would be expected, spending increased more quickly with stimulus, and steadily declined thereafter. Total expenditures rose by 31 per cent from 2005–10, but by only 8 per cent from 2010–15, despite the double-dip recession and weak recovery. The many line items that make up total expenditures reveal a similar pattern. Total transfers to persons, for example, grew by 30 per cent from 2005–10 and declined to 21 per cent from 2010–15. Similarly, total transfers to other levels of government were up 40 per cent in the initial period only to slow to 16 per cent in the latter. Total programme expenses ballooned by 40 per cent during the crisis and stimulus period, dropping to 11 per cent during the austerity period.

Over the ten-year period of 2005–15, public debt levels for the federal government and most provinces were also on the rise. Provincially, all governments except for Alberta, Saskatchewan, and Newfoundland and

Labrador saw their net debt levels increase between 2006 and 2015. Ontario's debt (and economy) is by far the largest of all provinces and it experienced the most significant percentage increase over this period, growing by 99 per cent. By 2015, the province's net debt was roughly half that of the federal government's. As a percentage of provincial GDP, Ontario's debt went from 27 per cent in 2006 to 40 per cent in 2015. The next two provinces of significance are Quebec and British Columbia; however, with Quebec's debt well below the Ontario level, and far above that of British Colombia, there is a notable discrepancy in provincial conditions. Between 2006–07 and 2014–15, Quebec's debt increased from 43 to 49 per cent. Ontario and Quebec account for most provincial debt: roughly 84 per cent as of February 2014 (Curry and McKenna, 2014).

Denmark

The Danish economy experienced serious structural challenges over the neoliberal period. The first shocks came with the end of the Bretton Woods regime in 1971, followed by the 1973 oil crisis – at that time over 90 per cent of Denmark's energy requirements were met with imported petroleum. The effects were dramatic, resulting in double-digit inflation for much of the decade. Denmark's national currency at the time, the krone, was devalued several times and eventually pegged to the Deutsche mark in 1982, which successfully reduced inflation and brought down interest rates. Economic growth recovered by the mid-1980s, although it was short-lived, averaging less than 1 per cent between 1987 and 1993 while unemployment peaked at 12 per cent in 1993. Signs of recovery began with current account surpluses beginning in 1990, generally sustained through to 2008. During this period, net foreign debt dropped from nearly 40 per cent of GDP in the late 1980s to –3.9 per cent by 2005. Unemployment and inflation also dropped, and long-term interest rate spreads between Germany and Denmark declined from 13 per cent in 1982 to 1 per cent in 1990 and were nearly on par by 2005 (Abildgren, 2007). Now a small open economy, not a member of the European Monetary Union but with its currency pegged to the euro, its politics feature frequent coalition governments that have often enjoyed political stability marked by pragmatic agreements, prudent economic policies, and an orientation toward social investment (Andersen and Ibsen, 2017).

Problems were brewing beneath Denmark's otherwise stable political system and healthy real economy. Its banking sector woes can be traced back to policy initiatives and private practices of financialization and privatization. Danske Bank invested heavily abroad: in Northern Ireland it created a commercial bank called Danske Bank UK in 2012 (formerly Northern Bank, one of the 'Big Four' banks in Ireland dating back to 1809), and in the Republic of Ireland it created Danske Bank Ireland in 2012 (formerly the National Irish Bank, also dating to 1809). Danish pension funds began investing in mortgage bonds as early as the mid-1980s when pension reforms came in, making private pension savings mandatory. The expansion of mortgage-backed securities made mortgage-based banks big players in the Danish system, eclipsing non-mortgage banks in domestic lending. In November 2003, mortgage banks were required to issue interest rate-only loans where ten years of an average 30-year mortgage involved paying only the interest, with many hoping to refinance their mortgage after that period to secure a better rate. By 2006, roughly half of all mortgages were wrapped up in this scheme. The bonds issued by the mortgage banks were then linked to the outstanding loans on their balance sheets. Danes were the primary investors in these bonds, with up to a quarter held by foreign investors. Non-mortgage banks were also able to raise more debt with less equity at this time too, and they began investing in commercial real estate.

When the global financial crisis turned into a credit crunch in the latter portion of 2008, interbank lending was squeezed and the lack of liquidity quickly exposed a serious deposit deficit in Danish banks (40 per cent of GDP) (Carstensen, 2013). Cutting interest rates would have been one obvious domestic solution to the credit crunch; instead the Danish central bank increased interest rates to protect the currency peg and dampen investment flight to euro- and US dollar-denominated bonds. Ultimately higher interest rates proved insufficient, its currency depreciated and its foreign reserves were inadequate to maintain the peg.

The Danish recovery was relatively slow compared to neighbouring countries including Sweden and Germany. Two types of measures were implemented in the wake of the crisis. The first set of measures attempted to stimulate flagging consumption via tax cuts for high- and middle-income earners along with moderate stimulus spending. The second set were austerity measures targeting benefits for the unemployed, early retirement regulations, public sector budgets, and wage growth, ostensibly seeking to reduce social expenditures. Both sets of measures were pursued largely unilaterally by the centre-right coalition that governed from 2001 to 2011. Input from the traditional social partners, the labour unions and employers' federation was not for the most part sought, as precedent urged. Consequently, inequality expanded, unemployment rates rose, and significant encroachment on some main elements of the Danish welfare state and tripartite corporatist arrangements was achieved (Hansen and Mailand, 2013; Madsen, 2013).

It is notable that the budget cuts and fiscal constraints imposed by the centre-right coalition in response to the crisis were less severe than the austerity strategies implemented elsewhere in the EU. In Denmark, austerity aimed not for deep cuts but instead to hold public expenditures steady through a zero-growth initiative. The 'automatic stabilizers' that characterize Denmark's high-tax, high social security economy did work to prevent some erosion in employment and economic growth. For that reason, Hansen and Mailand (2013) argue that even the strongest austerity measures in Denmark amounted to a resetting of reforms rather than a 'system redesign' (this is, quantitative rather than qualitative/structural changes to the public sector). However, one area of crisis management that can be construed as qualitative change implicates the government's strategic orientation on the tripartite social dialogue model, which was bypassed in favour of unilateral legislative action (see Chapter 5).

Ireland

In 1987, the Irish economy began to recover from a prolonged downturn and initiated a path of exceptional and unprecedented economic growth. The 'Celtic Tiger' had three phases to it: recovery from 1987 to 1993, boom from 1994 to 2001, and a credit bubble from 2001 to 2007. Economic growth averaged more than 6 per cent from 1987 to 2007 and was particularly high during the second phase when GDP growth began averaging over 9 per cent, eventually reaching double digits by the late 1990s (Kirby, 2002; Crafts, 2008). Unemployment, peaking at 17 per cent in 1986, had dipped below 4 per cent by 2001, and the labour force doubled from 1992 to 2007. GDP per capita increased rapidly. It is important note, however, that Ireland's tax haven economy renders spurious standard calculations of national income like GDP; instead, Ireland uses GNI* to account for new value added in domestic income. Sustained current account deficits were reversed during the 1990s and export growth averaged 18 per cent between 1995 and 2001 (Kirby, 2010: 35).

The Irish financial crisis was revealed when the decades-old property bubble burst. Some observers suggest that the Celtic Tiger era had been on the wane since 2001 when export-led growth slowed and housing-related activity became the primary engine of economic growth (Kirby, 2010; Ó Riain, 2014). For example, employment in construction increased almost 60 per cent from 2000 to 2008 and accounted for approximately 12 per cent of the total labour force in 2006 (Kirby, 2010). Household debt had soared to 236 per cent of net disposable income by 2007, and between 2003 and 2008 the total value of outstanding mortgages in Ireland more than tripled, fueling a rapid growth in domestic Irish banks' balance sheets and sending loan-deposit ratios to over 200 per cent. The decline in housing prices in late 2007 was followed by the near complete collapse of the construction sector due to lack of demand, plunging the Irish economy into a deep recession, with real GDP declining by over 4 per cent annually in 2008 and 2009 (since deflation had set in, the nominal rate of decline was even higher for 2009), while unemployment averaged close to 14 per cent between 2009 and 2012. Tax revenues evaporated and budget surpluses transformed into deficits that reached 32 per cent in 2010 despite significant austerity measures. Gross national debt rose from 24 per cent of GDP in 2007 to 120 per cent during 2012–13 (see Eurostat, n.d.).

Spain

Experiencing an economic boom between 1999 and 2007, the Spanish 'miracle' (Buendia and Molero-Simarro, 2018) saw real GDP per capita increasing by 20 per cent, average annual real GDP growing by 4 per cent, the elimination of the public deficit, and public debt cut to a healthy 36 per cent of GDP. Just prior to the global financial crisis, Spain enjoyed both a fiscal surplus and low public debt. Over the early 2000s, Spain became increasingly open to international markets and migrants, and experienced booms in housing and tourism markets with the lowest unemployment rates seen since its transition to democracy (Collado et al, 2004). The miracle economy, however, was based on thin arrangements, simmering intergovernmental conflict, and difficulties in coordinating the various levels of government (Colomer, 1998). As part of its remarkable economic performance, the country received some five million immigrants between 1995 and 2006 which increased labour supply, stimulated consumption, moderated wages, and contributed to Spain's economic success (Izquierdo Peinado et al, 2007). By 2007, Spain seemed to be on course to catch up with the average economic indicators of the EU. After the crisis, the country began its struggle with deep and enduring recession.

Between 2008 and 2013, real GDP fell by 9 per cent (Martí and Pérez, 2016), the unemployment rate reached 25 per cent in 2012 (Meléndez, 2012), and public debt increased to 94 per cent of GDP. Growth prior to 2008, as miraculous as it may have been, was reliant mainly on private consumption and low interest rates, large household debt and high population growth (Calvo and Paúl, 2009; Royo, 2009a, 2009b). It was evident by the early 2000s that a housing bubble was emerging. The resources allocated to investment in housing as a percentage of GDP had increased from 5 to 7 per cent, a much higher proportion compared to other countries that also experienced a real estate boom (Estrada et al, 2009). Spain's membership in the European Monetary Union and its Stability and Growth Pact also encouraged low interest rates – short-term interest rates dropped from 13 per cent in 1992 to 2 per cent by 2005 (Royo, 2009a) – and increased the availability of loan financing (Calvo and Paúl, 2009). The availability of funding and the desire for consumption stimulated the competition between financial institutions to relax loan conditions (García Montalvo, 2006). Although the Spanish financial system discouraged the use of risky repackaged subprime mortgages (Royo, 2013), banking institutions nevertheless made loans accessible to less creditworthy borrowers through other means, such as extended payback periods, substantially reduced debt-to-income ratios or down payments and the like. Altogether, these conditions encouraged property price inflation fuelled by excessive household and construction sector debt: by 2006, risky property loans accounted for 40 per cent of total loans to the productive sector (García Montalvo, 2006). With construction sector dominance also came limits to productivity growth, this averaging only 0.3 per cent between 1999 and 2009 (Royo, 2009a). Low productivity and competitiveness, increased consumption, and an appreciating euro led to a substantial trade deficit in Spain (Royo, 2009a). The bloom was off the rose for the miracle economy by 2007.

The ravages of the 2008 global financial crisis were initially more muted in Spain, given its relatively low exposure to subprime mortgages (Álvarez, 2008) with the majority of its banks' assets as mortgage loans and government securities (Quaglia and Royo, 2015) and a banking reserve regulatory framework in place since 2000 (Royo, 2013). When the domestic bubble burst, however, Spain's construction sector dependence on wholesale interbank funding, together with a deep recession (Quaglia and Royo, 2015), would spell disaster.

The institutional structure of the Spanish banking sector only exacerbated the crisis. One of two types of banks, the savings banks or *cajas*, would prove to be an especially weak link. The 'big banks' (Santander, BBVA, La Caixa), directly supervised and regulated by the Bank of Spain, were initially able to navigate the crisis by drawing on their fiscal reserves and relying on their geographical diversification (Royo, 2013), enabling them to relax loans provided to the insolvent borrowers during the economic boom. The *cajas*, on the other hand, were under limited supervision by the Bank of Spain (Royo, 2013; Quaglia and Royo, 2015). These *cajas*, the smaller regional savings banks, often had political parties and unions participating on their boards. Compared with the big banks, these institutions had fewer resources and their political affiliation encouraged less responsible lending behaviour (Royo, 2013). *Caja* lending also included a larger proportion of property developers (Quaglia and Royo, 2015). A serious crisis in the banks' balance of payments forced Spain to ask for a bailout from the EU that consequently served to increase public debt and deficit (Quaglia and Royo, 2015). In sum, as Royo (2009a, 2013) argues, Spain's economic crisis was not caused by domestically mismanaged public finances or even necessarily by the global financial crisis itself; instead the onus should be placed on the private sector debt that exposed domestic economic imbalances, and problems inherent to the EU that included low interest rates, inflationary consumption, dependence on foreign funding, and assumptions of international market stability.

Banking sector support and spending

A combination of domestic economic imbalances, financial and housing bubbles, and exposure to international economic downturn provide the fiscal–financial backdrop for banking sector outlays from 2007. In addition to monetary policy exhaustion through rock-bottom interest rates, exchange rate concerns (Canada and Denmark) and Eurozone monetary stability initiatives (Ireland and Spain), five themes to the shape of state-provided and crisis-borne banking sector support and spending initiatives emerge: 1) stimulus and guarantees (credit underwriting, insurance support and so on); 2) bailouts (asset taking, nationalization); 3) write-offs and taxpayer-borne risks; 4) partnerships and privatization; and 5) international pressures. Themes are not mutually exclusive or nationally unique even if the details are specific to each country. Themes are interrelated and overlap in some cases, although here they have been organized according to which category they best illustrate.

Stimulus and guarantees

The global financial crisis disrupted the Canadian economy through a world market-induced recession caused by slumping demand for Canadian exports, especially in the US and China. What Canada did not have to contend with, unlike much of the rest of the advanced industrialized world, was a significant crisis in its banking and financial systems. Indeed, its financial markets continued to operate relatively well (Lin et al, 2014). Banks did, however, experience losses exceeding $12 billion in 2008

(Loxley, 2009) given the generalized financial turbulence. Canadian banking sector stability is said to be the result of customary prudence, high standards and sound regulation. It is commonly held that Canadian banks, shunning the risky practices that led to crises elsewhere, neither required nor received a government bailout. Arguments such as these are misleading. Canada did implement banking sector support comparable in relative size and scope to its southern neighbour, an intervention that helps explain banking sector resilience throughout the crisis (da Silva, 2009; Walks, 2014). Bank assistance received much less attention than the economic action plan stimulus package despite the latter coming in at a fraction of the cost of the bailouts. The nature of bank support provided by government does, however, stand out for its characteristic guarantees provided to creditors (underwriting, co-lending, loans and the like) rather than asset taking (nationalization, privatization) like we see in Denmark, Ireland and Spain.

Canada began this banking sector intervention during the credit crunch of 2007, and continued, at much larger scale, once the crisis hit in 2008. Government support was aimed at forestalling bank failures and securing the flow of credit. Baragar (2015) argues that in 2007, the Bank of Canada, despite liquidity injections, also maintained its overall neoliberal monetary policy stance favouring market efficiency not Keynesian countercyclical theory. However, notable departures from standard neoliberal-era central banking in Canada include interest rate cuts following the Bear Stearns collapse and in light of international economic volatility, and the heavy use of purchase and resale agreements in 2008–10.

Interest rates were cut to near zero levels, increasing 'the supply of variable-rate credit while allowing the banks to earn risk-free profits by investing in government treasury bonds and banking the spread' (Walks, 2014: 268). Supporting liquidity, the government began to provide 'temporary loans against illiquid assets of questionable and unknowable value' (Walks, 2014: 269), through the Term Loan Facility and the Term Purchase and Resale Agreement, amounting to over $44 billion. The Extraordinary Financing Framework of nearly $220 billion was setup 'to guarantee the principal and interest of all new wholesale debt issued by the financial institutions' (Walks, 2014: 269). However, the largest source of financial assistance was the Insured Mortgage Purchase Program that allowed the Canada Mortgage and Housing Corporation, a state-owned enterprise, to purchase mortgage-backed securities up to $125 billion from financial institutions across Canada.

With low unemployment, a positive current account balance, and relatively low levels of public debt, Denmark appeared in a strong position for coping with the financial and economic crises (Kluth and Lynggaard,

2013). Weak global trade together with an end to the national housing bubble would go on to produce great difficulties for Denmark's financial system and its economy (Lin et al, 2013a). Denmark's response to the crisis was notable not just for its exceptional measures, but also for its collectivist character. Contrary to expectations that a country 'with a legacy of considerable public spending' (Kluth and Lynggaard, 2013: 774) would adopt a social democratic response, the government instead made collective commitments to the banking sector 'through considerable fees for guarantees and contributions to a fund covering losses from bank failures, which effectively ring-fenced the Danish financial industry and protected the public budget' (Woll, 2014: 140).

Crisis management responses in Ireland were significantly different from those of Denmark (Kluth and Lynggaard, 2013; Woll, 2014). Unlike Denmark, the Irish state played a dominant role in bailing out the financial industry, defying typical expectations for a liberal free market state compared with a coordinated market economy. Differences in absolute terms were also significant for emergency management. By the crisis period, financial industry assets in Ireland were triple the country's GDP, and if offshore banking and international funds are included, finance constituted seven times the national GDP. In Denmark, related assets were only twice the national GDP (Kluth and Lynggaard, 2013; Lin et al, 2013a; Woll, 2014).

Irish banks with the biggest exposure to property and construction markets were the first to fail. Anglo Irish Bank initially received government assistance through increased deposit protection. Concerned with the potential for cascading effects if this bank were to fail, other leading banks pressed the government to intervene. The Irish government, the Central Bank of Ireland and the Financial Regulator agreed to guarantee all deposits and much of the liabilities of six Irish-owned banks (valued at two times the GDP) for a period measured in years (Kluth and Lynggaard, 2013; Ó Riain, 2014; Woll, 2014). While the blanket protection at first involved no obligations, it was soon decided that banks would have to make contributions amounting to €500 million. Deposit guarantees were also offered to foreign banks; all but one declined on the basis of the terms given (Woll, 2014). The guarantees, depending on calculations, were valued at more than two to three times the Irish GDP (Kluth and Lynggaard, 2013; Woll, 2014). Next came recapitalization: €10 billion of public funds were made available, of which €5.5 billion was used to purchase preferential shares in three main Irish banks. This was followed by a full nationalization of Anglo Irish Bank (covered in the next section), and by injections of additional capital to important banks, making the government their largest shareholder (Kluth and Lynggaard, 2013; Woll, 2014).

With the housing bubble burst in Spain, 2009 brought rapidly rising unemployment and a major drop in industrial production – the economic crisis thus hit Spain's real economy harder than any of its European counterparts (Lin et al, 2013b). With its unique banking structure came unique implications for government intervention. As mentioned, pre-crisis Spanish banks consisted of many regional savings and loan *cajas*, and a handful of major banks. Given that the smaller savings and loans *cajas* were those primarily implicated in financing the housing bubble, they were the entities requiring subsequent relief and restructuring (Neal and García-Iglesias, 2013). The crisis response involved tackling liquidity issues, stimulating the economy, establishing a public authority to resolve failing institutions, and, later, stabilizing the banking sector with EU financial assistance. To revive economic activity, in 2008 the government introduced an €50 billion spending package, €8 billion of which was given to local authorities for public projects (Lin et al, 2013b). To support the automobile industry (10 per cent of the economy), the government also subsidized new car buyers by €2,000 (Lin et al, 2013b).

Bailouts

Canada's nation-wide stimulus programme, the EAP, was promoted as aid for individuals, housing construction, infrastructure and communities, though nearly half of these funds were 'used to bailout particular industries (including the automobile, forestry, and housing industries) and to support infrastructure projects being built mostly through private-public partnerships' (Walks, 2014: 269). Two of the 'Big Three' carmakers, General Motors and Chrysler, received $11 billion and $3 billion in assistance from the federal and Ontario governments respectively.

The Danish government's Rangvid Committee became an important actor in its banking sector bailouts. In September, 2013, this committee, led by Professor Jesper Rangvid, and open to input by the banking sector and academe but not the public, presented its findings on the causes of the financial crisis. The committee suggested multiple factors: Denmark, a small open economy with a pro-cyclical fiscal policy, had overly optimistic lending practices and liberalized mortgage lending rules, and thus experienced a housing price bubble. An especially serious problem emerged when Moody's downgraded the senior ratings of all Danish banks including Danske. The Committee also concluded that Danish banks should be better capitalized through tighter rules for the big banks, their strategically important financial institutions (SIFIs), Danske Bank being their main SIFI with double the Danish GDP on its books at the time of the crisis. Rangvid summarized the various banking sector packages as relating to: stability (state guarantees), credit (capital injections), exit ('haircuts' on unsecured senior loans and deposits over €100,000), and consolidation (with the Danish Deposit Guarantee Fund providing a guarantee against losses to a buyer bank). Notably, Denmark was the first European country to use a 'bail in' strategy in 2011, imposing losses on senior creditors after Fjordbank Mors and Amagerbanken failed. As context, the European Central Bank (ECB) blocked 'haircuts' for senior bondholders in Irish banks, with ECB president Jean-Claude Trichet telling Ireland that 'it had to go through with its fiscal austerity measures and imposing haircuts (or discounts) on investors could *not* be part of the plan' (Inman, 2011, emphasis added).

Thus, banking sector support in Denmark consisted of five packages ranging from depositor protections to bank exit. Government agreed to fully guarantee all deposits of reserve fund members in exchange for banks' contributions of DKK 35 billion. Designed to cover private losses beyond the DKK 35 billion, less than DKK 15 billion was needed in the end. Denmark also established the state-owned company Financial Stability Corporation (Finansiel Stabilitet – not to be confused with the Financial Stability Authority, which provides supervision), which 'authorized to arrange for take-overs of distressed banks by other banks and to support such take-overs with injections of share capital' (Andersen, 2011: 184). Any profits made by this company would be public. A recapitalization scheme, the second package, made available up to DKK 100 billion to allow the government to buy preferred stocks of applicant banks, with 65 per cent of these funds committed by the target date (Andersen, 2011). Another scheme was designed to encourage takeovers of distressed financial institutions or assets funded by the FS, along with a selective transfer of commercial real estate to FS and support for agricultural and export sectors (Woll, 2014). Roskilde Bank would be bailed out by government to the tune of DKK 9 billion by 2012.

Bank rescue package I was offered to all banks and aimed at unsecured creditors, mainly because of Danske Bank's liquidity trouble. Like Irish creditors, all were given a blanket guarantee. Introduced in October 2008, just after Lehman Brothers collapsed, most were able to keep operational funding through selling bonds, thus they did not actually need the emergency package at this early stage; however, the package I guarantee essentially kept Danske alive. The government began injecting money through hybrid financing (loans, not equity) in package II. Many mergers occurred as fallout, and 62 banks disappeared (mostly small banks). Package III (in 2010) was aimed at getting government money out. Like Ireland's decision to take over bad loans and property investments (see below), Denmark's Financial Stability Corporation took on troubled assets beginning in 2008.

Irish banking sector insolvency was addressed through the National Asset Management Agency (NAMA) that acquired toxic assets through government bonds (Kluth and Lynggaard, 2013; Woll, 2014). NAMA 'purchased the banks' toxic loans to cleanse their balance sheets and has since then managed them either by selling them on the market or by holding them to maturity' (Mercille and Murphy, 2015: 98). NAMA 'acquired 11,500 property development-related loans, with a nominal value of USD$92.5 billion (€72.3 billion) (46% of its GDP) at an average haircut of 58%, in return for NAMA bonds' (Lin et al, 2013a: 147), which the ECB accepted as collateral. NAMA's initial design, whereby banks and the government were to share ownership of the special purpose vehicles (51 and 49 per cent, respectively), was soon challenged; by 2011, the three major NAMA participants came under the control and guarantee of the state, making all their debt public (Woll, 2014). At the outset, as Woll (2014: 155) explains, the private sector 'did agree to contribute to NAMA', with its early participants being 'the pension fund managers Irish Life Investment Managers; New Ireland Assurance; and Clients of Allied Irish Banks Investment Managers, which are part of Irish Life Permanent, Bank of Ireland, and Allied Irish Banks respectively'. Yet, as 'all three of these banks had been under government control and guarantee by 2011, the debt of NAMA is now considered as government debt entirely' (Woll, 2014: 155).

These enormous bailout-related outlays pushed Ireland into a sovereign debt crisis by late 2010, forcing the government to request assistance from the EU and the International Monetary Fund (IMF). Within a week, these parties came to an agreement on an €85 billion rescue package, a large portion of which was allocated to the banking system (Woll, 2014). More specifically, beyond the €50 billion to fund the government, €10 billion was put towards the banking system (including €2 billion for 'credit enhancements that could allow Irish banks to sell packages of risky loans to private investors': Woll, 2014: 147), with €25 billion set aside as additional banking funds if necessary. Mercille and Murphy (2015: 98) calculate that a total of €64 billion (41 per cent of GDP) of public money spent was spent to rescue private financial institutions. The Irish Bank Resolution Corporation, created through the merger of Anglo Irish Bank and Irish Nationwide Building Society, received €35 billion, Anglo Irish Bank (and its subsidiary EBS) took €21 billion, Bank of Ireland got €5 billion, and Irish Life & Permanent received €4 billion. As Lane (cited in Woll, 2014: 162) notes, 'while the public capital injections into Bank of Ireland and AIB may be viewed as financial investments that may ultimately yield return, the capital poured into Anglo Irish Bank and Irish Nationwide Building Society are effectively write-offs'. The Irish situation was one of the worst in Europe, with only Iceland suffering a higher sovereign debt impact (Woll, 2014).

In Spain, the privately funded deposit guarantee scheme, the traditional resolution mechanism, provided liquidity and asset protection (Huerta, 2019: 28). One of the first government interventions targeted Caja Castilla-La Mancha after it failed to meet its capital requirements. Recognizing that the existing systems may not be able to provide adequate financial stability, Spain created its 'bad bank', the Fund for the Orderly Restructuring of the Banking Sector (FROB – Fondo de Reestructuración Ordenada Bancaria) in June 2009, a resolution authority tasked with supporting both voluntary and mandated restructuring of failed banking institutions in cases where the deposit guarantee scheme fell short. The fund began by providing public assistance through the purchase of preference shares, and continued with capital injections and contingent convertibles. In total, the FROB bad bank took over almost €57 billion in diverse capital instruments (Huerta, 2019). These funds included €39 billion 'for the recapitalisation of eight credit institutions under restructuring or resolution', a €2 billion stake in the Asset Management Company for Assets Arising from Bank Restructuring (SAREB) to buy part of its subordinated debt (roughly 200,000 toxic real estate assets shifted to SAREB at a cost of €5.1 billion) (Huerta, 2019: 32). FROB funds were well above the €20 billion privately financed deposit guarantee scheme and 'the €178,000 million of liquidity support to banks (through State guarantees and liquidity facilities)' (Huerta, 2019: 34).

Write-offs and taxpayer-borne risks

Canada's 2009 budget touted the fiscal advantages of banking sector support, explaining that the Insured Mortgage Purchase Program (IMPP) would not affect the size of the federal debt given that, 'the borrowings and associated interest costs are matched by an increase in revenue-earning assets. Other borrowings undertaken to strengthen the financial system are also offset by interest-earning assets' (Government of Canada, 2009: 229). Yet Igan et al (2019: 50) note that 'Canadian authorities have not released any bank-level information on aid disbursed through the IMPP, and bank annual reports confound any such estimations by embedding these securities' sales in other financial information, preventing a straightforward calculation of the associated risks borne by the authorities.' Parallel supports for capital reveal troublesome implications. Not only did direct fiscal benefits from automobile sector bailouts not materialize, the rescue effort was never fully repaid either.

Recovering only $10 billion from loan repayments and the sale of General Motors shares, Canadian taxpayers in effect absorbed nearly $3.5 billion in losses (Keenan, 2015). And, in late 2019, General Motors announced the closure of a large assembly plants in Oshawa, Ontario – the provincial and federal bailouts a decade earlier having won the battle but largely lost the war for jobs in Canada's automobile sector. Not only was this a shameful betrayal on General Motor's part, it also indicates short-sighted government support for capital without any strings attached.

With Denmark's Trelleborg Bank and Roskilde Bank facing liquidity problems early in the crisis (2007 and 2008, respectively), the government provided liquidity through the Danmarks Nationalbank, and, when this proved insufficient, it facilitated a private takeover worth DKK 750 million whereby the Danish government would guarantee any losses beyond this amount (Woll, 2014). It was soon evident, however, that 'the government's responsibility would be far above the industry's contribution, reaching DKK 6.6 billion in 2009 and well over DKK 9 billion in 2012' (Woll, 2014: 157). By 2012, Financial Stability Corporation had taken ownership of roughly 60 banks, anticipating a net profit for taxpayers given that assets were to be arbitraged: strategically returned to the market at a later date and a higher value. Andersen (2011: 186) suggests 'DKK 15 billion collected from the banks and savings banks will probably turn out to be substantially more than what has been spent on the rescue or unwinding of the handful of collapsed banks and savings banks.' Overall, in Eurostat's assessment, and as described by Woll (2014: 162), the Danish bailout was 'the most profitable in Europe in 2011, helping the Danish government to reduce its fiscal deficit by 0.3 per cent of GDP over 2008–10 [...] equivalent to €0.7 billion in absolute terms'. This interviewee agrees: "[the bailout] was funded through the interest, and it did end up making the state money again. Again, I think it's worth stressing that because there is a story here about success of this policy" (Danish academic researcher, 2018).[1]

State support for the Irish banking sector, initially promoted as the 'cheapest bailout in the world' (Mercille and Murphy, 2015: 76), became one of the most expensive in history. Here we quote Mercille and Murphy (2015: 77) at length for their explanation of the magnitude of the bailout and its relative costs:

> The government guaranteed all liabilities (excluding shareholders' equity) of the six largest Irish banks for an amount of €365 billion, almost 2.5 times Ireland's Gross National

> Product (GNP); injected €64 billion to recapitalise them and pay bondholders, many of which were foreign financial institutions; and bought the bad loans issued by financial institutions through NAMA, for which the state is responsible for any shortfalls. This strategy proved extremely costly, but this was incidental given that much of the expenses were shifted onto taxpayers. Indeed, the International Monetary Fund (IMF) surveyed 147 banking crises since 1970 and concluded that Ireland had 'the costliest banking crisis in advanced economies since at least the Great Depression' of the 1930s [...] The bank rescue was the costliest in Europe, reaching a stunning 25 per cent of Gross Domestic Product (GDP), or €9,000 per capita, compared to an average of only €192 per capita in other European Union (EU) countries.

Further complexity is added by this Irish private sector union staff interviewee who points to other scandals associated with profiteering from taxpayer-funded NAMA:

> '[NAMA] sold land on which 50,000 social houses could have been built. That land was sold to help them recover, as I say, the billions lost by the banks. But it was passed over to people who are now making profits, huge profits, from developing on those lands.
>
> 'The bailout meant that something in the order of 74 billion [euros] in toxic debt, effectively, was transferred to the taxpayer, to the public, through this setting up of NAMA. Since then, the government, led by, as I say, a right-wing party called Fine Gael, decided that it was going to do everything as instructed by the Troika: the ECB and the IMF and the European Commission. Not only that, but they actually agreed, having campaigned during the election in 2011, that they would not cover unsecured bondholders or banks in Europe that had recklessly lent to the Irish banks. Because the banks were borrowing on the European ... financial system. When the crash came, the bondholders, particularly European but also American banks, demanded that they get paid [...] – even though they were unsecured in many cases.' (Irish private sector union staff member, Dublin, June, 2018)

While the early banking sector interventions in Spain had a net positive return (2009 and 2010), significant losses would soon be revealed, especially through its bad bank SAREB: roughly €36 billion of SAREB's €40 billion remains outstanding. With some recovered from bank sales, repayments and dividends, the rest is likely unrecoverable (Huerta, 2019).

Partnerships and privatization

Despite neoliberal arguments of the inherent superiority of the private sector having been tarnished through the subprime mortgage market meltdown that implicated both private capital and surveillance, private authority was nevertheless quickly turned to for help and guidance by the state. Representatives of the Danish banking industry, anticipating distress, established a private alternative to government-mandated deposit insurance, the Private Reserve Fund for Distressed Banks (or Private Contingency Association, depending on the English translation), in 2007 (Andersen, 2011; Kluth and Lynggaard, 2013; Woll, 2014). Though it would soon prove insufficient in the face of the large losses, particularly those of Roskilde Bank, it took on a central role in Denmark's crisis management system (Woll, 2014).

> 'So the idea here, behind this Financial Stability Corporation, was to bring in expertise from the industry. We need the know-how of industry to get these things sorted – to get these banks closed down in a good way. But that's interesting, too, right. That the industry is being dealt with [...] So it's a pretty tight-knit thing. But their main job was to sell off these assets and land and liabilities.' (Danish academic researcher, Copenhagen, June, 2017)

Another interviewee indicates the problems posed by the cozy public-private revolving door governance structure in Denmark:

> 'Basically the "too big to fail" argument was extremely strong and we have some huge problems with the state institutions that control the banks [...] [instead, the state institutions] are controlled by the banks [...] [the] same people are sitting in high positions in the state institution. So it's really not very independent.' (Danish academic researcher, Copenhagen, June, 2017)

On the creation of the National Asset Management Agency, Ireland's bad bank, one interviewee confirmed "NAMA was done secretly" (Irish retired union confederation staff member, Dublin, June, 2018). After NAMA took on the country's toxic property debt, "The leadership of NAMA [decided to] sell it off to these big hedge funds [...] they went on road shows." (Danish academic researcher, Copenhagen, June, 2017). Thus, NAMA

> 'became a vehicle which has enriched a small number of both global and local business people, finance people, real estate people, lawyers as usual, and other professionals, accountants, liquidators, receivers ... vast amounts of money ... have been flipped ... transferred from public ownership, through NAMA, into the hands of private global vulture funds in the case of many billions [of euros].' (Irish private sector union staff member, Dublin, 2018)

International pressures and investment

Whereas Blyth (2013) describes austerity as originating with German authorities and within the European Central Bank in the lead up to the June 2010 G20 meeting, Irwin (2013) locates its return slightly earlier at the G7 finance ministers' meeting in February of that year. Canada played a lead role, with austerity foreshadowed by comments such as those of its finance minister:

> 'We'll continue to stimulate the economy this year but what is the plan and the Canadian situation to get back to balanced budgets. We're working on that. I know that [...] thought is shared by other members of the G7, including the United Kingdom and the United States.' (Curry and Carmichael, 2010)

Canada is not only a source of international pressure, the country is also swayed by the pressures of international markets, tethering its interest rate policy to exchange rate concerns and voluntary harmonization with key trading partners like the US.

For Denmark, monetary policy was aimed at defending the euro–krone pegged exchange rate regime. To elaborate on the dynamics, when the crisis hit, rather than lowering interest rates to ease economic recession, the Danish central bank increased rates to stave off pressure on the krone. Pressure only mounted as investors sought safe haven in euro- and USD-denominated government bonds. Danish foreign exchange reserves were inadequate to fend off such a sudden decline in the exchange rate and thus interest rates became the main policy tool for maintaining the peg. Attempts by Danmarks Nationalbank to counter the pressure on the krone through a foreign exchange swap market failed in September and early October 2008. The interest rate spread between Denmark and the Eurozone hit 1.75 per cent in October 2008 despite the Danish central bank raising rates several times in response to continuing capital outflows (Sørensen, 2010). The impact on Danish homeowners was immediate – by December 2008, nearly 8 per cent of Danish households needed to refinance their mortgages (Andersen and Malchow-Møller, 2015). Andersen and Malchow-Møller (2015) argue that the housing bubble and/or 'overheated' economy explanations cannot account for the disproportionate decline in private consumption expenditures towards the end of 2008, and that policy choices made in the context of defending the peg must be considered primary explanatory variables in accounting for the subsequent slow recovery.

Although not part of the Eurozone, some might ask why Denmark as an EU member did not go to the European Central Bank for support, like Spain and Ireland. This interviewee downplayed the issue of the krone or other EU dynamics, instead pointing to the structure of Denmark's banking sector:

> 'That's probably the main reason [why Denmark didn't go to the Troika]. Danske Bank survives. Had Danske Bank not survived, then it would have been a completely different story. And the reason why in Ireland the programme was so bad – it was because these large two or three banks, they failed. We have one very large bank. We have also Nordea which is like a Swedish bank, right, but Danske Bank survives. I think that's the main point. And why do they survive? That is because it was not as bad as in Ireland. There's probably not much more to say in some sense. The situation was bad, but it was not as bad as in Ireland. So again, those banks that failed – and there are many of them – but they were all small, and that means it's certainly manageable.' (Danish academic researcher, Copenhagen, June, 2018)

As a member of the Eurozone, Ireland took full advantage of European Central Bank (ECB) support, although in this case one might reasonably ask in whose interest this support was secured. On the ECB and Ireland, interviewees describe the following:

> 'Essentially what the ECB did was they printed a whole lot of money and they gave it to the government so the

> government could pay off the bond holders in Anglo Irish, but the government got stuck with the bill and has to pay back the central bank.' (Irish private sector union staff member, Dublin, June, 2018)

> 'In fact, it got so bad that the American Treasury Secretary [...] said if Ireland didn't pay the bondholders they would go to hell in a basket. So pressure came from the US administration, as well as the ECB and the European Commission, to insist that everything would be paid back. That, of course, resulted in what you might call a deep austerity programme which involved cutting pensions and salaries for the public service, across the public service. It involved a series of emergency budgets. It involved – what would you say – cuts to the minimum wage. It involved punishing the people who had nothing to do with the crash, who weren't at the scene of the car crash when it came, and bailing out those who were responsible.' (Irish private sector union staff member, Dublin, June, 2018)

In 2012, economic slowdown and a loss of investor confidence limited the Spanish government's capacity to raise funds and stabilize the banking sector. Turning to the EU for support, up to €100 billion was made available for the recapitalization of its financial sector as part of the European Stability Mechanism, though only roughly €40 billion was used. The associated Troika-inspired restructuring of the Spanish financial sector led to the elimination of locally owned and public saving banks and their acquisition by larger banks, outcomes unpopular with the public (Medina and Correa, 2016). "The ECB policy to provide almost unlimited liquidity to these banks, and to purchase public debt in secondary markets, reduced the risk premium on Spain and facilitated adjustments in the banking sector" (Think tank official, Madrid, May, 2018) – in short, throughout the crisis, the banks could have never made it on their own, but some ended up much richer for it.

Comparisons and conclusions

The fiscal–financial backdrop for banking sector measures featured a combination of domestic economic imbalances, financial and housing bubbles, and exposure to international economic downturn. Some countries struggled with exchange rate concerns (like Canada with its reliance on international trade and Denmark because of its currency peg with the euro) and with supranational rules and impositions (like Eurozone monetary stability initiatives and bailout conditions for Ireland and Spain). In addition, there was monetary policy exhaustion through rock-bottom interest rates for all (albeit with some notable differences, like Denmark's defence of its currency peg through interest rate targeting). Commonalities continue through five themes that shape state-provided and crisis-borne banking sector support: 1) stimulus and guarantees such as credit underwriting, insurance support, co-lending, and other liquidity measures; 2) more direct bailouts through asset taking, and nationalization (often via bad banks); 3) various write-offs and taxpayer-borne risks associated with toxic assets and nationalization; 4) partnerships and privatization that include direct private sector participation in political decision-making processes and newly created government agencies; and 5) international pressures, namely the conditionality of the Troika but also ideological suasion or voluntary harmonization. As mentioned, these themes are not mutually exclusive nor nationally unique even if the details are specific to each country.

By way of additional comparison, without unduly repeating what was already covered earlier, a few trends in the saga of banking sector bailouts become clear. First, most notably, all governments established institutions to resolve bad debt. Canada handled its banking sector support through the Canada Mortgage Bond and the Insured Mortgage Purchase Program's mortgage-backed securities schemes with a purchase plan 'strikingly similar to the original US TARP (Troubled Asset Relief Plan) bailout proposal [...] to directly purchase poorly performing mortgage loans from the big US banks' (Walks, 2014: 271). In Denmark, the state-owned enterprise Financial Stability Corporation was tasked with settling claims and bank resolution. The Irish government established the National Asset Management Agency (NAMA) to remove risky or toxic assets from banks. As discussed, though initially the ownership of its assets was supposed to be shared 49 to 51 per cent with the private sector, its assets became fully public once the state took control of NAMA's participants. In Spain, SAREB, the Asset Management Company for Assets Arising from Bank Restructuring, handled troubled assets purchased with senior debt (lower-risk debt, often with collateral that can be used to prioritize its repayment).

While the state was integral to crisis resolution, providing liquidity and reinforcing confidence in the financial system, support also varied among the four countries, with banking sector rescue going beyond the state to include supra-national authorities in some cases. Canada was exceptional, not because of its avoidance of any systemic problems or a conventional bailout, but through its proactive absorption of 'securitized mortgage assets, many of which were issued under compromised lending standards from Canadian financial institutions' (Walks, 2014: 277). The response in Denmark, consistent with its 'negotiated economy' involving decisions and responsibility shared among private and public actors (Kluth and Lynggaard, 2013; Woll, 2014), was made evident through the design of its Private Reserve Fund for Distressed Banks and, later, in the Financial Stability Corporation, as institutions key to crisis management. Moreover, the government was willing to limit its support for failing banks, which lead to a downgrade of Danske Bank and five other lenders, 'making funding costs soar for the Danish industry' (Woll, 2014: 160).

In Ireland and Spain, the restructuring drew on a significant amount of public funds, with limited prospects for return on investment. In Spain, for example, 'FROB's accounts already estimate a scant recovery of its investment' (Huerta, 2019: 34). Both countries also conducted nationalizations, with the Irish government taking over Anglo Irish Bank and becoming a major shareholder in most Irish banks, and with Spain creating Bankia, an entity formed by merging several failed *cajas*. Moreover, with Ireland experiencing a sovereign debt crisis and Spain facing a crisis of confidence and real economy collapse, both requested and received EU assistance with its associated terms and conditions.

Governments also clearly played a role in economic stimulus, with some strategies including bailouts for non-financial businesses like in the automobile industry and for infrastructure. Canada focused on the nationally important automobile industry, and Spain supported car buyers. Ireland, on the other hand, saw its government using stimulus to guarantee deposits and other liabilities in the financial sector. While all stimulus packages involved some degree of national variation, Ireland's blanket guarantee (drawing on its national pension sovereign wealth fund for stimulus) is a distinction worth highlighting.

All four provided liquidity support. Spain provided liquidity resolution through its deposit guarantee scheme; deposit guarantees increased in Ireland, Spain and Denmark, and Canada relied on existing state-owned enterprises like the Canada Deposit Insurance Corporation and Canada Mortgage and Housing Corporation. Asset resolution involved writing down tens of billions in losses. Distressed assets were commonly transferred to the public sector in all four countries, though in Denmark this featured public-private ownership. Bank capitalization was conducted in Spain through state guarantees and liquidity facilities (the deposit guarantee scheme and EU-funded recapitalization); Denmark used its Danmarks Nationalbank; Ireland purchased preference shares and drew on EU support; and Canada used its Insured Mortgage Purchase Program.

Nationalization occurred in Ireland and Spain, bank mergers in Denmark and Spain.

Government debt run up is an important component of banking sector protection and recovery. In the aggregate, over 2007 to 2017, Canadian gross government debt to GDP rose from 87 to 109 per cent, peaking at 115 per cent in 2015; Danish debt went from 35 to 48 per cent, peaking at 61 per cent in 2012; Ireland saw debt rise from 27 to 77 per cent, with a high of 132 per cent in 2013; and Spanish government debt to GDP went from 42 per cent in 2007 to 116 per cent in 2017, with a high of 119 per cent in 2014 (see Figure 1 in Chapter 1).

Low interest rates in the 2000s, together with capital mobility, led to easy lending, producing housing and construction market inflation, and credit bubbles. Vulnerability to world markets and exchange rate pressures, domestic and regional institutional disequilibria, and secondary market investment either encouraged or ignored by national regulators, indicates a combination of policy choices and structural pressures ready to boil over. The subprime meltdown, credit crunch (particularly in interbank lending) and Great Recession were serious pressures unto themselves, but equally they served to expose already-existing crises. In class terms, footloose finance emerged through a long-run concerted effort by the state in all four countries to encourage risky banking, debt-fuelled consumption and investment, along with asset and property market inflation. When the house of cards collapsed, state commitments to capital proved resilient. Timid and temporary stimulus was dwarfed by massive commitments to banks and investors. Trenchant austerity completes the picture. How exactly these austerity measures were justified rhetorically will be examined in the next chapter, on the politics of public budgeting, which looks at the discourse of public sector finance in the crisis period.

Returning to Table 1 in Chapter 1, with regard to the issue of debt and finance, we see institutionalization through the mobilization and reconfiguration of existing public sector agencies/monies in Ireland through the National Asset Management Agency, its public pension plan-cum-blanket banking guarantee mechanism; and in Canada through the

Table 2: Varieties of austerity – dynamics or degrees of debt and finance

	Institutionalization	Insulation	Insinuation
Debt and finance	Exceptionalism: mobilizing new or existing government or public-private agencies for private sector debt relief and the socialization of toxic assets by the state	Bailouts and guarantees: size of contribution, 'haircuts', terms and conditions	Return on bailout

Canada Housing and Mortgage Corporation, a state-owned enterprise once taking care of social housing and first-time homebuyers, now involved in mortgage-backed securities and helping with underwriting and liquidity, together with other guarantees for banking through similar state-owned enterprises like the Canada Deposit Insurance Corporation. Denmark saw public-private forms of asset nationalization through the newly created Financial Stability Corporation and guidance by the Rangvid Committee. In Spain the existing deposit guarantee scheme operated alongside the bespoke Fund for the Orderly Restructuring of the Banking Sector and the bad bank agency SAREB. We consider these measures to be 'exceptional' in three ways: as unique and urgent in the face of the 2008 global financial crisis, as massive in scope and scale, and as demonstrative of the preferential treatment given to banking and finance particularly when contrasted with the deleterious implications of austerity within the public sector, and for social services, the labour force and vulnerable communities living already precarious lives (explored in subsequent chapters).

Whether the banking protections at issue were large or small, public or private, nationalized bailouts or more limited forms of liquidity support, altogether this chapter has shown that just as most countries around the world were poised for austerity reforms and cutbacks, the banking sector was being insulated for the most part from toxic collateral damage of its own making. The exact terms and conditions of public contributions, along with nature of haircuts imposed (Denmark) or not (Ireland) on bondholders, are of course important details, but the fact remains that banking and finance were never reformed to any profound degree in the decade that followed – even the much-maligned global derivatives market (Helleiner et al, 2018). Taken together, not only have some countries (Denmark) trumpeted making money from banking sector support, but overall these developments indicate that austerity programmes, having emerged so quickly on the heels of crisis-era bailouts and stimulus, insinuate that public sectors, staff and programme recipients are to blame for state debt run up and economic fragility – letting the banking sector culprits off the hook. As the next chapter indicates, selling austerity involved dodging the realities of tremendous spending commitments made to capital in the early period of the crisis.

3

Selling Restraint

Public budgets might be thought of as technocratic documents that set out planned revenues and expenditures for the fiscal year. But with fiscal policy connected to all aspects of government activity, budgets hold significant repercussions for a wide range of actors including the state, private enterprise and labour. Budgets focus the relationship between government and economy: where and for whom spending and revenue are directed or diverted, implicating existing institutions, empowering (new or established) agencies, insulating or exposing particular segments of society, and insinuating degrees of blame and responsibility for both the good and bad times. Budgetary analyses must therefore consider the political economy context of fiscal crises, revenue and spending, and the relationship between state expenditures and private enterprise. The (re)allocation of public money by the state reflects the political priorities and choices of government.

The normative dimension of budget allocation is a prime expression of its politics. Consequently, the pre-eminent position of ministries of finance within the state ought to be no surprise. Likewise, monetary policy, commonly the preserve of independent central banks, affects not only the money supply but also interest and exchange rates, conditioning the behaviour of many economic sectors and government departments. Other strictures like balanced budget legislation and cost control equally pressure public decision makers, often with more to say on expenditures than revenues (especially revenue beyond taxation).

In this chapter on selling restraint through the politics of public sector budgeting, we analyze the fiscal narratives of Canada, Denmark, Ireland and Spain through a political economy lens that understands fiscal policy, public sector spending, cuts and reallocations to be intrinsically political activities, which fundamentally delineate the contours of the state–society relationship through changes (or lack thereof) on both revenue and expenditure sides of the ledger. In terms of national snapshots of how these countries got to austerity, we note diverse exposure to the 2008 crisis and thus diverse post-crisis financial sector support, stimulus and social spending.

To reiterate some of what was covered in the previous chapter, Denmark's banking sector and more generally the economies of Spain and Ireland were hit hard by the global financial crisis. Ireland's banking sector was in meltdown by 2008–09 and the government responded with dramatic protections for creditors and assets. Ireland was the only country in the Eurozone to provide a blanket guarantee – sovereign protection of its six big banks (Boyle and Mulreany, 2015: 284). The blanket guarantee turned potential paper losses for private investors into substantial public debt, with roughly €64 billion shifted to taxpayers through its bad bank scheme to nationalize toxic private sector assets. Carswell (2010) describes this manoeuvre as 'social[izing] the cost of decades-long misadventures of runaway banks whose managers and private shareholders enjoyed the spoils of bumper profits through the boom'. Ireland used its National Pensions Reserve Fund to finance the banking sector guarantee. Established during the 'Celtic Tiger' boom years and funded by Exchequer contributions aimed at social welfare and public service pensions, its €32 billion fund was gutted by the bank guarantee.

Spain also suffered a serious banking sector crisis and bailed out several banks, leading to a run up of public sector debt and deficit. Spanish banks had been borrowing en masse through the interbank market mainly for the purpose of funding the construction sector through property development and mortgage loans, and the credit boom soon produced a property market bubble (Quaglia and Royo, 2015: 489–91). Their investments were not focused on what later became toxic debt in derived financial products or off-balance sheet loans; liabilities were mainly due to defaults on property-related loans through the collapse of the construction sector with nearly 60 per cent of bank loans tethered to the real estate market (Quaglia and Royo, 2015: 493, 500). Bank bailouts and nationalization soon followed; Spain created a bad bank to absorb toxic assets in the real estate sector, and centralized banking sector governance by shifting this away from regional authorities. Similar reforms continued even though Spain required less than half of the Troika funds received and loan repayment began much earlier than expected. The national government voluntarily extended the EU's Bank Recovery and Resolution Directive in 2015, eliminating locally owned and public savings banks.

Like Ireland's Celtic Tiger, Denmark was also heralded as an economic 'miracle' in the 1990s (Andersen, 2011). Growth in the 1990s led Danish banks to borrow from international financial markets, acquire foreign banks and assets, and lend with exuberance domestically. This produced a housing bubble in the years leading up to the crisis. When the global financial crisis turned into a credit crunch in the latter portion of 2008, interbank lending was squeezed and the lack of liquidity quickly exposed a serious deposit deficit in Danish banks (40 per cent of GDP) (Carstensen, 2013). The government introduced stability and bailout packages between 2008 and 2010, which included guaranteeing deposits and unsecured debt at distressed banks, toxic asset acquisition and liquidation, and government loans for distressed banks. In 2011, two regional banks failed, and systemically important financial institutions were bailed out.

Unlike many other countries around the world, Canada did not suffer a banking sector collapse and thus did not have to bailout its banks through the nationalization of toxic assets (for nuance, see Chapter 1). The federal government did, however, provide $200 billion in banking sector guarantees through the temporary Business Credit Availability Program overseen by state-owned agencies. In the automobile sector, the federal and Ontario governments provided General Motors and Chrysler, two of the 'Big Three', what was initially described as up to $4 billion in short-term repayable loans (Department of Finance Canada, 2009: 173), but which would later amount to a $2.6 billion write off – a taxpayer-funded bailout by any name (Beeby, 2018).

The issue for this chapter becomes how these governments sold austerity to the general public so quickly after massive outlays for capital. We politicize austerity by examining the discourse of government budget framing, focusing on the immediate crisis period of 2008–13 that set the stage politically, ideologically and economically for the entire decade (2008–18). Three sections make up the chapter: the austerity initiatives announced by each state in this early period; thematic trends in the political economy of public sector budgeting, reflecting the political priorities and discursive choices of government; and comparison/contrast by way of conclusion.

Post-2008 budget cuts and public sector reforms

Austerity is often institutionalized to varying degrees through structural (not only cyclical) changes in budget spending and associated programme reforms that insulate or expose certain segments of society to the ravages of crisis and retrenchment. Irish austerity from 2009 forward postponed public sector pay increases, reduced social welfare payments, imposed health levies and higher taxes on public sector pensions, increased VAT and sin taxes (alcohol, tobacco and gambling), and slashed spending on education, health, child benefits and social welfare. Enhanced outsourcing at the local level and higher user fees deeply affected municipal governance. Not only a reaction to 2008, an Irish policy window was forced open by motivated austerians. The 'Wright Report' blamed tripartite social partnership and government programme spending under coalition governments for overwhelming the government's budget process, undercutting flexibility and responsiveness (Wright, 2010). The government's National Recovery Plan 2011–2014 laid out a strategy whereby the 'budget system will be comprehensively reformed and updated to bring greater sustainability to the management of public finances; to achieve maximum value for money in public expenditures; and guard against the emergence of structural budgetary imbalances' (Government of Ireland, 2010: 59). The Irish Government Economic and Evaluation Service was also established in 2012 to ensure 'value for money' and assist with policy and programme reform.

Troika-related restructuring has also been blamed for Irish austerity and its deleterious effects, evidenced by the infamous Trichet Letter, wherein then-European Central Bank leader Jean Claude Trichet told Ireland in November 2010 that it must apply for a bailout, spelling out Ireland's subordination to the Troika – no EU assistance without an Irish state restructuring plan. However, Troika-imposed austerity was foreshadowed domestically by the Department of Finance's 'McCarthy Report', which recommended broadly similar forms of restructuring – public sector spending cuts, redundancies, labour market reforms, marketization, and privatization (McCarthy et al, 2009). Irish austerity would endure for years, until at least budget 2015 which brought some modest reversals through extra spending and tax cuts.

Spanish austerity involved imposing debt controls on regional governments; greater discipline through new budget rules for regional governments such as standardized accounting; public reporting procedures; forced rationalized plans; risk assessments; central approval for long-term operations; and adjustments applied to fiscal transfers from the centre (Zapico-Goni, 2015: 219–20). Changes also affected important pillars of the welfare state, namely pensions and labour market policies, 'with a potential[ly] "transformative" effect' (Guillén and Pavolini, 2017: 141). Spain had relatively low levels of public debt going into the crisis and was thus in a stronger economic position than other Southern European countries. Its fiscal accounts were buoyed by the property market bubble that enabled increases in public spending, without deficit, through tax revenue and economic growth, and public sector compensation was largely controlled in the period leading up to the crisis (Di Mascio and Natalini, 2015: 142). When the bubble burst in 2008, deficits grew and revenues dropped off. Economic deterioration initially prompted stimulus measures but by 2009 this turned to austerity through the Stability

Programmes (2009, 2011), the Law of Sustainable Economy (2011), a constitutional change capping future deficits at 0.4 per cent (2011), cuts in public sector spending, increased personal and corporate income tax, and value added tax. By 2012, balanced budget requirements were imposed on all subnational governments and public spending was cut once more. Pensions were de-linked from inflation and indexed to the structural position of the social security budget. Centralization through nationally determined deficit reduction goals and public sector rationalization are a clear legacy of this era.

Danish stimulus, introduced in 2009, was followed by austerity through budget cuts and welfare reforms in 2010, involving reforms to early retirement, disability pension, and the flex-job scheme, along with cuts to unemployment benefits, municipal public sector budgets, wage growth and some taxes. Consultation with traditional social partners in the labour movement and employers' federation dwindled. Like Spain, Denmark also introduced balanced budget legislation for municipalities. Annual Financial Agreements negotiated between the Ministry of Finance and the municipalities embedded cost controls and fiscal allocations that reflected limits imposed by the ministry. If municipalities overspent or otherwise did not comply with Financial Agreements, they were subject to a financial penalty the following year (Mailand, 2014: 422). Given that municipalities were free to prioritize spending however they liked and to allocate funds accordingly, some greatly underspent in 2011 and 2012, suggesting the internalization of budget discipline: municipalities were spending less than they could for fear that their costs would exceed revenues. Self-imposed austerity meant both less spending than budgeted and less than allowed for under the Financial Agreements (Mailand, 2014: 423).

Some say the crisis created a policy window in Denmark, similar to Ireland, by providing 'an opportunity for launching not only structural labor market reforms that had stalled amid party politicking for years, but also institutional reforms of the budgetary framework' (Jensen and Davidsen, 2015: 174). Danish municipalities were especially targeted for budget reforms and spending restraint in the wake of 2008. Of the three levels of budgeting in the country – state, regional and municipal – it is the local governments that are charged with providing public services relating to welfare, schools, day care, elder care, administration, care for disabled people, other aspects of health care, and environmental stewardship (Mailand, 2014: 420). Municipalities are the single largest employer of the three levels of government despite structural reform in 2007 cutting the number of municipalities to a third of their original size by amalgamating 273 into 98. Roughly a fifth of municipal budgets were cut by over 4 per cent in 2011, and almost a tenth were cut by over 7 per cent (Mailand, 2014: 421, 425). Subcontracting was also promoted with a non-binding target set in 2011 that over a third of public services would be exposed to competition (Mailand, 2014: 420).

Canada's crisis was mainly one of proximity, owing to its long-standing reliance on the US economy for exports and investments, and its vulnerability to world prices, with Canadian interest and exchange rates largely tethered to market dynamics abroad. Budget surpluses at the federal level were common in the years leading up to the crisis, but with global economic deterioration the federal surplus turned to deficit when tax revenue declined and spending on social services and income support rose (as automatic stabilizers). The government initially denied Canada's exposure to the global financial crisis, then implemented a timid stimulus plan with the bulk dedicated to automobile sector bailouts and liquidity support for banking (through underwriting and co-lending if required) (McBride and Whiteside, 2011). In 2010, the federal government signalled its intention to terminate spending on extraordinary measures as quickly as possible. The politics of austerity in this country were not strictly fiscal in nature given that the federal government announced it was seeking to balance the budget 'without raising taxes, cutting transfers to persons, including those for seniors, children and the unemployed, or cutting transfers to other levels of government that support health care and social services,' and nominal government spending had increased by 2013 (Whiteside, 2016a: 349). The climate of austerity and purported aim of balancing the budget were instead leveraged to justify privatization and structural reform of public sector programmes, pensions, benefits and civil service employment.

While all four countries experienced and reacted to the global financial crisis in different ways, Canada is nonetheless an outlier. Not only was the recession relatively mild in Canada, the banking system remained stable, and there were no supranational directives to follow. Yet Canada did pursue fiscal consolidation, public asset sales, public sector redundancies, restructuring and cuts. Examples include the federal budget 2010, which sought to save $17.6 billion over five years through government department spending cuts and freezes to some operating budgets; likewise, budget 2012 introduced cuts totalling $5.2 billion, targeting the federal public service in particular through the elimination of roughly 19,000 jobs. In Canada's largest subnational economy and population centre, Ontario, budget 2012 introduced cuts to 11 of 26 departments, and targeted public sector wage restraint and pensions in a bid to pay down a deficit incurred through economic downturn. Public sector union officials called these initiatives a 'slap across the face' given that business, not labour, was clearly responsible for the economic woes of government at the time (CBC, 2012).

What happened next and how: selling public sector austerity

A government's budget can be construed to be a technical document rationally setting out the planned revenues and expenditures for the fiscal year to come and beyond. A century of budget studies, however, suggest the budget is much more complex and is shaped by political, economic, social and cultural factors and forces (Frank, 2006). Budgets and budgetary policies are not isolated 'but are rather connected to all socio-economic spheres of government activity, and consequently have important repercussions for a wide range of actors' (Damhuis and Karremans, 2017: 1272). As such, government budgets 'are the outcome of complex policy processes involving the nature of the decision-making institutions, the preferences of decision-makers (organised by political parties), and informational signals from a changing environment' (Jones et al, 2009: 61).

Examining budget speeches or their equivalent at the height of the crisis (roughly, 2008–13) illustrates how budget allocations are framed and how winners and losers in society are presented, thus connecting to the dynamics and degrees of insinuation involved with austerity measures. Exogenous forces shape and inform these choices along with ideological predilections and the prevailing balance of political and economic forces. In short, concepts in the budget are political statements not simply of who or what is getting how much in public monies but a representation of the mind of the state and, of course, the power relations that compose a particular way of knowing and meaning making. Budget speeches and qualitative explanations of budget arcana are also significant because this is one of the rare moments in political economy where the sentiments of the general public are appealed and attended to. Six thematic trends dominate the budget discourse of these four countries during the height of post-2008 austerity: 1) fiscal narratives and budget framing; 2) how the nation is characterized; 3) justifications for crisis management via austerity; 4) establishing the priorities of crisis-era governance; 5) rationalizations of reform beyond merely cuts; and 6) appeals to European citizenship.

Fiscal narratives and budget framing

The international crisis is presented as an external force or raging storm, an exogenous shock to Denmark's otherwise healthy public and private sector economies. 'It presents us with challenges. Tailwind has for the time being been replaced by headwind' (Rasmussen, 2009: 2), it is a source of 'pressure' (Thorning-Schmidt, 2011: 2); although, 'we have weathered the crisis better than feared' (Rasmussen, 2010: 1). Government must have a strong hand at the helm: 'we must bring Denmark safely through the crisis' (Thorning-Schmidt, 2012: 1). Turbulent economic times ahead are a certainty. Slow growth is inevitable and unemployment is 'unavoidable' (Rasmussen, 2009: 2). Denmark is asked to prepare for this, and its government is at the ready.

In Ireland, the economic crisis is characterized as turmoil caused by both global economic factors and previous domestic mismanagement. Ireland is frequently described as a 'small open economy' exposed to international volatility in trade, finance and British monetary devaluation. However, the emphasis from the finance minister is on domestic miscalculations. 'With the benefit of hindsight, it is clear that more should have been done to contain the housing market. We [government] became too reliant on the construction sector for growth and tax receipts' (Lenihan, 2009a: 1).

The diagnosis by late 2009 is that 'the economy went into reverse' because Ireland lost competitiveness during its boom years, through the property bubble bursting, and via an international banking sector crisis that led to a worldwide recession (Lenihan, 2009b: 3). While responsibility is domesticated, and located mainly within the public sector, with many aspects of this 'reversal' the responsibility of particular banks or private sector investors and agents is glossed over and chalked up to the impersonal vagaries of the market. 'Restoring our competitive edge' is all that is left for governance purposes given that the banking sector guarantee is a fait accompli and the bubble has already burst in property markets (Lenihan, 2009b: 4).

Austerity for government and internal labour market devaluation are the only options given the monetary union and Ireland's reliance on export markets. 'The single currency has provided huge protection [...] but membership of monetary union also means devaluation is not an option. Therefore, the adjustment process must be made by way of reductions in wages, prices, profits, and rents', wages being the obvious focus of government policy; 'put simply, we have priced ourselves out of the market' (Lenihan, 2009b: 4). As if Ireland overindulged during the holidays, the economy needs to 'work off the excesses of the boom' (Lenihan, 2010: 3), that is, doing what markets do best: self-correcting. The change in government in 2011 added blame for the previous government's 'reckless spending' to the list of crisis causes (Lenihan, 2011: 9). By 2012, with the economy on the uptick, government had completely reversed the cause of the crisis. No longer a capitalist crisis, or even one associated with a bubble, international banking or export competitiveness, if 'the Irish financial crisis could be summarised in one word – debt – national debt and personal debt' would be the culprit (Noonan, 2012: 5).

By 2013, the Spanish government presented the crisis as one of debt and spending recklessness, not international political and economic dynamics with the prime minister stating, 'we are paying a very high price for learning that we can not spend what we do not have, that we can not live on loan for ever and that we have to count slowly all the money we borrow' (Rajoy, 2013), and the budget minister hoping to 'prolong our effort to clean up public finances' (Minder, 2012).

Despite avoiding the worst of the global financial crisis (no banking sector meltdown, no housing market collapse, and no need for very large bailouts), enacting a moderate stimulus package in the face of deteriorating conditions abroad, and not being part of a monetary union, Canada also avoided any budgetary, ideological or other structural constraints associated with EU-style considerations. The crisis is thus presented as a moment when Canada is 'outperforming our peers', recognizing that 'the global economy remains fragile [...] [and] traditional trading partners face serious long-term economic challenges' (Flaherty, 2012: 4). In this context, Canadians were asked to 'plan for the future' (Flaherty, 2012: 4).

The budget narrative story becomes more checkered for subnational Canadian governments. Government of Ontario budget speeches beginning in 2007 trumpet their fiscal conservatism, gloating that cuts exceeded campaign slogans, 'we promised to save $750 million but we actually saved more than $800 million' (Ontario, 2007). And after securing re-election in 2008, one of the first statements put out by the Liberal government celebrated cutting business taxes and eliminating debt under its previous mandate. By 2009, Ontario found itself 'in the middle of a global economic and financial storm' (Ontario, 2009), and the portent was ominous: revenue was down and a near-$4 billion deficit was in store. After a brief foray into stimulus spending in 2009–10, austerity loomed. Under the banner of 'Responsible Government', government connected public sector job and spending cuts with preserving public sector services in this tough economic time (Ontario, 2009). In comparison with previous economic crises, Ontario's share of Canadian job losses rose from 30 to 36 per cent in the period 2008–11 (Chan et al, 2011: 14).

Characterizing the nation

The Danish 'character' – that is, the internal or national feature of the public at large and of the public and private economies – was presented as resilient, responsible and self-sacrificing. Danes were encouraged to 'dig deep down into ourselves and find the Danish resilience that will bring us safely through the storm' (Rasmussen, 2009: 2). The crisis was a moment where Danes are asked to 'work hard' and 'make difficult choices' but 'we can do it when we stand together' (Thorning-Schmidt, 2011: 1–2).

Ireland, by contrast, was characterized as having a 'false sense of invincibility' through previous economic success, and 'a lot has changed since then' (Lenihan, 2009a: 10). Ireland was now 'facing the challenge of this nation's life', one of 'adversity', a 'downward spiral' and 'economic distress' (Lenihan, 2009a: 10). Fiscal policy was the mechanism to transform the 'way in which we do business in this country' (Lenihan, 2009a: 10). The personalization of the crisis as being the fault of Irish mismanagement only deepened as time went on: 'our self confidence as a nation has been shaken' (Lenihan, 2009b: 1). But Ireland could be proud that structural reform measures were 'commended' by international bodies and international markets (Lenihan, 2009b: 1). Austerity was the way for Ireland to 'start believing in itself again', to 'rediscover our optimism and our self-belief', healing the trauma of crisis and overcoming a recession that 'has knocked us off our stride' (Lenihan, 2009b: 12). The road to recovery involved government acknowledging its 'mistakes' and correcting them through austerity (Lenihan, 2010: 10).

Buoyed by circumstance, Canada boasted of having 'banks [that] are the soundest in the world' and a *Forbes* magazine ranking of 'the best place in the world for businesses to grow and create jobs' (Flaherty, 2012: 4). Government celebrated having 'the lowest overall tax rate on new business investment among major advanced economies' (Flaherty, 2012: 4). Confidence in the future required 'a return to balanced budgets' (Flaherty, 2012: 5). Yet, historical Canadian figures can also be leaned on here; austerity was not merely a current need but a policy with recurring appeal. The finance minister quoted a cabinet minister from the first decade of the 20th century: 'in times of prosperity prepare for trouble' (Flaherty, 2013: 4). In his subsequent budget speech, Flaherty positioned austerity as foundational to Canada itself: 'nearly 150 years ago, Canada was founded with fiscal responsibility as its cornerstone' (2014: 1).

Avoiding national humiliation through an EU bailout 'at all costs' became essential for Spain. Government switched from earlier welfare and socially oriented crisis management to 'an epic rhetoric based on the ideas of necessity, responsibility and collective effort' (Ortega and Pascual-Ramsay cited in Dellepiane and Hardiman, 2013: 12). The emergency budget of 2010 dealt with the crisis through cuts to public sector salaries, pay freezes, changes in pension entitlements, elimination of dependency benefits and grants to infants (Dellepiane-Avellaneda and Hardiman, 2014).

Justifying crisis management via austerity

Of utmost importance, fiscal discipline and low debt were characterized as the 'responsible' orientation for Denmark's government, and fiscal balance constituted a 'sound' public economy (Rasmussen, 2009, 2010; Thorning-Schmidt, 2011). This held in both good times and bad. Rasmussen (2009: 4) added, 'We met the crisis with a sound public economy, because we spent the good years paying off debt.' And long run prudence meant that Denmark 'can pay the bill from the crisis in a responsible and proper manner' in contrast with other European countries having to take drastic measures (Rasmussen, 2010: 1; see also, Thorning-Schmidt, 2012: 3). Fiscal consolidation in its first few years was 'common sense' (Rasmussen, 2010: 12) or 'necessary' (Thorning-Schmidt, 2011: 2). By 2012, a familiar narrative was struck, that fiscal consolidation, modernization, rationalization and efficiencies within the public sector were necessary in 'safeguarding confidence in the Danish economy' (Thorning-Schmidt, 2012: 1).

Ireland and Denmark were strikingly similar in their orientation to public debt. 'We will consolidate, not indebt the economy. We will not pay debt with debt' (Rasmussen, 2010: 2). Lessons learned from the crisis related not to capitalist greed, banking sector fragilities, Troika overreach or vagaries of the market, but that austerity is of enduring benefit: 'a new realization that rests on old virtues. Well-managed and orderly finances. Living within one's means. Personal responsibility' (Rasmussen, 2010: 1). Danish prime ministers were silent on the banking sector bailouts and mainly ignored housing market dynamics (Thorning-Schmidt, 2011: 1).

Ireland was described as being in need of restoration and renewal. This was to be accomplished through public fiscal stability (aiming to restore investor confidence), fixing damage to the banking sector (credit being cast as the life blood of the Irish economy), regaining competitiveness by ending 'over-reliance on domestic spending' by 'driving down costs' locally (reducing public sector spending as a way of boosting exports), addressing unemployment through retraining, and improving a tarnished reputation within the EU and abroad (Lenihan, 2009a: 2–3). Living 'within our means' was now necessary; tax increases had 'reached the limit' (Lenihan, 2009b: 4). 'Excessive public sector spending on the back of the enviable but transient taxes of the boom added to the overheating of the economy' (Lenihan, 2010: 10).

Structural reforms to the Irish public sector shifted into prominence through austerity management: 'the problem is our expenditure base is too high and our revenue base is too low' (Lenihan, 2009a: 4). In conjunction with the European Commission, obligations were struck to ensure structural reform through a five-year consolidation plan that targeted long-lasting reform. A 'permanent reduction in the cost of the public payroll is an essential element of this plan' (Lenihan, 2009a: 5), to be accomplished through cuts in government salaries, workers, banning recruitment and promotion, a public sector pension levy, scaling public pensions down to match private pensions, and cuts in public service spending. A change in government in 2011 brought some renegotiation with the Troika, but ultimately government continued the push for domestic fiscal consolidation just as before.

Public sector employees and public services were put in the crosshairs: 'given that Public Service Pay and Social Welfare each account for about one third of all day to day spending, reductions in these two areas are unavoidable' (Lenihan, 2009b: 6). In this fashion government would 'secure our [Irish] economic future' (Lenihan, 2009b: 7). This is what a responsible government should do. Examples include pension reform (downward harmonization with the private sector, a higher minimum age of eligibility). 'The Government is determined to meet the immediate fiscal problems Ireland faces and, at the same time, to make far-reaching reforms for the future' (Lenihan, 2009b: 7). The choice was between 'safeguards' through cuts or 'put[ting] it all at risk' (Lenihan, 2009b: 7).

Despite Canada's relatively strong position, the national government nonetheless adopted an austerity stance in 2012. The finance minister justified fiscal restraint by saying, 'we have a rare opportunity to position our country for sustainable, long-term growth. Our government chooses prosperity' (Flaherty, 2012: 4). It would be 'short-sighted', 'dangerous' and 'irresponsible' to 'squander Canada's advantage' by raising taxes or increasing government spending (Flaherty, 2012: 5). With 'significant risks ahead' for trading partners and the global economy, Canada's stance of fiscal responsibility would avoid the reckless governance practices seen elsewhere: 'in uncertain global economic times, the most important contribution a government can make to bolster confidence and growth in a country is to maintain a sound fiscal position' (Flaherty, 2013: 3). In 2014, government trumpeted its 'record of strong, sound and consistent fiscal management', of paying down federal debt, lowering taxes on families and businesses, and 'mak[ing] sure our fiscal house was in order" especially important when 'few could see dark clouds on the horizon' (Flaherty, 2014: 1). Austerity, in other words, is needed in good times and bad; unlike stimulus, it is not extraordinary; unlike bank nationalization, it is not temporary.

In the Canadian province of Ontario, public sector pensions and public administration were targeted. The 2012 Drummond Report (Commission on the Reform of Ontario's Public Services), conceived at the height of cyclical economic problems but reaching deep into the realm of long-run public sector restructuring, was unambiguous: 'we cannot count on robust economic growth to resolve our fiscal challenge' (Commission on the Reform of Ontario's Public Services, 2012). Even once the budget was balanced, a sustainable fiscal environment was needed and this would come in the form of health, education and social service reforms, and wide-ranging adjacent changes to other aspects of government like immigration, natural resources, justice, labour relations, state-owned enterprises and intergovernmental relations. The guaranteed fund for public sector pensions was derided as out of step with the rest of the world. In all, 362 reforms were recommended to balance the books. Drummond was characterized by critics as unnecessarily gloomy and broad in scope, as if Ontario were Greece and overspending was the cause of the government deficits that emerged during the global financial crisis (examples can be seen in Stanford, 2012; Weir, 2012).

Austerity initiatives were justified by the Spanish government in several ways including the claim that the changes left the essential pillars of the welfare state untouched. However, there were deep cuts in child welfare, home care for older people, freezes on pensions, and pay cuts for civil servants, and while credit markets welcomed the news, other pointed out that the economically weak were paying the price (Tremlett and Moya, 2020).

A few months later, in July 2010, Zapatero described the switch from stimulus to austerity in 2010 as being 'necessary and indispensable' for the Spanish economy, particularly by appeal to the new international consensus: 'if during 2009 most of the experts and international bodies agreed on the need for fiscal stimulus packages, since May 2010 there is a need for fiscal consolidation and additional measures to foster growth' (Zapatero, 2010). There was a notion that being in the EU meant 'co-responsibility' – the need for all EU members to adopt harmonized fiscal practices – following the initiation of a financial rescue package for Greece, and because national 'specificities' of the Spanish economy led to domestic imbalances. An outdated growth model inherited from 1990s, when Spanish initiatives aimed to promote the construction sector and private indebtedness, was targeted 'because the crisis, although it was originated in the international financial system, it definitely showed the serious weakness of our Economy' (Zapatero, 2010: 5).

Prime Minister Zapatero equally invoked notions of collectivity and fairness to rationalize public sector austerity:

> this call to collective effort has to be accompanied by equity and justice in its distribution. These are the criteria we bore

> in mind when we agreed on the adjustments last May: we freeze pensions to avoid [...] their reduction; we reduced public wages [to not cut] social benefits to the rest of the citizens; we limited pharmacy benefits [to avoid] the calls for co-payments. (Zapatero, 2010: 11)

The subsequent Spanish finance minister, on the other hand, invoked neoclassical logics of crowding out private sector spending familiar to early roll-back neoliberalization of the 1970s/1980s:

> this is a financial crisis and a financial crisis cannot be solved with an increased deficit. We have to inexorably reduce public deficit, we must reduce it without hesitation, we have to reduce public deficit without delay because its need for financing is limiting the credit made available for the rest of the society. [...] Thus, there is no other way, there is no shortcut. This must be a straight path; we have to reduce public deficit. [...] Thus, achieving a balanced public budget is an absolute priority for unblocking the financing our country's economy. (Montoro, 2012: 4)

Priorities of crisis-era governance

With public and household economies cast as synonymous by Danish authorities, there was no room for discussion of Keynesian multipliers, or of the opportunities and wellbeing created by government debt, despite a clear emphasis on the welfare system in Denmark. Capitalist economic growth was framed as the basis of wellbeing: 'in reality it is quite simple: we must continue to be one of the most affluent countries in the world in order to be able to maintain and finance one of the best welfare societies in the world' (Rasmussen, 2009: 5). Rasmussen (2010: 2) claimed, 'It is quite simple. The prosperity of society is derived from private enterprises only.' Even a change in government in 2011 did little to alter the refrain. No socialist vision seems to have informed the Social Democrat party, whose leader considered reforms were needed 'so that we can afford welfare' (Thorning-Schmidt, 2011: 1), and that 'a well-run public sector is a cornerstone of Danish community and solidarity, of our welfare society' (Thorning-Schmidt, 2011: 10).

The crisis was transformative, and affirmative, providing the prime minister with a platform from which to foreshadow a shift in fiscal policy, 'the financial crisis should, if anything, have taught us that we must earn the money before we share it out. We must be razor-sharp in how we prioritise. We must ensure sound public finances' (Rasmussen, 2010: 2). He continued, 'in today's stern reality – after the global economic crisis – we cannot improve our welfare in the same way we have done previously' (Rasmussen, 2010: 5). And, by 2011, the cart was put before the horse, the crisis was transformed into one caused by public imbalance. Bringing public balance sheets into the black was touted as preventing the economy from 'spin[ning] out of control again' (Thorning-Schmidt, 2011: 3).

Things were fundamentally different after the crisis.

> It is no use longing for the good old days. The 2010s are new times compared with the 1990s and 2000s. And we must use these new times as a springboard for new opportunities [...] Therefore, the Government will introduce an expenditure ceiling for the state, municipalities and regions. (Thorning-Schmidt, 2011: 10)

The Danish national government, over several years and with different parties in power, consistently and with greater compassion than the other countries, acknowledged the scourge of unemployment. But even here, it was not capitalism or a capitalist crisis that was to blame but job seekers. The government set out 'strong initiatives to prevent unemployment', such as practical training: 'knowledge and education are the best defence' (Rasmussen, 2009: 2). Parents were held responsible for youth unemployment through a change in the child benefit scheme, the young person would only receive funds if they were in work, school or another similar activity. Municipalities were held responsible as well; they were to oversee the personal education plans of youth aged 15 to 17, echoes of the nanny state liberal economies were once warned about.

Fiscal, structural, programme and legislative changes were targeted under Irish austerity, 'provid[ing] the basis for a renewed economy that will lead to job creation' (Noonan, 2012: 2). Doing more with less and efficiency gains were needed in Ireland, taking the form of using private finance, public-private partnerships, asset sales, sale and leaseback arrangements and so on, to cut direct public outlays for infrastructure (Lenihan, 2009a: 6). Despite being ambitions that have either been sought or actively pursued for a long time (see the reports by McCarthy et al, 2009, and Wright, 2010, both described earlier), it is only now that reforms could be described as imperative, unavoidable and the path to sustainability. The crisis opened the opportunity to conduct an efficiency review of local authorities, local authorities being 'a key driver of cost for business' (Lenihan, 2009b: 9).

The corporate tax rate, Ireland's tax haven status, was never touched, this being 'a key aspect of our inward investment strategy' (Lenihan, 2009a: 6). This narrative was maintained even after a change in government: 'much of Ireland's growth at present can be attributed to the attractiveness of Ireland for inward investment [...] The Government have [*sic*] successfully protected this [12.5%] rate even under international pressure and given our fiscal state' (Lenihan, 2011: 3). Other tax increases were part of the austerity package, mainly regressive taxes such as hiking the VAT and multiple rounds of sin tax hikes on alcohol, tobacco and the like. Municipalities were now enabled to collect property tax for the first time through the Local Property Tax Act 2013 and encouraged to use tax space in a competitive fashion from 2015 (Noonan, 2012: 7). New fees on water metering were also to be a source of service funding for local authorities (leading to much social strife; see Chapter 7). A capital gains tax incentive was also announced, encouraging property market recovery (and making the same mistakes as before?), along with enabling legislation for commercial property and real estate investment trusts (REITs) (Noonan, 2012: 4). There is a connection here to the National Asset Management Agency (NAMA) discussed in Chapter 2, as described by an interviewee:

> 'One of the senior executives in asset management in NAMA, left NAMA in 2012 – late 2012, early '13 – and set up what's called Hibernia REIT, which is the first Irish REIT, and is now involved in again a lot of those properties that are being developed on the Docklands.' (Irish private sector union staff member, Dublin, June, 2018)

The unique blanket guarantee offered to the largest Irish banks was, however, explained as being in the interest of all:

> our sole objective is to ensure that households can access credit for homeloans and consumer credit, that small and medium sized businesses can fund their enterprises, that deposit-holders can have confidence that their money is secure and protected, and that international investors are satisfied about the stability of our banking system. (Lenihan, 2009a: 7)

> We took these measures not for the sake of the banks but for the sake of our economy. (Lenihan, 2009b: 3)

While the Irish government came to own 25 per cent of the large banks, this was cast as 'radical' and temporary – pre-privatization, with assets to be resold over time (Lenihan, 2009a: 8). Enhancing the surveillance capacities of the Central Bank of Ireland was offered as the major salve to prevent a similar meltdown in the future, there is no significant structural reform of the banking sector offered. Given that the country's sovereign wealth fund, the National Pensions Reserve Fund, was gutted to save the banks, the government offered the following justification: 'it is not credible to suggest we could have retained a sovereign wealth fund while expecting others to make resources available to us' (Lenihan, 2010: 3) – this, despite major creditors in Irish bank assets being non-nationals: US, British, German and offshore investors.

The crisis, it appears, did little if anything to dislodge the Irish commitment to neoliberalism; in fact, they doubled down on their embrace. There was no new path as described by Denmark; instead, Ireland sought to regain the glory days of Celtic Tiger labour flexibility, international competitiveness in exports and capital investment (as a tax haven), and light touch regulations. Ireland focused on getting back to 'mid-1990s [drivers of growth]: flexibility and adaptability in the labour market' (Lenihan, 2009a: 8; 2011: 9). The priority was for the 'economy [to] return to being driven by sustainable export-led growth, rather than by domestic demand. To do so [...] price and cost structure must fall relative to [Ireland's] trading partners' (Lenihan, 2009a: 8). Government spending was 'out of control' before the crash (Lenihan, 2010: 3). By 2010, the Fiscal Responsibility Law was going to 'ensure that the principle of keeping the public finances on a sustainable footing is binding in law' (Lenihan, 2010: 10).

For Canada, government spending restraint and redundancies, a 'leaner and more efficient' public sector, was only 'common sense' (Flaherty, 2012: 5). As such, budget 2013 'contained the smallest increase in discretionary spending in nearly 20 years' (Flaherty, 2013: 3). Consolidation featured government cuts, of 'getting our own fiscal house in order' (Flaherty, 2014: 3). Government employment and the internal configuration of the bureaucracy and programme provision were considered distinct from the rest of the society: 'we did not do this [austerity restructuring] on the backs of ordinary Canadians or Canadians in need, or at the expense of our provinces and territories' (Flaherty, 2014: 3). However, even with its relatively healthy position, any deviation was thought to be unwise: 'a return to surplus is not a license to spend recklessly' and taxes must be kept low (Flaherty, 2014: 4). Ontario's budget speeches linked budget balancing with long run growth, charting a 'path to balance' (Flaherty, 2012, 2013).

In Spain's 2012 debate on the Organic Law 2/2012 of Budget Stability and Financial Sustainability, the speech by Minister of Finance Montoro described why balanced budget legislation was needed and the centralization of budget authority was justified:

> we are all in the same in Spain, the State of the Autonomies, without hesitation, without nooks and no alternative approaches. This is what we do with this Law' […] [the law is] necessary to regain confidence [and to] restore the credibility of Spain in the eyes of our European partners, it is also a very important step for Spain to become a leading country, a trustworthy partner in the international community and the international finances. In short, it is a step to restore confidence and then to make possible Spain's economic recovery. (Montoro, 2012)

Public ministries were forewarned: the budget law 'prevents any of the public administrations [from jeopardizing] the financial solvency and credibility [of] the rest' (Montoro, 2012). Other measures provided by the Law outlined by the speaker were: public debt repayment was prioritized above all other public expenditures and public debt (not only deficit) was now included as an element of financial sustainability (adopting a 60 per cent threshold of public debt in line with EU dictates).

Rationalizations of reform, beyond merely cuts

A unique refrain in Denmark surrounds the belief that government's key role is to ensure an adequate labour supply – this is 'a core aim of Danish governments' according to Thorning-Schmidt (2011). Rule changes such as eligibility tightening for welfare recipients were part of the austerity package but justified using paternalistic or moralistic reasoning, sometimes even demonization by suggesting some are benefiting at the expense of those who really need support.

The flex-job scheme was reformed for moral reasons, again set within an austerity context. An example of a moral appeal was Rasmussen's rhetorical question:

> Is it right to tell a girl of 23 that she will never be able to take care of herself? […] Flexi-jobs must be targeted at the people who need them […] Those capable must take responsibility for themselves, so that those in need of a helping hand are taken care of and can move on with their lives. (Rasmussen, 2010: 7)

The disability pension was reformed for equally moralistic concerns, 'so that everyone has a chance to contribute what they are able to'; likewise, with the cash benefits scheme and activation programme, 'we must train the unemployed for jobs, not to find their inner owl' (Thorning-Schmidt, 2011: 4). Personal blame was set against common resolve to deal with the crisis as a collective: 'We will change the rules for cash benefits with the aim of ensuring that people do not become dependent on public welfare year after year' (Thorning-Schmidt, 2012: 3).

Additional corporate tax was out of the question, as this would 'weaken [Danish] opportunities in the world of globalised competition' (Rasmussen, 2009: 3). Similarly, greater tax for higher-income brackets 'will stifle enterprise' (Rasmussen, 2009: 3). Deregulation and greater 'freedom' and 'rights' for recipients of major areas of welfare provision such as day care, elder care, health care, were bundled into austerity era reforms (Rasmussen, 2009, 2010). In this view, 'it is freedom that makes ideas bloom. And responsibility that makes people grow' (Rasmussen, 2010: 5). Absolute spending on health care did rise in this period; much like Canada this was a protected area of spending, with DKK 5 billion in additional spending on health care in 2011–13.

Morality also featured prominently in Irish narratives: government must 'lead by example' (Lenihan, 2009a: 3). Government must not 'condemn our generation and the next to the folly of excessive borrowing' (Lenihan, 2009a: 4). Public debt was cast as 'dead money that should be used to improve vital public services' (Lenihan, 2009a: 4).

Particular programmes, such as the Child Benefit, which saw annual increases in the past, may have been 'right when times were good' but 'now that we are in recession, we must look to [...] [offer only] protection to those in most need' (Lenihan, 2009a: 5). Included here are tighter eligibility requirements and means testing for workers and families receiving benefits from the state. Bringing minimum wage workers into the tax system was justified as being fair now that Ireland was no longer experiencing 'good times' (Lenihan, 2009a: 7). The Maternity Benefit was also restructured as taxable income.

Reputation was particularly important for Ireland, given needed to attract foreign investment (Lenihan, 2009b: 10). Ireland sought to avoid pandering to 'sectional interests', spreading around the pain, 'if we work together now and share the burden, we can deliver sustainable economic growth for all' (Lenihan, 2009b: 3). The common good was not supported by targeting responsibility in a progressive manner. Changes such as those made to the Child Benefit were done not only because it was 'unaffordable' but because it would be 'unfair' to not make changes to contribution levels (Lenihan, 2009b: 7). Even more ominously, 'everybody pays' (Lenihan, 2010: 9). The ethos of the public sector was relied on to justify long hours for less pay and with fewer supports: '[going] above and beyond the call of duty, [as] shown by civil servants who have accepted significant pay cuts' (Lenihan, 2010: 5).

Welfare supports in Canada were framed as emergency measures, to be 'there when [people] need them' (Flaherty, 2012: 6). Concerns such pension plan and social programme sustainability were taken up in the crisis context and adjusted accordingly – like in Ireland, the national public pension plan was harmonized with private schemes, the age of eligibility for Old Age Security pension is increased, insurance for the unemployed was refocused on those 'who are eager to work' (Flaherty, 2012: 6). Government pursued 'the most ambitious trade expansion plan in Canadian history', signing nine trade agreements between 2006 and 2012 (Flaherty, 2012: 8). Funding and support for public-private partnership infrastructure was enhanced through the Building Canada Fund, aimed at commercializable public works projects that involved private finance and profit making.

Economic prosperity in Ontario was rhetorically connected with fairness in society:

> what we will do to help create a more prosperous Ontario [...] what we will do to help build a more fair society. These two issues are closely linked. When our government speaks about a fair society, I want to be clear about what that means in the context of our economy. It means ensuring that everyone has the opportunity to find a job. Because Ontario's economy is stronger when everyone has the opportunity to be gainfully employed to participate in the life of their communities [...] and to contribute to the prosperity of our province. It also means they have access to important public services. (Ontario, 2013: 12)

This fair society with austerity at its core would allow for broad economic prosperity, enable middle-class jobs, enhance pathways for youth employment, favour health care spending, and even help to resolve centuries-old racial tensions by 'ensur[ing] Aboriginal [*sic*] people can work and thrive' (Flaherty, 2013: 16). Even stimulus spending on small infrastructure projects was conceived of in austerian terms. Public investment should not be about 'building more government', it should be about 'building more opportunity' (Flaherty, 2013: 6).

The deep and multifaceted economic crisis in Spain was used as a justification for wide-ranging structural reform of government: a budget law that centralized decision making and imposed balanced budget rules; labour market reforms, tax and pension systems restructuring, banking supports (not only for large international or nationally oriented banks but also for the local system of community-based credit); and New Public

Management reforms of the public sector that included redundancies and promoting competitiveness in key sectors like services, energy, innovation. As Prime Minister Zapatero put it:

> I say to all citizens: to create employment, to keep and to improve our welfare standards and to ensure them [for] our children, we need to achieve growth on solid basis, we have to do it without increasing public expenditure, and [to grow] like that we have to implement the reforms to improve our productivity. (Zapatero, 2010: 7)

Objectives of the 2010 Spanish labour market reforms were twofold. First, to 'increase our capacity to generate employment in parallel with economic recovery and, structurally, to contribute to modernising our industrial relations framework by easing its adaptation to changing market environments', by bringing in changes in employment relations aimed at intra-firm flexibilization (some examples are the modification of working conditions and opting out clauses) and sectoral flexibilization (as in easing the enactment of redundancies for companies in difficulties) (Zapatero, 2010). Financial incentives encouraging open-ended contracts targeted 'high temporary rates and employment instability' in Spain: 'The high turnover generates great employment instability, discourages investment in training and hinders the introduction of new technologies' (Zapatero, 2010: 8). Structural reforms made to labour markets were applauded as underpinning a new economic growth model by 2013 (Rajoy, 2013).

Pension system reforms (for example, raising the age of retirement and increasing the pension contribution rate) were connected to 'fiscal consolidation and budget stability in the mid and long term' associated with not only the economic crisis but also changes in demography and promoted as a way of harmonizing with other EU benefit structures. Public sector reforms were chalked up to competitiveness, public administration and public services were blamed for inflation differentials compared with other Eurozone countries, and public sector reforms were explained as efforts to encourage innovation and the internationalization of companies. Competitiveness was invoked in the early stages of the crisis by Prime Minister Zapatero (2010) just as it was after the double-dip recession by Prime Minister Rajoy (2013). However, 'competitiveness' also became a catchall, even taking on a mercantilist tone, 'the best indicator of the imbalances of an economy is its balance of payments deficit' (Rajoy, 2013), particularly relevant in the context of Eurozone pressures for internal transformation given the common currency.

European citizenship

Monetary policy was an area of paradox. Despite Ireland and other hard-hit Eurozone countries having to adopt forms of internal devaluation given their use of a common currency, the Danish prime minister argued 'the economic crisis has underlined that it will be to the advantage of Denmark to participate in the euro area', the only thing holding back such ambitions being the public budget disequilibrium which meant that 'for a period of time, [Denmark] cannot meet the accession criteria for membership in the euro area' (Rasmussen, 2009: 11). Denmark came to play an important leadership role internationally by heading up the EU 2012 presidency and its introduction of a fiscal compact, the Compact for Growth and Jobs, called a 'key Danish priority' (Thorning-Schmidt, 2012: 9). Canada played a similar leadership role in restoring the global austerity narrative in 2010 when the country hosted the G7 (under Finance Minister Flaherty).

Budget documents indicate Ireland's enthusiasm for the euro. Rather than pushing Ireland in a new direction,

> events over the past year have underscored how interdependent the world is and have reminded us that our fortunes are deeply intertwined with those of our European partners. We are a small trading nation on the edge of Europe, but our best interest is served by remaining at the heart of Europe. (Lenihan, 2009a: 10)

However, the blanket banking sector guarantee was, ironically, described as offering Ireland 'a new start' (Lenihan, 2010: 9).

With a change in government during the crisis, Prime Minister Rajoy (2013) used the concerns of EU members to justify tough reforms, stating that when he first came to power Spain had lost face given that many countries felt there was a 'lack of will to carry out the necessary structural reforms'. As he described, almost wistfully, 'I found myself within a Europe where the dominant discourse was limited to just one word: adjustment' (Rajoy, 2013). The Spanish government's efforts were therefore aimed at convincing other EU members that financial hardships and crisis dynamics were not confined to a single country but instead a problem of the Eurozone as a whole, demanding a common response from European institutions: 'my idea [on] the future of the Europe consisted of five points: public deficit reduction, structural reforms at [the] national level, reforms in Europe, stabilization of financial markets and also advancing towards a truly economic and monetary union by means of a fiscal and monetary union' (Rajoy, 2013).

As for the role of the European Central Bank in terms of common-cause 'European citizenship', as one interviewee put it,

> 'The ECB don't give a shit about ordinary people or democracy. [...] The ECB board should actually have to look beyond monetary policy, the mandate is all wrong and it must be changed to be like the US Fed to have employment and also in my view, social Europe.' (Irish retired union confederation staff member, Dublin, June, 2018)

Comparisons and conclusions

The budget speeches and associated official commentary on fiscal affairs in Canada, Denmark, Ireland and Spain reveal several distinct narratives of crisis and justifications offered for the (re)normalization of austerity after 2008. Six thematic trends are highlighted here as ways that these governments sold austerity to the public in the midst of a Great Recession and on the heels of massive banking sector supports: 1) offering fiscal narratives and budget framing; 2) relying on characterizing the nation; 3) justifying crisis management through austerity; 4) outlining priorities of crisis-era governance; 5) rationalizing reforms beyond budget cuts; and 6) appealing to European citizenship. The crisis was framed as either ineluctable or external stormy weather (Denmark, Canada), or the result of pervasive and reckless mismanagement of a previous boom (Spain, Ireland). Either way, whether the result of an exogenous shock or imprudent politicians, austerity was presented as the solution for maintaining or regaining competitiveness internationally and achieving sound health domestically for all four countries. Citizens were called on to sacrifice now for a better day tomorrow, for unity and a common resolve in the face of tough times. Thus, the nation, its founding myths and claims of character, were invoked as though suffering through budget cuts would be an experience akin to the wartime grit and determination of yesteryear. While these were certainly tough times for many, the justifications offered for austerity as fiscal cuts, public sector restructuring and labour market reforms were surprisingly non-economic (at least as presented to the public in the official public documents examined here). Governments presented austerity as ethically necessary, the only responsible course of action, a plan for restoration and renewal, and an enabler of long-term betterment. Narratives of austerity as a means of protecting the welfare state and social services cast cuts as moral, equitable and socially just.

The global financial crisis of 2008 was often portrayed as a transformative watershed moment, not for what it revealed about the problems associated with neoliberalism (privatization, financialization and liberalization), but because it eliminated the status quo ante in public sector management and provided lessons that were to be heeded – with little if any formal acknowledgment of the pre-crisis domestic ambitions of public sector restructuring that were suddenly made possible under the cover of emergency management (Ireland, Denmark). The climate of post-2008, for these governments, meant prosperity through restraint, job creation through redundancies, reaffirming neoliberal commitments, common sense austerity, and trustworthy government that kept a steady hand and tight lid through the tough times. Crisis management involved no new solutions for a new time – despite being dubbed the 'Great Recession', there was no John Maynard Keynes theorizing a better way out or Franklin Delano Roosevelt-style New Deal Coalition this time around – instead it meant doubling down on commitments to a previously established class vision of state and economy. For all four countries, though to different extents, austerity reforms were rationalized by way of competitiveness, the reputation and integrity of government, and intergenerational fairness.

The challenges of currency union were equally important structural considerations for Eurozone countries (Spain, Ireland). However, though it uses only a currency peg, not the euro, Denmark behaved as if it were in the Eurozone; Canada, despite being a clear outlier in terms of its exposure to crisis and its central bank independence, demonstrated consistent concern for its relative and competitive position in international markets (especially vis-à-vis the US economy), effectively hampering monetary policy autonomy. As we shall in see in the chapter that follows, all four, in spite of clear differences in domestic and international circumstance, have been austerity enthusiasts for some time, regardless of structural position, political party or institutional configurations.

Moving to the next row in our Varieties of Austerity table (Chapter 1), the saga of selling austerity in the early period of the crisis involved

Table 3: Varieties of austerity – dynamics or degrees of public money

	Institutionalization	Insulation	Insinuation
Public money	Decision-making agencies: empowering particular agencies or departments and actors to make crucial decisions about who gets what, when, and how (fiscal allocation)	Degree of autonomy from centralized or supranational decree; budgetary ring fencing	Target of debt/deficit: responsibility and repayment

mobilizing particular narratives and structures with regard to the redistribution of public money. We see institutionalization through both imposed and voluntary cuts, restraint and reorganization under particular national plans and agencies. Ireland's National Recovery Plan 2011–2014 and Irish Government Economic and Evaluation Service are notable examples, as are Spain's Stability Programmes and the Law of Sustainable Economy. Ministries of finance, monetary authorities and central governments are especially important decision makers in budgeting exercises, and their narratives and implications.

Insulation – or in this case exposure – became obvious through centrally imposed decree such as Denmark's Annual Financial Agreements wherein the Ministry of Finance threatened overspending municipalities with sanctions and penalties in future budgets. Spain's new budget rules imposed mechanisms on regional governments like standardized accounting, public reporting procedures, forced rationalization plans, risk assessments, central approval for long-term operations, and adjustments applied to fiscal transfers from the centre. In other instances, there are both domestic and international origins to austerity programmes, Ireland's dual Troika-imposed austerity evidenced through the Trichet Letter and previous Department of Finance 'McCarthy Report' being a prime example. More generally, the insulation of banking through supports and guarantees described in Chapter 2 can be readily contrasted with the exposure of the public sector to the ravages of austerity detailed here. And a slightly more nuanced view of these austerity measures reveals the insulation of those deserving of social supports set against those individuals and programmes 'justifiably' exposed to market forces through the narrowing of spending generosity.

The six thematic trends that dominated the budget discourse of these four countries as justifications for early austerity encapsulate the degree of insinuation involved with selling austerity by blaming the state for reckless spending and unworthy assistance recipients for draining the coffers, along with self-congratulatory praise for digging deep to weather the storm, prioritizing tough measures now for better days tomorrow, and reaffirming commitments to European and national communities through prudence. In the next chapter, we examine the longer-run nature of the austerity phenomenon in relation to the public sector and the transformations witnessed over decades of austerity-oriented restructuring.

4

Transforming the Public Sector

Austerity means a lot more than less. Cutting public sector budgets and staff holds long-run implications for the capacities and orientation of the state. When fiscal cuts are connected with particular normative programmes, transformation rather than erosion becomes the watchword. The purpose of this chapter is to put post-2008 public sector restructuring in its historical context by examining some of the central strategies for reform connected to the longer-run trend of New Public Management (NPM). Rooted in neoliberal ideas, particular sets of economic theories, managerial strategy and normative assumptions of efficiency and expenditure, NPM has been altering the internal workings of the state for several decades, not only post-crisis. By merging elements of neoclassical economic theory and private management studies (Hughes, 2003: 3), including an emphasis on value for money, competition and market mechanisms, NPM is a rather broad agenda that generally consists of government doing more steering than rowing through the privatization of state-owned assets and the marketization of service delivery using public-private partnerships (PPPs).

NPM has been covered extensively in the public administration literature (see Hood, 1991), indicative of the context in which post-2008 austerity and public sector reforms emerged. Contemporary developments are easily traced to decades-old ideational, structural and policy changes that have transformed public administration into public management, with significant ramifications for staffing, spending, procurement, the workplace, planning, public works and service delivery, and other core elements of the public service and public sector (on NPM and privatization see Whiteside, 2015, 2019). By the early 1990s, the OECD was publishing on the widespread nature of this new paradigm among member states, and advising of the benefits of this good managerial approach (Holmes and Shand, 1995). Public management replaced public administration through a reversal of nearly all earlier tenets: stressing results rather than procedures or public interest ideals; disaggregating the bureaucracy and letting the managers manage; fostering competition within and between units in the public sector; importing private sector management styles; encouraging the recruitment of private sector employees and hiring business schools graduates; adopting strict cost control and fiscal discipline. With that historical perspective in mind, it is clear that austerity (historical and recent) is simply not a phenomenon running parallel to neoliberal restructuring – austerity was and is a means for that transformation of policy and bureaucracy.

Applying these insights to Canada, Denmark, Ireland and Spain, this chapter will historicize post-2008 reforms by briefly summarizing their experiences of NPM over the past few decades, followed by national snapshots of state restructuring up to 2008 and the relevant austerity measures affecting public sector employment and programmes. While each country is unique several varieties of austerity in relation to public sector restructuring after the global financial crisis are discernible, with common features centring on: 1) changes in public sector employment (insinuation); 2) increased centralization of political decision making (institutionalization); and 3) the endurance of PPPs (insulation). New agencies have also been created to enact austerity-driven reforms through the institutionalization of NPM, most notably the Irish Fiscal Advisory Council and Department of Public Expenditure and Reform (DPER), and the Spanish Commission to Reform the Public Administration (CORA – Comisión para la Reforma de la Administración Pública). Further, expanding on what was as noted in Chapter 3, within government we see the privileging of logics of fiscal discipline, with implications for the centralization of authority and imposition on subordinate levels of government explored in this chapter. Along the way, staff cuts and miserly programme reforms exacerbate the exposure of some workers and recipients to market forces, while insulating others like those associated with PPPs. Insinuation is clear over the decades: the public sector is profligate and must be brought to heel through thorough (and continual) reform.

Exposed here is a dichotomy of temporal implications for the public sector. In the more immediate term, austerity cuts erode the capacities of the state. In the longer term, when austerity is paired with the normative ideals of marketization, privatization and partnerships, such restraint-era restructuring transforms the nature and purpose of the state. For the past three decades, NPM largely colours this transformation (to varying degrees, nationally). For the past decade, post-2008 spending restraint has meant fewer employees (whether through early retirement, outright redundancies and/or the outsourcing of key functions) and/ or a privileging of particular departments and staff (namely, finance and economics), the hoarding of power and decision making at the centre, the privatization of commercializable state-owned enterprises and partnerships for other areas of programme delivery. PPPs for infrastructure finance and provision are a leading procurement policy that largely spans the crisis, stimulus and austerity periods. And some public corporations remain important market actors in supporting profit making in areas like housing and mortgage markets (see Chapter 2 on the public sector institutions orchestrating banking sector bailouts and assistance).

NPM and public sector restructuring

It is said that the Keynesian welfare state eroded productivity, produced inefficiencies, encouraged special interests, was ineffective in its goals, displaced the role of the family and community, and that democracy was hampered through the build up of its bureaucracy (Pierson, 1998: 45). Something new politically and administratively was emerging in the mid-1970s as

> [e]conomic crises, fiscal scarcity, demographic change, immigration, and the resultant concerns with the financial appetite of the welfare state gave impetus to public policies emphasizing government retrenchment and efficiency. Public management-cum-private management came to be viewed by neo-liberal reformers [...] as a means [...] for achieving more frugal, more efficient [...] more effective [...] governments. (Lynn, 2006: 104)

Thus, the NPM movement arose as the public administrative expression of the new right's broader political agenda to refashion the post-war order and squash the redistributive welfare state.

The public sector was asked to do more with less, requiring state managers to critically assess their structures, budgets and service delivery models. NPM encouraged responsibility, downloading and a transition to privatized models of service provision. A managerial approach to public services delivery was encouraged through the increased use of markets and competition to allocate public resources, and the importing of private sector management techniques into the delivery of public services (Hood, 1991). NPM was developed not to tinker: it sought to transform the public sector and its relationship to government and economy, 'aim[ing] at the replacement of the traditional model altogether' (Hughes, 2003: 50). Its spread was therefore 'a complex process, going through different stages and packaged in different ways in different countries, with each country following its own reform trajectory within a broader framework' (Christensen and Lægreid, 2007: 3–4). NPM is less a coherent doctrine than a 'label under which private sector disciplines can be introduced to the public services, political control can be strengthened, budgets trimmed, professional autonomy reduced, public service unions weakened and a quasi-competitive framework erected to flush out the natural inefficiencies of bureaucracy' (Pollitt, 1990: 49). There is within NPM a conviction that private sector management is superior to public administration. The solution, therefore, is to transfer government activities to the private sector through privatization, marketization, contracting out and PPPs. The deficiencies of the just-in-time and for-profit model of delivering public services was fully exposed when the COVID-19 pandemic struck in 2020. Inadequate supply of vital equipment and the exposure of health care workers to risks that should have been unnecessary, disease transmission due to precarious employment practices, and higher death rates in overcrowded for-profit long-term care facilities were widely noted and attributed to austerity policies.

NPM initiatives emphasize a common approach; but we are also cognizant of the differences emphasized in the varieties of welfare state literature. The four countries we examine here are typically assessed as falling into unique categories. Spain is characterized as a South European or Mediterranean welfare state (Ferrera, 1996). Denmark is most often classified as a social democratic welfare state. Canada is considered a liberal welfare state (Amable, 2004; Greve, 2013), but with its universal benefits structure and fairly comprehensive welfare programmes, some call it a social liberal welfare state (Cox, 2013). As indicated in Chapter 1, we opt for liberal welfare state. Ireland's regime of welfare state is ambiguously hybrid (Andreosso-O'Callaghan et al, 2014: 328) with corporatist social partnership labour relations of tripartite bargaining at the national level modifying its basically liberal structure.

With both the normative project of NPM and the varieties legacy in mind, we now turn to what became of actual public sector restructuring in the four countries at issue here, both prior to and in the face of the 2008 global financial crisis and through its fallout. We see as much overlap as we do distinct trajectories of restraint and restructuring. In some cases, the state response to crisis is not only an issue of public sector administration (NPM, or otherwise) but also owing to the constraint of public sector workers and their unions. Historical legacies in terms of party strength, trade union membership and social movement mobilization (much of which is explored in greater depth in Chapters 5 and 7), all contribute to the extent of public sector restructuring in the aftermath of 2008.

Denmark

Marketization began in Denmark in the 1980s when market provision and competitive logics were introduced to supplant government-produced and provided goods and services. Schwartz (1994a, 1994b) describes these efforts in Denmark as being hatched by austerity-oriented fiscal bureaucrats on the left (under the Social Democratic party) attempting to reform the welfare state rather than simply privatize it, with antecedent austerity and restructuring efforts dating back to the 1960s. Despite a shift in government to a centre-right coalition in 1982, Danish reforms were relatively muted when compared with how other small economies were busy implementing NPM in the 1980s, but important changes were nonetheless introduced, notably in public sector budgeting techniques which reoriented spending around output rather than inputs supervision by shifting from gross to net budgeting, and from line item budgeting to block grant-style global budgets with allocative flexibility awarded to local governments (Schwartz, 1994a).

In the mid- to late-1990s, the finance ministry provided the leadership in a campaign to divest the state of various assets and started selling off big commercially oriented infrastructure owned by the state – the Copenhagen airport, national telephone company, national postal bank and national energy company (Christoffersen and Paldam, 2006) – and initiated subcontracting at the local level, based mainly on management- and efficiency-related arguments, not austerity according to Danish interviewees (Danish trade union and political party adviser and a think-tank activist, 2017). These sales were furthermore justified on the basis that they would not have a negative impact on welfare (Danish public administration expert, 2017). And yet, for this Danish think-tank activist (Danish interview, 2017), "the Ministry of Finance is key to understanding Denmark". Since the 1990s, the Ministry of Finance has assumed the role of 'great coordinator' (Andersen, 2011: 91).

In its 1999 budget report, the Social Democratic government introduced a policy framework for PPPs (Ministry of Finance, Denmark, 1999). The Liberal-Conservative coalition in 2001 focused on structural transformations to the public sector such as shrinking the number of municipalities (from 271 to 98) and regions (13 into 5), arguably the most drastic example of structural reform among the Nordic countries over the past few decades (Greve and Ejersbo, 2016). These changes were part of a major reform programme introduced in May 2002 when the Liberal-Conservative coalition released a comprehensive framework for public sector modernization, aimed at 'ensuring that the public sector is grounded in the citizenry's freedom of choice, is open, straightforward, and responsive, and provides value for money' (Ejersbo and Greve, 2014: 16).

In 2002, the Ministry of Economics and Business Affairs was given partial oversight over PPP policies, but the bulk of responsibility was effectively devolved to the Danish National Agency for Enterprise and Construction that has specialized in advocating for PPPs. By 2010, only three of the ten PPP projects that had been initially proposed were operational and only a handful of others were under way. Early PPP contours in Denmark included the EU's 2004 competitive dialogue procurement directive (which was announced after the early pilot programmes in the UK, Ireland and the Netherlands), restrictive regulations on local PPPs requiring municipalities to place on reserve an amount equal to the value of the contract (to avoid the potential for debt/default, instituted after a scandal with the municipality of Farum), and complex tax legislation related to the legal ownership and tax treatment of PPP contracts (Petersen, 2010).

Plans for labour market reforms (flexibilization) and tax cuts in the post-2008 period pre-date the crisis period and were promised to strengthen welfare and enhance labour supply (Danish trade union and political party adviser, and a think-tank activist, Copenhagen, June, 2017). In fact, as one interviewee described, there is no Danish word that captures the concept of austerity as indicated in English; instead, the translation refers to 'strengthening' and 'tightening' (Danish think-tank activist, Copenhagen, June, 2017), as opposed to prudence, frugality, parsimony or thrift as is commonly depicted in English media (Mercille, 2014). Cost containment may be novel in the Danish case, but the shift away from pro-welfare policies in the post-2008 context is not (Andersen, 2011: 139).

As was explained in Chapter 3, municipalities were hit particularly hard by budget changes and spending restraint in the wake of 2008: 20 per cent experienced spending cuts of 4 per cent or greater and 7 per cent experienced cuts of more than 7 per cent (Mailand, 2014: 421–5). The single largest public sector employer, subcontracting at the municipal level was also promoted with a non-binding target set in 2011 that 32 per cent of public services would be 'exposed to competition' (Mailand, 2014: 420).

Ireland

Ireland's NPM-style reforms can be traced to several initiatives in the 1990s, along with earlier pressures. Collins and Cradden (2007) point to a mix of neoliberalism, increased international competition, the end of protectionism, and fiscal and debt crises during the 1970s and 1980s. NPM takes on 'a uniquely Irish flavour' (Collins and Cradden, 2007: 27) through cherry-picking reforms, leading some to categorize Ireland as being closer to the Nordic and Continental models of public sector reform (see Hardiman and MacCarthaigh, 2008). In 1990, performance-related pay was introduced for some senior civil servants together with independent administrative budgets and multi-annual capital programmes for the majority of departments in 1991 (MacCarthaigh, 2017).

The ratification of the Maastricht treaty in 1992 provided further impetus for public sector reform by promoting standardized regulations and programme evaluations across the EU and by making Irish civil servants more familiar with prominent reform trends elsewhere. Meanwhile, the economic miracle that was to become the Celtic Tiger of the 1990s generated incentives for the inclusion of growth-supporting administrative changes, often along NPM lines, in the negotiations between the social partners. The 1994 Strategic Management Initiative (SMI) was the first comprehensive reform agenda for Ireland's civil service (Hardiman and MacCarthaigh, 2011). The SMI (later relabelled the Public Service Modernisation Programme) was concerned with NPM-oriented enhancements in productivity through managerial flexibility, as well as greater public accountability for the administrative system. The Delivering Better Government programme of 1996 would further extend reforms through initiatives in management structures, human resources, and financial management systems aimed at service delivery and at transforming management practice in the civil service (Boyle, 1997). Policy makers and policy execution would be further redeveloped through the Public Services Management Act 1997 (see MacCarthaigh, 2017: 38–9).

Ireland introduced PPPs to tackle pressing needs in infrastructure, with a pilot programme launched in June 1999 for roads, the environment, schools and public transportation. It was claimed that projects would be delivered quicker and with greater value for money than what had been obtained under the traditional public procurement process. Support for PPPs as a component of infrastructure delivery also came through the Programme for Prosperity and Fairness pact (2000–03), which outlined a key role for PPPs in implementing the third National Development Programme for large-scale infrastructure expenditure. As the Irish economy continued to expand during the mid-2000s, these objectives were overshadowed by calls within the public service for better employment terms and conditions. Reports published in 2002 and 2007 as part of social partnership negotiations indexed public service pay against their private sector equivalents and led to public sector pay increases accordingly. The relative gap between public and private sector workers had almost doubled (from 14 to 26 per cent) between 2003 and 2006 alone (Kelly et al, 2009).

Austerity-related cuts and conditions began in 2009, as explained in Chapter 3, and led to greater outsourcing at the local level and user fees in municipal governance. Tripartite social partnership and government programme spending under coalition governments were blamed for overwhelming the government's budget process (Wright, 2010). The pressure for restructuring in Ireland can in large part be attributed to the Troika (European Commission, European Central Bank and the International Monetary Fund). For a more nuanced view, we can turn to Irish key informants who provide a different framing. The deal with the Troika "was broadly similar to what they [government] would have done anyway" (Irish politician, 2017). Troika involvement made austerity "easier to sell" domestically, and Ireland voluntarily undertook austerity to act as a "good European"; "everybody knew what the Troika would want" and "most of the measures taken were [already] proposed" (Irish public administration expert, 2017). Troika-imposed austerity was also pre-staged domestically by the Department of Finance's 'McCarthy Report', which recommended public sector spending cuts, redundancies, labour market reforms, marketization and privatization (McCarthy et al, 2009). According to several interviewees, the Troika would have also allowed for alternative forms of fiscal consolidation, making the specifics malleable and subject to Irish domestic political will (Irish social activist involved with Troika submissions, 2017; Irish politician, 2017; Irish economics expert, Dublin, June, 2017). Despite widespread public opposition to the government's austerity proposals and the largest anti-government demonstrations in decades, little progress was made in tripartite negotiations and the government unilaterally withdrew in March 2009, introducing an emergency budget, the Financial Emergency Measures in the Public Interest Act 2009. The following month brought across the board pay cuts and pension levies (a 'pension-related deduction') for public sector workers (Doherty, 2011).

Spain

Spain is unique among the cases presented here in that liberal democratic institutions were only in the process of being rebuilt, following 36 years of dictatorship, after the death of Franco in 1975. The fragile state of democracy in combination with the economic crisis of the 1980s provided the backdrop informing the construction of the post-Franco state. The first part of the 1980s was centred on the consolidation of democracy, economic recovery, income moderation policies, and the containment of working-class discontent (Royo, 2000; Guillén and Gutiérrez, 2008; Molina, 2014). The institutional and legal framework was thus established to regulate industrial relations, increase profitability and sustain employment growth (Royo, 2002). Critics of this framework have contended that the actual result was a prioritization of macro-economic stability at the expense of labour conditions (Molina, 2014). Deep economic crisis and deindustrialization in the 1980s saw unemployment climb to 20 per cent. In response, policies of labour market reforms aimed at flexibilization, market liberalization, neoliberal macroeconomic policy (focusing on monetary stability and inflation fighting), austerity and privatization were adopted. As part of this programme, state-owned enterprises and assets in industries related to energy, telecommunications, automobiles and electronics were privatized in the 1980s and 1990s (McVeigh, 2005: 99–103). In the 1990s, modernization would focus on the public as client, and NPM reforms proceeded apace. An iterative, not always smooth and successful, process of administrative reform linked to public service marketization and contracting-out continued until 2008. Public sector reforms should not be exaggerated, although some areas such as the health sector have been more substantially marketized through contracting out and privatization (Alonso and Clifton, 2013: 37).

Austerity has been implemented through several iterations in Spain. Beginning in 2010, the Zapatero government brought in a 5 per cent pay cut for public sector workers (and an 8 to 15 per cent pay cut for higher-ranking officials) and imposed cuts on local and regional public spending; a second adjustment package in July 2010 consisted of cuts in overall public spending amounting to 8 per cent and a further 5 per cent cut in public employees pay for 2011. A new government in 2011 undertook a series of reforms under the Stability Programme, which included a more aggressive austerity agenda that would affect all public services and especially the regional governments, apply cost containment measures to income maintenance programmes, and design economic policy in pursuit of flexibility and competitiveness in order to stimulate growth (Secretaria de Estado de Communicacion, 2012: 3). Key austerity measures included wages freezes and reductions in the public sector workforce (10 per cent in 2012), eliminating several public sector agencies and other organizations, and reductions in individual ministry spending (17 per cent in 2012) (Secretaria de Estado de Communicacion, 2012: 4). Public sector employees' working time was increased, and a zero per cent replacement rate introduced. However, 2012 saw the most drastic austerity package. Announced by the Rajoy government, this phase aimed for €27 billion in budget cuts and tax hikes, a freeze on public sector pay and limits placed on public employee replacement after retirement. The 2013 austerity initiatives featured an increase in the value added tax, a reduction in unemployment benefits after six months, additional cuts to public employees' pay by eliminating the Christmas bonus payment for that year, and the third consecutive pay freeze for the public sector.

Canada

In reference to the 1990s, Tupper (2000: 143) writes that, 'under the weight of New Public Management principles and expenditure restraint, the Canadian public service has been broadly, deeply and constantly reformed over the last decade.' He describes all manner of changes, including for-profit oriented partnerships between business and government, new vocabularies for public servants (now serving customers and clients rather than citizens), and austerity- and market-oriented programme expenditure and design restructuring. Canadian federal and provincial governments became early adherents to NPM-style public sector restructuring – well before the 2008 crisis. As early as 1984, the Canadian federal government was reviewing its options for fiscal consolidation, public sector redundancies and market-oriented public management reform (Whiteside, 2017a). In 1993, the federal government introduced a number of service agencies – special operating agencies and alternative service delivery (ASD) agencies – which separated policy and service delivery functions (Glor, 2001). ASD mechanisms included special operating agencies, service agencies, PPPs and contracting out (Kernaghan, 2009). The 1995 federal budget restructured and eliminated programmes, and cut programme expenditures to levels not seen since the 1950s; with budgets consistently in surplus or balance for the next 12 years (Good and Lindquist, 2015: 59). In 1996, several federal transfers to the provinces (health, welfare, social programmes) were rolled into a single block-grant funding scheme that not only reduced federal oversight and permitted neoliberal-style experimentation by subnational governments (such as tighter eligibility requirements, lower benefit levels and the introduction of user fees) but also brought a dramatic reduction in federal spending. The Canada Health and Social Transfer merger of health, social services and welfare spending dramatically reduced transfer payments: 1996–98 cash transfers to the provinces alone declined by 33 per cent (Vogt, 1999: 193).

Through the late 1980s and beyond, the federal government privatized a series of government services including airports, air navigation, ports, the government printer, public service training and a number of Crown corporations including part or all of Petro-Canada, Canada Post, Canadian National Railways and Air Canada (Glor, 2001; McBride, 2001). Government spending on external policy consulting grew as a share of total government expenditures between 1982 and 2001, from 0.35 per cent to 0.97 per cent (or from $239 million in 1981–82 to $1.55 billion in 2000-01) (Perl and White, 2002), occurring alongside a declining federal workforce: between 1991–97, the federal public service shrank by 21 per cent (Glor, 2001). Employee buyouts and attrition were most common features of the downsizing process (Rose et al, 2000). The reduction in operational and administrative support staff created the fiscal capacity to support a greater share of government expenditure towards policy consulting to enhance efficiency (Perl and White, 2002).

Varieties of public sector restructuring

Having charted the long run public sector restructuring trajectories, we now highlight the particular varieties of austerity that characterize post-2008 public sector reforms affecting employees, services and delivery: 1) changes in public sector employment that involve both/either redundancies and privileging particular departments (insinuation and exposure); 2) the increased centralization of political decision making through quasi-authoritarian control at the centre amid the downloading of austerity responsibilities to sub-nationals (institutionalization); and 3) privatization, enhanced use of PPPs, contracting out or otherwise marketizing programme delivery (insulation) (with institutionalized market support through some state-owned enterprises like the National Asset Management Agency and Canada Mortgage and Housing Corporation, previously noted in Chapters 2 and 3).

Changes in public sector employment

At both the national and municipal levels, there has been a steady decline in the number of public sector jobs in Denmark, from 750,000 just before the crisis to a little over 710,000 in 2017. Proportionally, however, Denmark still has a relatively high rate of public sector employment, hovering at over 30 per cent. Danish unions acquiesced to wage freezes during 2011 bargaining as part of the regulation mechanism that tied public sector wages to their private sector counterparts, but they also managed to limit claw-backs for pre-existing benefits and bargained enhanced employment security as compensation for wage restraint (Hansen and Mailand, 2013). Thus, despite their relatively weak position after the crisis, the unions were not forced into accepting any structural changes to employees' rights, working conditions, or any other primary feature of the Danish labour relations model.

The rescue of Ireland's banking sector through a blanket guarantee (Chapter 2) sits in stark contrast to the country's public sector austerity measures. Through a series of negotiations that were essentially foisted on the public sector unions after the abandonment of social partnership, the Irish state managed to freeze public sector wages and eliminate 18,700 public sector positions as part of the Croke Park agreement (2010). With economic conditions worsening in 2013, the government sought an additional €1 billion in savings over three years by renegotiating the parameters of the original Croke Park deal through pay cuts on public sector employees earning over €65,000 (ranging from 6 to 10 per cent), a reduction of overtime pay, and an increase in the allowable distance of job redeployment (from 45 to 100 km). Although the leadership in the largest public sectors unions (the Services Industrial Professional and Technical Union and IMPACT (Irish Municipal, Public and Civil Trade Union) recommended that their membership accept the so-called Croke Park II agreement, and others like the Irish National Teachers' Organisation made no recommendation, it was roundly rejected by a majority of public service union members in April 2013, despite the government threat to impose an across-the-board 7 per cent cut in pay on all public servants if the deal was not ratified. The government responded in May 2013 with a set of watered down proposals called the Haddington Road Agreement (HRA) that nevertheless maintained the central pay cut provisions of Croke Park II and enacted pay cuts on the highest-earning civil servants, backed by amended financial emergency legislation (FEMPI) that would impose harsher measures on those unions that rejected the deal, including unilateral pay cuts more severe than those in the HRA. Almost all public unions accepted the deal, which was recommended by the majority of union leaders, with the notable exception of the Association of Secondary Teachers' Ireland, which rejected the terms by a majority of 63 per cent and voted to engage in industrial action starting in October 2013 (ASTI, 2013). Public service numbers were slashed by 10 per cent by 2014; by 2015, the public sector had been reduced by more than 40,000 workers and the public wage bill had declined by €3.1 billion, coming close to the original targets set by the Croke Park agreement.

Within public administration, the first wave of austerity cuts in 2011 involved a plan to reduce numbers in the public service without compulsory redundancies (favouring early retirement); a second wave, however, saw a new public service reform programme in 2014 that involved redeployment to fill gaps and shift staff. Government also

> 'created an Irish government economic and evaluation service, and they have been recruiting a number of young graduate economists primarily into the system [...] to essentially get training in the central departments – in the departments of public expenditure and reform, department of finance – then go out and work in the line departments, many of them, and be placed there and help them to do evaluative type activity [...] reviewing the estimates [...] and so on.' (Irish public administration expert, Dublin, June, 2017)

Canadian public sector redundancies, restructuring and cuts include examples like the federal budget 2010, which sought to save nearly $18 billion over five years through government-department spending cuts and freezes to some operating budgets; and likewise, budget 2012, which introduced cuts totalling $5.2 billion, targeting the federal public service in particular. An important component of the Conservative government's efforts to downsize the state consisted of cutting tens of thousands of federal public sector jobs. Between 2011 and 2015, roughly 26,000 jobs were eliminated – a 9 per cent drop in the size of the federal public sector (Government of Canada, 2016).

Spain's 2010 austerity budget implemented a 5 per cent pay cut for public sector workers and announced a hiring freeze, 'with only one in ten employees leaving the public sector being replaced' (EPSU, 2013: 27). By 2011, this was extended to a near-total ban on new hires. Additional measures in subsequent years include cuts to sick leave pay, and cuts amounting to one-month's pay at Christmas time (amounting to roughly 5 to 7 per cent of an individual's salary). Public sector employment fell every quarter from 2011 to 2012, or 9.4 per cent over 15 months, with the public sector employing 300,000 fewer employees at the end of 2012 than it had at the end of 2011 (EPSU, 2013: 28).

Increased centralization of political decision making

Denmark's post-crisis efforts to increase the centralization of public sector administration reversed its earlier trajectory of concentration and devolution. As mentioned, prior to the crisis, various municipalities and regions were amalgamated, and municipalities were tasked with greater oversight and responsibility for education, childcare, elder care, health, traffic and so on (Mailand, 2014). In the 2011 austerity period, the central government reasserted control over the municipalities through their prerogative over municipal budgets, undermining their previous autonomy (Hansen and Mailand, 2013). By imposing a tighter budget regime, many municipalities felt forced into restructuring and cutbacks, although the institutional framework within which this was accomplished had already been established prior to the crisis.

Despite the Social Democrats having lost power in 2015, the incoming Liberal party (Venstre) did not reassert the restructuring objectives of earlier centre-right governments in any significant way. Reintegration remained the order of the day, and the 2017 reform plan of the finance ministry emphasized the coordination of service delivery across sectors and municipalities. NPM-style plans were established to address the red tape of government by reducing bureaucratic fragmentation and eliminating regulations in order to provide civil servants with more time to focus on core duties, while promoting more timely and effective service delivery through the integration of new digital technologies, in line with the previous administration (Regeringen, 2017).

As in other cases, the Irish finance ministry provided a leadership role in advancing austerity-oriented restructuring. In 2011 the government split the Department of Finance in two: one entity kept the original title and its responsibility over taxes and budgets, while the other took the name 'Department of Public Expenditure and Reform' (DPER) and was tasked with public service reforms. The DPER held significant authority over crisis management since it was given the triple task of overseeing industrial relations, expenditure allocation and public service reform (Hardiman and MacCarthaigh, 2017). By linking together departmental budgets and administrative reforms, the DPER was able to virtually guarantee the implementation of reform objectives and spending cuts. The DPER released a Public Service Reform Plan in 2011 that outlined staff reduction targets (which were achieved in 2014), an expanded rationalization of state agencies (up to 48, with 46 targeted for further review), the cancellation of the decentralization programme that had been in place since 2003, and a number of other initiatives such as shared services models and new business models for non-core service delivery (DPER, Ireland, 2011). In 2017, the DPER was subsequently merged with the Department of Finance once more amid public criticism that this was an anti-democratic reform. Likewise, an 'economic management committee' was also created to impose central mandates on local economic policy decisions, with some labelling this too as anti-democratic (Irish public administration expert, 2017; see also Whelan, 2014). Through the Troika assistance programme, Ireland committed to establishing an independent council to monitor fiscal policy and performance. The Irish Fiscal Advisory Council was created in 2012 (through the Fiscal Responsibility Act 2012) to assess the soundness of government fiscal finance, provide independent budget commentary and analysis vis-à-vis targets and objectives, and assess compliance with fiscal rules.

Agency reform also paved the way for agency elimination as the state attempted to address the separation of policy making and implementation, with the minister of finance announcing a wide review of public sector bodies to identify targets for mergers and termination. In line with NPM rhetoric, the minister argued, 'the real benefit from the rationalisation of state agencies will be a less crowded administrative landscape resulting in greater democratic accountability, less duplication of effort and clearer lines of responsibility for the citizen', and promised, 'savings of €20 million in enhanced service efficiencies and value-for-money' (Merrion Street Irish Government News Service, 2012). Forty-seven measures were planned for end of 2012, with all manner of agencies affected, from Education and Skills, to Tribunals, to Environment, Community and Local Government, and a public sector expenditure ombudsman act; these run the gamut, across arts and culture, economics and finance, tourism, defence, child and family services, and so on. Not only is the rationalization of state agencies an example of concentration and centralization, the force behind these efforts is the threat of austerity of a most severe variety: the warning in 2012 that 'no funding would be made available in 2013 estimates for bodies not rationalised' (Merrion Street Irish Government News Service, 2012).

With Spanish austerity came the imposition of debt controls on regional governments, and greater discipline through new budget rules for regional governments such as forced rationalization plans, central approval for long-term operations, and adjustments applied to fiscal transfers from the centre (Zapico-Goni, 2015: 219–20). Regional and municipal governments made up half of all public spending at the time, making such measures highly significant (Lopez-Laborda cited in Zapico-Goni, 2015: 208). Changes were also introduced, affecting important pillars of the welfare state, pensions and labour market policies, 'with a potential "transformative" effect' (Guillén and Pavolini, 2017: 141). Local governments subsequently introduced NPM delivery methods including contracting out, the creation of public agencies, and cooperation with other municipalities and private companies in the delivery of public services (Pérez-López et al, 2015). Their response to the crisis led to a form of recentralization and reflected a change in the policy-making process. External influence and legitimation needs have become necessary while internal ones have consisted of persuading the electorate of the absence of alternatives to harsh austerity.

Restructuring the Spanish public sector accelerated after 2012. The 2012 National Reform Programme created the Commission to Reform the Public Administration with the aim of enhancing efficiency and quality of services delivered. Four main guidelines for reform were identified: avoiding overlapping competencies among levels of administration; simplifying administrative procedures; re-establishing centralized management in those cases where there are common resources and gains to be achieved; and revising existing legal entities and the activities they carry out. The overall objective of this reform plan was to move beyond the short-term cost-saving goals imposed during the crisis toward a more ambitious modernization of public administration (read: NPM).

Lecours (2017: 57) notes the exceptional character of the Canadian federation: it involves both centralization and decentralization in various ways, complicating a straightforward analysis of austerity in that country. The provincial governments remain constitutionally endowed with responsibility for key areas of socioeconomic concern like health, education and natural resources. The federal government is able, however, to use the uneven development amongst the provinces, and its ability to raise substantially greater revenue than any one province alone, to set the tone for pan-national programmes, even if ultimate control remains within provincial jurisdiction. Thus fiscal–federalism matters significantly in Canada and in the previous section we noted the dramatic changes in 1990s-era budget transfers and funding formulae in areas of social and health programmes. Since 2009, the Canada Health Transfer and Canada Social Transfer are mostly distributed on a per-capita basis to fund provincial programmes in these areas, not in proportion to a province's economic performance, or its rates of poverty and unemployment. The federal government can thus exert a significant degree of centralized authority through fiscal means, even where constitutionally hamstrung.

Another Canadian centralization dynamic worth noting, this one in relation to the federal government itself, can be traced to the privileging of budgets relating to PPP infrastructure and natural resources in an effort to continue 'growth-first' priorities for this export-driven economy (Stoney and Krawchenko, 2013: 34). The delivery of 'omnibus budgets' equally raises issues of transparency. Bill C-38, the Jobs, Growth and Long-Term Prosperity Act was tabled as the 2012 budget but it is over 420 pages, and amends, repeals or introduces 70 federal laws, which Stoney and Krawchenko (2013: 52) describe as being, 'presented to the House of Commons in a manner that may be without close precedent in Canadian parliamentary history and has made proper parliamentary scrutiny impossible in the time available'. Cabinet, the Central Bank and Ministry of Finance rule the roost when it comes to Canadian federal decision making.

Privatization and reliance on PPPs

State-owned enterprises were historically employed in Ireland to develop domestic production and labour markets in key sectors like telecommunications, air and ocean transport, shipping, agriculture, industrial manufacturing, insurance and banking. With the onset of the neoliberal era, these were largely privatized in the 1980s (Barrett, 1998, 2006; Palcic and Reeves, 2011). Along with targeting commercially oriented enterprises, privatization has also been a feature of the Irish hospital sector since the 1980s (Mercille, 2018). The expansion of for-profit health care in hospitals through two-tier health care, public subsidization of private health insurance, and the growth of private for-profit hospitals all became part of this new landscape. Nursing homes suffered a similar fate over the years given that a mainly public system has been largely replaced with a for-profit one through state-provided tax incentives and austerity measures that have circumscribed the public role and encouraged global investors such as multinational nursing home corporations and for-profit PPP service providers (Mercille, 2018).

PPP procurement was vastly expanded over the following decade, and by 2013 there were nearly one hundred projects at various stages of procurement and delivery in Ireland (Reeves, 2013). Among European countries, Ireland had one of the highest increases of PPP use as a percentage of GDP from 2005 to 2009, after Spain and the UK (Kappeler and Nemoz, 2010: 17). In an examination of PPP procurement in water services and the housing sector, Reeves (2013) found that value-for-money tests carried out during the procurement phase had been contracted out to consultants who overestimated the cost savings in comparison to traditional procurement, due to the inherent complexities and uncertainties of the infrastructure projects. In almost all of the cases examined, PPP procurement transferred risks to the end user rather than the private sector, contracts bids were less than competitive, and many projects were abandoned over the same period of time. For Reeves (2013), such cases demonstrate the fallacies of advocates' claims about benefiting the public interest by speeding up infrastructure delivery and providing value for money. A similar analysis of Canadian PPPs can be found in Whiteside (2015, 2016b).

The economic crisis initially cut into Irish infrastructure spending but stimulus spending reversed these trends and reasserted the central place of PPPs as a primary instrument in building infrastructure. In 2011, the Infrastructure and Capital Investment Framework 2012–16 prioritized closing these infrastructure gaps; and the July 2012 stimulus package highlighted the use of privately financed PPPs to avoid and augment

Exchequer funding (Reeves, 2014: 74–5). By 2013, nearly three quarters of Ireland's almost one hundred PPPs were in water and wastewater sectors (Reeves, 2015: 471). At the height of the austerity period, Reeves (2011, 2013) called PPP the only game in town for Irish water services and infrastructure as local authorities have largely ceded responsibility for this once-public service. The 2018 iteration of the National Development Plan, a ten-year blueprint for Building Ireland's Future, put PPP centre stage for social infrastructure like housing and education.

Canadian privatization trends are strikingly similar to those of Ireland. State-owned enterprises had been used since the 1820s to guide economic development and the transition from a colonial to national economy, to build up internal linkages, and to overcome foreign domination. Public enterprise was common mainly in areas that supported, not rivalled, capital accumulation, such as transcontinental transportation, export ports, mail and insurance, electricity and telephones – most of which have since been sold (like Air Canada, Canadian National Railways, Ontario Hydro, Manitoba Telephone Systems) or commercialized (like Canada Post) (Whiteside, 2012).

Use of PPP by austerity- and marketization-oriented Canadian provincial governments has led to a proliferation of PPP hospitals in particular, both before and after 2008, making up half of the more than 230 PPP infrastructure projects developed in the country since the early 1990s (Whiteside, 2016b). Policy infrastructure akin to the Irish examples has existed for some time, with provincial agencies providing PPP best-practice guidance, methodological harmonization, and standardized tendering and procurement practices. In 2014 the New Building Canada Fund was introduced within Infrastructure Canada, requiring all provinces, territories and municipalities seeking money for infrastructure projects over $100 million to participate in the PPP screening process. The government also created a $1.25 billion PPP Canada Fund, subsidizing the development of PPP projects across Canada (Infrastructure Canada, 2014; West, 2015). PPP Canada was replaced in 2015 with the Canada Infrastructure Bank, created to link global institutional investors' funds to local infrastructure projects and provide procurement and financing support (underwriting, co-lending, guarantees, and the like) (Whiteside, 2017b). Proving that privatization is a policy for all seasons, some of these developments were excused as responses to austerity, others as stimulus efforts; private finance is cast as both augmenting and replacing government expenditure.

In other areas, the Canadian federal government, including Human Resources and Skills Development Canada, began expanding the idea of social finance and social innovation. Collaborating across different levels of governments, charities, the not-for-profit and private sectors to address common social issues, social finance in Canada has aimed to mobilize private capital for public good. Tools such as social impact bonds combine pay-for-performance element with an investment-based approach, allowing for private investors to pay upfront, and get their principal investments back by the government if results are achieved (HRSDC, 2013; ESDC, 2018; Government of Canada, 2019). In 2018, the federal government established a social finance fund which was allocated $755 million over ten years and the capacity-building investment and readiness fund was given $50 million over two years (CSI, 2018). Collaboration, in this example, expands the role of the private sector in social service delivery, ultimately blurring the lines between public and private, and awards contracts to private investors instead of investing money in public services.

Spain has had a long tradition of private concession projects – from roads to water – since the 19th century. However, both mainstream political parties initiated intense periods of privatization — the PSOE (Partido Socialista Obrero Español, the Spanish Socialist Workers' Party) in the 1980s, and the PP (Partido Popular People's Party) from 1996–2004. In 2008, the government established a PPP unit, the CECOPP (Centro Espanol de Excelencia y Conocimiento de la Colaboracion Publico Privada), to promote their use and provide technical assistance.[1] During the crisis years, the PSOE shepherded one the most ambitious privatization processes undertaken by any Spanish government in recent history: the partial sale of AENA (Spanish Airports and Aerial Navigation), one of the largest airport operators of the world. After an interruption due to the crisis, divestiture was concluded in February 2015 by Rajoy's PP government, and AENA started trading on the stock exchange. The privatization process raised public controversy when under-valued public assets led to a dramatic loss of potential gains. On the same day of the Initial Public Offering, the share price increased by 20 per cent (and the gap only increased over the next few months), representing a significant private gain.[2]

Spain has also been described as 'one of Europe's most enthusiastic users of PPP since 2003', opting for this form of privatization to meet EU fiscal targets and address local budget constraints (Allard and Trabant, 2008: 1). The transportation sector was initially targeted by the national government, along with health by regional governments, followed by a series of other sectors at the regional level, from waste, railways and airports, to other public infrastructure like prisons, convention centres and courthouses. Use of PPPs during the Great Recession provides additional evidence of government enthusiasm: PPP deals in Spain worth €4.3 billion were in place by 2010, an amount greater than, for example, that of the UK, France, and Portugal (Irimia-Dieguez and Oliver-Alfonso, 2012: 612). Its Spanish Transport Infrastructure Plan (in effect until 2020) requires that at least 40 per cent of public infrastructure renewal financing come from the private sector (for projects such as highways, railways, airports and so on) (Irimia-Dieguez and Oliver-Alfonso, 2012: 612). All that said, it remained the case that Spain is 'one of the countries that has demonstrated least interest at an official level in informing, monitoring, regulating and following up projects to ensure that their deepest benefits are being achieved' (Allard and Trabant, 2008: 1). In addition to an ideological commitment to neoliberalism on the part of both major parties, Spanish enthusiasm for PPP can be explained by different factors. These range from the view that PPP is the most efficient way to deliver public services, to being forced into fiscal restraint policies through euro membership, to the expected drop in EU Structural Cohesion funds following the enlargement of the EU to Eastern Europe countries.

Comparisons and conclusion

The country cases underline, much like NPM itself, the specificity of national-historical trajectories while also pointing to commonly shared experiences of public expenditure constraint, privatization, marketization and public sector reforms across the spectrum. While the 2008 crisis clearly pushed Spain and Ireland into radical fiscal consolidation with particularly harsh consequences for the public sector, in Denmark and Canada the 2008 crisis was not as significant and thus public sector reform was more protracted. For Denmark and Ireland, the crisis provided cover for austerity and public service reforms that had been long since planned. In Canada, the 1990s were a more important watershed moment for austerity and NPM changes to public sector spending, programmes and staff (although, as always, with Canada there is an important subnational dynamic given the decentralized nature of its political federation). For Spain, the concentration and centralization of government power extended beyond the budget to the public service and local authorities. Understanding the implications of austerity for the public sector thus requires knowing both short-run and long-run dynamics of restraint and restructuring. Changes quite often accompany cuts sooner or later, given the intrinsic support for markets played by the public sector, no matter what variety of capitalism or welfare state.

Moving to the next row in our Varieties of Austerity table from Chapter 1, varieties of austerity with respect to the public sector are revealed in several ways. First, as a form of institutionalization, the increased centralization

Table 4: Varieties of austerity – dynamics or degrees of public sector restructuring

	Institutionalization	Insulation	Insinuation
Public sector restructuring	Scope of changes in public spending and decision making: PPPs, devolution, downloading and centralization	Nature of the contribution of public services and the public sector; nature of budget imbalance; contribution to income support	PPPs and value for money; NPM and efficiency, effectiveness

of political decision making became prominent in all four countries after 2008. Centralization can take the form of quasi-authoritarian power grabs by particular agencies within government or of central governments exerting pressure on subordinate units through forced restructuring and/or austerity downloading. Institutionalization through austerity-era agencies like the Irish Fiscal Advisory Council and the DPER, or the Spanish Commission to Reform the Public Administration, is equally significant for both centralizing and enforcing restraint and reforms.

Second, we see changes to public sector employment. Change implies difference, not merely loss, and thus some groups are more insulated whereas others are more exposed. While all countries see some cuts to staff, quite often the story is one of qualitative rather than quantitative shifts; not simply fewer public sector workers – instead austerity involves privileging and hiring in areas like finance/economics, or moving staff around to meet new priorities (often of an NPM flavour), or more precarious working conditions (see Chapter 5).

Finally, austerity-era reforms – recently after the 2008 crisis and over decades of neoliberalism – go hand in hand with the privatization of state-owned enterprises and programme delivery through PPP, contracting out and marketization. Not only can this be construed as a type of institutionalization, it is also a form of insinuation. Infrastructure and finance PPPs are now common to all countries and appear to largely weather all storms: they are popular in times of stimulus and restraint. Noted in Chapter 2 on bailouts and guarantees for capital, where state assets are retained, public corporations are frequently called upon to play important stabilization and financing roles during crisis and its aftermath. The NPM toolkit, which emulates market-oriented efficiency and effectiveness, are subtle or not-so-subtle indictments of a public sector oriented toward collective need rather than profitable ends. For what all this restraint and restructuring means for labour in particular, we now turn to labour market flexibilization.

5

Class Struggle from Above

At the time of the global financial crisis all four of our national cases had experienced several decades of neoliberalism, together with the embrace of the global economy and the need to adapt to the new context it wrought. The degree of transition and its pace varied but a general trajectory was common. Each of the countries retained their own institutional profile of labour relations and labour market policies, the product of distinct historical and sociological development. Even the highly integrated EU consigns jurisdiction in these areas to the national level meaning that adjustments to preferred international options are subject to delay and take specific forms at the national and subnational levels. The starting points in terms of the 2008 financial crisis and its longer-term impacts were different, as were the experiences of the crisis itself. Yet each faced in its own way the structural, political, and ideological pressures emanating from the international political economy and its governance structures. Here we highlight a number of features that relate to labour relations and labour markets in particular. That done, we present snapshots of these countries' labour profiles at the onset of the crisis, and subsequent comparative developments since the turn to austerity in 2010, paying due attention to the factors involved in the institutionalization, insulation and insinuation schema outlined in Chapter 1.

Underlying national responses to the crisis and longer-run institutional patterns held different configurations of class relations. Often cited indicators of working-class power include trade union density and collective bargaining coverage, strike activity and the existence, or not, of a dependable political ally – usually in the modern period, a social democratic party notionally more pro-labour than other parties. Union density in 2007 varied with Ireland and Canada around 30 per cent, Denmark much higher at 68 per cent, and Spain lagging at 16 per cent. In all cases they were lower than they had been a decade earlier – losing a per cent or two in the case of Canada and Spain, but experiencing more dramatic falls in the case of Denmark (from 75 per cent in 1997) and Ireland (from 44 per cent). Collective bargaining coverage varied according to the industrial relations system, closely tracking union density in Canada, but deviating in the other countries. Thus, three quarters of Spanish workers were covered by collective agreements despite its low-density rate; and in both Denmark and Ireland coverage was higher than union density largely as a result of social partnership arrangements. In these cases, the voluntarist nature of the arrangements indicates unions' reliance on cooperation with other social partners. In the case of Spain, it shows a dependence on the state-constructed system of collective bargaining. Those structures were enacted during the transition from fascism to democracy and reflect the calculations of the state and various social forces at that time. Strike activity, of course, is not really class conflict, being confined normally to localized or sectoral sites and frequently reflecting particular rather than general or systemic issues. Nonetheless it does provide one lens into the overall relations between employers and workers. Compared to the statistics a decade earlier, the number of strikes had declined in Canada, Denmark and Ireland. In Spain, the number remained constant. Days lost declined more rapidly in all four cases. Taken together, these trends could constitute evidence of a weaker trade union movement, one less inclined or able to wield its muscle.

Similarly, in none of our cases did organized labour enjoy the benefits of a reliable political ally. In Canada and Ireland social democratic parties were weak and unlikely to be influential in government at the national level. In Canada, where they had achieved power at the provincial level, they had proved as likely to engage in anti-labour policies as any of their notionally more conservative rivals (see McBride, 2005). In Denmark, the social democrats were often in government but, as indicated in Chapter 4, had energetically pursued policies based on New Public Management, with negative effects for labour. In Spain the traditional associations between the trade union centrals and left political parties, had been broken in the 1980s and 1990s as the PSOE (Spanish Socialist Workers' Party) revealed itself as an instrument of labour market flexibilization.

In this chapter we examine labour market flexibility and restructuring through three sections. First, we look at class struggle from above, as indicated in the 'best practices' that aim to cut labour costs (insinuation). Next, we provide national snapshots of labour market dynamics just as the 2008 crisis was about to hit (institutionalization). Third, we detail the actions and themes that make up the post-2010 austerity response: creating insecurity; attacking labour and collective bargaining;

imposing outcomes on bargaining; bypassing (or effectively abolishing) social dialogue; and controlling unit labour costs in the name of competitiveness (insulation and exposure, institutionalization). We conclude by once more summarizing how this relates to our varieties of austerity framework.

Class struggle from above (or recommended 'best practices' to achieve lower wage costs)

Post-2008 austerity was operationalized within the longer-term context of neoliberalism. Neoliberalism had different goals to the full-employment ambitions of its Keynesian predecessor, which it displaced between the 1970s and 1990s. Its immediate goals involved balanced budgets, high real interest rates to fight inflation in the 1980s and 1990s, deregulation and privatization, and, for labour markets, various supply-side initiatives to encourage the operation of the market and to accept rather than modify its distributive outcomes.

From this perspective, the actual level of unemployment was caused within the labour market itself by market imperfections that reduced demand for labour or prevented the labour market from clearing. Examples of such imperfections or rigidities include strong trade unions, and state interventions in the labour market such as employment protection legislation, social safety nets and unemployment benefits, which, by this interpretation, increase unemployment above its natural level. Such rigidities also prevent wage flexibility and thus impeded the adjustments necessary, within the conventional economic wisdom, to achieve competitiveness. Measures to reduce or eliminate rigidities would serve to intensify the commodification of labour on terms advantageous to employers. In the name of flexibility, this approach to labour issues was embedded in the policy advice and recommendations of various international organizations including the OECD (OECD, 1994: 66–9; see also McBride and Williams, 2001), to which all our case countries belong, and the European Union, of which three are members (see McBride and Mitrea, 2017). Crespy and Vanheuverzwijn (2017) demonstrate the consistency in EU messaging on structural reforms after 2011 – liberalization of product and services markets, deregulation of labour markets and public administration reform. The micro labour market rigidities argument calls for labour market deregulation through cutting unemployment assistance, reducing employment protection, and increasing the retirement age; for example, we can look to the Directorate-General for Economic and Financial Affairs' *Labour Market Developments in Europe 2012* (European Commission, 2012). In addition, a subsection on wage bargaining frameworks in *Labour Market Developments in Europe 2012* called for member states to: decrease statutory and contractual minimum wages; decrease bargaining coverage; decrease (automatic) extension of collective agreements; reform the bargaining system in a less centralized way; introduce/extend the possibility to derogate from higher-level agreements or to negotiate firm-level agreements; and promote measures that result in an overall reduction in the wage-setting power of trade unions.

Expressed in technocratic terms, in often obscure policy documents, it is absolutely clear that the content of such recommendations focus on reducing the power of and rewards flowing to labour. The format might be technocratic and even genteel, reminding one of the seminar room rather than the picket line, but it nevertheless represents a systematic campaign to enhance the power of one class over another.

Initially presented with a rationale that implementation of such recommendations would produce more employment, the argumentation was increasingly coloured by the notion of enhanced competitiveness. Indeed, the role of the state in a global economy was depicted in academic literature as a competition state (Cerny, 2000). Welfare state policies based on the premise that most labour market problems were systemic rather than individual were abandoned. There was a consensus that the primary determinant of competitiveness is flexibility, whether in labour, production or process (Jessop, 1993). Labour flexibility was built around the concept of internal devaluation to re-establish export competitiveness and correct external balances by lowering unit labour costs. The means of achieving it included weakening and decentralizing collective bargaining institutions, and activating increased labour market participation for individuals dependent on social or unemployment benefits.

Thus, major themes established in international bodies and willingly endorsed by national political elites were:

1. supply-side measures to reduce rigidities within the labour market;
2. measures to weaken collective bargaining institutions;
3. imposing outcomes on bargaining; and
4. reducing or bypassing the influence of social dialogue institutions.

All these are seen as central to increasing competitiveness and controlling unit labour costs. These themes occupy most of the chapter and implicate the insinuated targets of blame. First, however, we present snapshots of the four labour relations systems as they had developed prior to the crisis.

National snapshots on the eve of the crisis

Canada

Canada is a liberal market economy (LME) and has a liberal-residual welfare state (see Chapter 1). Its federation is one of the most decentralized in the world. Industrial relations, collective bargaining and most associated policy areas, though regulated, were firmly within this highly decentralized mode. Nationally, a rather limited Keynesian posture was adopted in the post-war period but, as early as 1975, there began a (contested) drift toward neoliberalism that was certainly complete by 1995, if not earlier (see McBride, 1992; McBride and Whiteside, 2011). Canada's austerity moment long preceded the crash of 2008. In the mid-1990s fiscal austerity was introduced together with significant decentralization of some areas of social and labour market policy.

Most labour policy, social policy and collective bargaining is jurisdictionally decentralized (provincial legislation covers far more workers than federal). Collective bargaining is further decentralized since it typically occurs locally – local union by local union – with most locals consisting of a specific workplace. Despite decentralized jurisdiction most provincial collective bargaining systems emulated federal policy established in a period of wartime centralization (McBride, 1987), though some differences emerged over time. In addition to collective bargaining, in areas like employment standards, health and safety, workers' compensation and employment equity, most Canadian workers (around 90 per cent) are covered by provincial regulation, with unemployment insurance as the major exception to the rule of provincial primacy – it is exclusively the responsibility of the federal government (see McBride, 2017, chapter 2, for a fuller discussion).

At the provincial level major confrontations with labour and legislative assaults on collective bargaining preceded the global financial crisis. They can be viewed as a key element of neoliberal policy but not ones triggered by the crisis of 2008. For example, in Ontario they were the product of the Conservative government's 'common-sense revolution' of the 1990s, and, in British Columbia, of the Liberal (neoliberal) government's first term in office, from 2001.

When the crisis struck in 2008, Canada had long fitted the decentralized model being recommended by international organizations. Neo-corporatist institutions of social dialogue or social partnership have left traces, but have played a very limited role in comparison to our three other cases (McBride, 1995). Quebec constitutes a partial exception but, even there, there is the view that the model is now fragile in the face of neoliberalism (Graefe, 2012). Elsewhere, Canadian governments have dealt with social actors by receiving lobbying delegations from various interest groups: through pluralism rather than through social dialogue or partnership. As a result, and given the weakness of Canada's social democratic party, the New Democratic Party, labour was poorly represented in the policy-making apparatus.

Thus, Canada entered the crisis period with a highly decentralized collective bargaining and employment standards system, low union density and collective bargaining coverage, weak social dialogue institutions, a politically weak labour movement and, according to OECD measures, a high degree of compliance with its flexibility recommendations (see McBride and Williams, 2001).

Ireland

Ireland represents a hybridized version of a liberal market economy and welfare state (see Chapter 1). Elements of neo-corporatism and social dialogue, and the influence of the Catholic church in social policy, render it more complicated than the purer Canadian liberal version. Ireland is often regarded as a competition state, and its just-in-time production process, combined with heavy reliance on foreign direct investment, institutionalizes pressures towards cost control. It approaches labour market policy with a light touch ideology, highlighting lax regulation, weak oversight, and encouraging union-free workplaces to enable Ireland to compete on costs rather than quality (Murphy, 2017). Employment protection legislation is low for regular and temporary contracts (Papadopoulos, 2016), and the country has tended to opt for a modified form of US-style flexibility rather than European flexicurity (Sultana, 2013). Consistent with this, the Irish industrial relations system often has been considered as voluntarist, meaning there was minimal legal intervention into collective bargaining relationships between capital and labour. As a result, Ireland had one of the most flexible labour regimes in the world, lacking such basic features as statutory collective bargaining and union recognition rights (interview, Irish union official, Dublin, March, 2013).

There were exceptions to the voluntarist depiction. There was some legislative attention to strengthening the individual rights of workers, often in response to EU directives (Maccarrone et al, 2019: 315). In addition, it was estimated that in 2009 about 8 per cent of employees in the private sector were covered by registered employment agreements (REAs), mostly in the construction and electrical sector, and another 15 per cent, mostly in low-skilled service sectors, were covered by employment regulation orders (EROs). These wage-setting mechanisms were different from those found in other LMEs (Duffy and Walsh, 2011; Doherty, 2014) and were ultimately subject to the jurisdiction of the labour court. Both types of regulated agreements were found to be unconstitutional by 2011 and 2013 Supreme Court decisions (Maccarrone et al, 2019). This produced a significant restructuring of employment relations. However, the roots of these challenges lie in employer pressures in the pre-crisis period – a reminder that labour restructuring is not always tied to austerity or to economic crises, but rather to a longer-term neoliberal project.

Another modification was a degree of coordination produced by national-level tripartite agreements or social pacts covering wages and also a variety of social and economic issues. This was peak level bargaining, through the National Economic Social Council (NESC), between the Irish Confederation of Trade Unions and the Irish Business and Employers Confederation, with other groups representing farmers and voluntary associations sometimes involved. The arrangements were in effect between 1987 and 2010, and had a longer history dating back as far as 1973 (Roche, 2007; Hogan, 2010). Under NESC's auspices seven tripartite programmes were negotiated from 1987 to 2008, most including triennial pay agreements that outlined permissible wage increases and traded income tax relief for wage restraint. The programmes also encompassed various policy targets and commitments regarding economic and social issues, including poverty reduction, welfare reforms, and the creation of active labour market policies. Thus, while the system was voluntarist, it was not uncoordinated. An interviewee (trade union official, Dublin, March, 2013) described it as having been highly successful in achieving labour peace and boosting investor confidence by guaranteeing there would be little wage drift, even when unemployment was low. However, the system collapsed in the wake of the crisis and the ensuing recession (Maccarrone et al, 2019: 316)

Spain

Like Ireland, Spain is difficult to classify in terms of varieties of capitalism and type of welfare state (see Chapter 1). Some argue it is shifting towards a liberal market economy (McVeigh, 2005). Others depict a Mediterranean capitalist country and type of welfare state with a rigid labour market, regulated product markets, underdeveloped financial markets, and weak corporate governance (Amable, 2004). Spain's industrial relations system is heavily state regulated. The origins of this lie in the Franco period, though its content evolved with the transition to democratic institutions. Bargaining takes place at national, sectoral, provincial and company levels. Which of these is most important often depended on the sector involved (interview, Spanish academic, Barcelona, May, 2018). Low levels of unionization and union density are combined with high levels of union representation and collective bargaining coverage. Representation at the firm and sectoral levels is provided for by law, through elections to workers councils, and agreements are extended to cover those who are not union members. This feature explains the high coverage of collective bargaining in Spain and simultaneously gives rise to a free-rider problem in terms of union density. Other factors behind low union density rates are associated with the evolution of the labour market with characteristics like widespread unemployment, high segmentation of working conditions, and precarious employment, affecting particularly women, young people and migrants.

With respect to collective bargaining, before the crisis Spain was among the highest for collective bargaining coverage in Europe. Collective bargaining from the 1980s to 2010 covered 80 per cent of the workforce, underpinned by two major trade union confederations, the Worker's Commissions and the General Union of Workers, both of which have worked closely in their strategies to develop collective bargaining. Three of the basic principles within the system are: legitimacy of the most representative unions to participate; the principle of statutory extension (application to all workers forming part of the geographical/sectoral activity); and *ultractivdad*, meaning that a formally expiring collective agreement remains valid if it is not reviewed or renegotiated. Apart from the free-rider problem mentioned above, trade unions in Spain also have relatively low structural power due to high unemployment and temporary contract rates, and the constant restructuring of the Spanish economy since the 1980s that has affected core industrial sectors with traditionally strong union presence (López-Andreu, 2019).

Following the transition from fascism, an extensive system of social dialogue and bargaining was built. The main tripartite body is the Spanish Social and Economic Council (Consejo Económico y Social), a consultative body created in 1991 that submits reports to the government before laws and royal decrees are enacted and analyses various issues under its own initiative. There are equivalents at the autonomous community level (that is, political and administrative entities based on region and/or nationality), and other tripartite bodies operate at the sectoral level in various industry sectors and in the construction sector.

The system operated fairly smoothly from 1997 to 2008 as various tripartite agreements were signed and annual bilateral national agreements on collective bargaining were concluded. Indeed, the main strategy of trade union revitalization in Spain was based on participation in social dialogue institutions with the aim of widening the bargaining agenda beyond immediate items of wages and working conditions, thus enhancing union legitimacy.

Denmark

It might be said that, at the onset of the crisis, Denmark enjoyed a low unemployment rate, a coordinated voluntary bargaining system through social dialogue institutions, and a widely admired flexicurity system within the labour market. To some extent this presents an idealized picture. In fact, serious reform of the social security and welfare provision had occurred in the 1990s under social democratic leadership. The reforms rendered welfare provision more flexible and decentralized while entrenching active labour market policies, ostensibly in order to reduce the burden on the state's social security institutions. This era of social security restructuring saw an erosion of the principles of universalism and decommodification, and a stark shift towards workfarist insurance initiatives along with the growing involvement of the private sector in welfare provision. Still, in comparative terms, the Danish welfare state continued to resemble the social democratic model, certainly to a greater extent than our comparators. Denmark is positioned, among our sample countries, as a coordinated market economy and a social democratic/Nordic welfare state (see Chapter 1) and displays much higher levels of coordination and social policy development than our other cases.

The prominent role of the social partners in reaching neo-corporatist class compromises has resulted in high institutional stability and low industrial conflict with flexibility of the labour market moderated by the concept of flexicurity. Flexicurity is also referred to as the golden triangle that confers flexibility for employers who can hire and fire with relative ease, security through adequate levels of income support for those laid off, and active labour market programmes to reattach the unemployed to the labour market (Madsen, 2006).

The roots of the Danish industrial relations system itself go back over a century to the conclusion of the September Compromise in 1899 and the introduction of collective labour law institutions in 1910. In the public sector things are much more recent, dating to 1969. Most collective bargaining in Denmark is at the sectoral level. Negotiations in the industrial sector generally set the trend for the other negotiations at this level. The Danish collective bargaining system is often regarded as an institution that helps to create a thriving economy in relation to the flexicurity model, strengthening productivity and competition and maintaining total employment in society. Implicit in this idea is that both Danish flexicurity and collective bargaining produce a harmonious system that serves employers, employee and society as a whole (Lind and Knudsen, 2018). Most collective agreements are 'framework' agreements, whereby wages and scheduling of working hours are set at the workplace, changing from standardized provisioning in national agreements to a flexible pay and working system negotiated at company level. This is often coined 'centralized decentralization', as interest representation was centralized through the Confederation of Danish Industry and the Central Organisation of Industrial Employees while bargaining capabilities were decentralized, although in a coordinated way (Andersen, 2008). Although Denmark has traditionally achieved a high degree of coordinated collective bargaining in both private and public sectors it is founded on the principle of voluntarism. In the private sector this means that most issues are settled by negotiation between representatives of capital and labour, with limited state regulation. That said, there is a labour court that handles issues not covered by industrial tribunals established by agreement between the parties, and there is a state role in areas like employment policy, pension regulation, employment standards, and education and training. Collective bargaining coverage is around 65 per cent in the private sector and close to 100 per cent in the public sector. Union membership is high, partly as a result of union involvement in the unemployment insurance system – the Ghent system (Lind, 2019: 151–2). However, there has been a decline in union density due to changes in occupational structure, a less generous unemployment benefit system, and legislation designed to weaken the connection between the unions and the administration of the funds.

Collective bargaining in Denmark is separated into private and public negotiations taking place every two to three years. In recent decades, wage setting has become more decentralized through sectoral framework agreement even as bargaining authority was increasingly centralized, leading some to depict the trend as one of centralized decentralization (Due et al, 1994; Elvander, 2002).

Comparing our cases, we can identify institutional patterns that map only poorly onto established categories in the literature on comparative political economy. On the eve of the crisis Ireland and Denmark had voluntarist industrial relations/collective bargaining systems, though Denmark had very levels of unionization and collective bargaining coverage. Both had established mechanisms of social dialogue that achieved economic coordination to differing degrees. Spain had established social dialogue processes and works councils within the context of a high degree of state regulation. This produced very high levels of collective bargaining coverage, but low levels of union density. Canada, like Spain, had a regulated system. But unlike Spain it was less complete and also significantly decentralized – to subnational levels of government and also largely to workplace level. Canada had medium levels of unionization in the private sector (higher in the public sector) and, outside Quebec where agreements were sometimes extended by decree to cover an entire sector, these corresponded almost exactly with coverage.

Responding to crisis, the 2010 turn to austerity and its consequences: actions and themes

The result of the institutional picture outlined above, and underpinned in each case by different configurations of social forces and balance of class power, was that policy makers charged with implementing best practices of labour restructuring, or class struggle from above as it might more accurately be depicted, faced different circumstances. On balance, however, given the agenda they were to pursue, they enjoyed the advantage that labour was weaker than it had been in the past. The measures they would take, albeit informed by a common perspective shared by both international and national elites, would vary considerably in detail. What follows speaks to each state's efforts to institutionalize austerity and diminished the insulation of labour through enhanced market exposure.

Creating insecurity

One of the themes identified earlier in the chapter reflected official terminology in speaking of supply-side measures to reduce rigidities within the labour market. It is, of course, a case of one class's rigidity being another's security. Measures to reduce rigidities, like increasing the supply of labour, or using tools that 'activate' those outside the labour market, should be understood for what they are. Reducing the limited decommodification that social programmes might provide means recommodification for individuals. And the impact on the labour market is to increase the supply of often poorly skilled labour, with the obvious effect of reinforcing a regime of low wages or labour costs.

Ireland provides one of the most explicit examples of the trend to supply-side activation, and a focus on removing rigidities. This could be viewed as ironic given that Ireland was already a highly flexible labour market with few protections for workers, other than those provided by the voluntary agreement reached by the social partners. By 2008, Ireland ranked seventh among 29 OECD countries on flexible labour market regulations (OECD, 2009: 84)

Under the general rubric of labour market policy, the Irish government implemented reforms with the partial guidance of the Troika and OECD advice. In return for financial assistance, Ireland signed a memorandum of understanding (MOU) with the Troika and agreed to detailed monitoring of its economic and social policy. However, this is not a picture of international imposition on a recalcitrant national government. Government officials interviewed indicated that the Troika accepted the general lines of what the Irish government had already decided on. That said, the Troika pushed hard on some issues – the need to implement activation within Irish labour market policy was one. Such pressure was not unwelcome. It created a rationale for actions that some sectors of the Irish government had long wanted to implement. One academic (Irish academic, Dublin, April, 2018) referred to Ireland's failure to implement previous OECD recommendations on activation as having been an "implementation deficit disorder". In regular interrogation sessions the Troika acquired a deep knowledge about Irish policy and administration and used it to push for its objectives. But many of the Irish participants were willing ones. Thus, international pressures, in the shape of the Troika, brought discipline to the responses to the crisis and served to legitimate unpopular measures – along the lines of 'we had to do it because the Troika made us'.

After an early attempt to reduce the national minimum wage, later reversed, international pressures via the Troika focused on four areas. These were activation of the unemployed and other supply-side measures, partial privatization of service delivery, targeting some programmes to particular groups such as those who were long-term unemployed and youth, and competitiveness through controlling labour costs. The context was one of extremely high rates of unemployment in Ireland following the crisis. At the height of the crisis in 2012, the unemployment rate had tripled to just over 15 per cent, almost double the OECD average (Gurría, 2016; OECD, 2020d).

A series of changes were introduced targeting public spending and unit labour costs, including flexible hiring and firing practices for employers. The government introduced legislation enabling it to implement pay cuts that averaged between 5 and 15 per cent. This also sent a signal to the entire economy that there were few obstacles to downward wage flexibility (Regan, 2012).

Similarly, the government introduced an 'inability to pay clause', which allowed employers who could prove financial difficulty the ability to opt out of wage minimums set by registered employment agreements or employment regulation orders in their industry (Hickland and Dundon, 2016). With already weak employment legislation compliance, employers have taken advantage of this and increased the precarity of employment in Ireland (Murphy, 2017; see also Roche, 2017). Mandate trade union General Secretary John Douglas condemned the anti-union behaviour of big, foreign owned employers such as Tesco, Lloyds Pharmacy, Ikea, Aldi and Lidl, and called for stronger legal protections for workers in the form of statutory collective bargaining and enforceable access to workplaces for unions. The call for statutory protections reflected unions' beliefs that the voluntarist industrial relations model was broken. ICTU General Secretary Patricia King agreed in October 2019 that ICTU would lead a campaign to achieve better collective bargaining rights across all economic sectors and increase trade union rights at work (ICTU, 2019).

The Irish coalition government was explicit about its reliance on supply-side rather than demand-side measures. One of its Labour Party members, Joan Burton (2016), describing one programme, Pathways to Work (in her capacity as deputy prime minister and minister for social protection) commented "these reforms broadly aim to ensure that the supply side of the labour market is supportive of employment growth". To spearhead the Pathways to Work reforms, the Department of Social Protection created a centralized service provider, Intreo, to coordinate the administration of benefits, the design and supervision of active labour market programmes, and job matching and job placement (OECD, 2011, 2015b). Failure to engage in activation processes could result in reductions of social welfare payments. The trend to social welfare was driven by central government departments with responsibility for finance and spending (on activation see O'Connell, 2017). Some bureaucratic, local and political resistance was apparent (Irish government official, Dublin, February, 2013), partly because activation in a context of very high unemployment was seen as punitive. As unemployment began to rise, active labour market policies (ALMP) spending per unemployed person was reduced under austerity measures implemented from 2011 onwards, and activation services were contracted to two private sector companies. The work-first Irish activation model is structured based on the notion that any job is better than no job, and this has reinforced the sustainability of low-paying jobs by forcing people to accept them. Penalties for non-compliance were increased. Eligibility and entitlement criteria implemented from 2009 onwards has made it harder to qualify and often excludes the most low-paid and precarious workers (like youth, lone parents and women) from social protection (Murphy, 2016, 2017).

Thus, a significant part of the Irish response to the crisis comprised a structural reform agenda articulated as 'a strategy to remove remaining structural impediments to competitiveness and employment creation' (IMF, 2010: 8). This meant internal devaluation by way of reduced labour costs. The minister for enterprise and trade went further in revealing the government's thinking: 'let us be clear: labour market reform is a prerequisite for Ireland's long-term economic recovery. Unless steps are taken now to address labour market inflexibility, it is likely to inhibit job growth in Ireland and lead to a loss of competitiveness in coming years' (O'Keeffe, 2010).

In Canada, at the federal level, training policies continued to evolve according to a logic that favoured the supply side and employer needs. New programmes such as the JobFund training programme reflected this long-standing trend that cannot be tightly associated with the crisis or with austerity, but which nevertheless reflect continuity within neoliberalism (Wood and Hayes, 2016). However, training policy was never a very robust feature of the Canadian labour market system. Provincially, British Columbia (BC) and Ontario were in the vanguard of the drive for labour flexibility through attacking employment standards and trade unions. In both cases these developments long preceded the 2008 crisis taking place in the 1990s in Ontario under the Conservative government of Mike Harris, and in the early 2000s in BC under Gordon Campbell's Liberal Party. The legacy of Mike Harris was ameliorated slightly by succeeding Liberal governments but it was not until much later, in 2015, under a new Premier, Kathleen Wynne, that the Liberals introduced a series of progressive reforms to the Employment Standards Act 2017, and also increased the minimum wage. However, these were short lived as an incoming Conservative government reversed most of these changes in 2018 and froze the minimum wage increase.

Austerity was part of BC's policy priorities throughout the neoliberal era, with particular emphasis from 2001 and the election of a hard-line neoliberal government. Its project of public sector restructuring involved removing job security from public sector workers, contracting out public sector work, and allowing employers to avoid union succession rights by firing and rehiring workforces between contracts (Lee and Cohen, 2005: 9).

As is often the case, Quebec, though far from immune from these trends, presents a somewhat different picture. There, labour standards are guided by legislation originally adopted in 1979 and administered jointly by unions and employers' representatives in the Committee on Standards, Equity, Health and Safety (CNESST: Commission des normes, de l'équité, de la santé et de la sécurité du travail). This legislation underwent a major reform in May 2018 following the requests of unions, employers and social groups to adapt labour standards to the new realities of the job market. Though the reform was requested by unions and employers for several years, the triggering event occurred in October 2016, when a coalition of trade unions and social movements started the campaign Coalition 5–10–15.

Against the national trend, Quebec's 2018 reform addressed several aspects of labour standards: the balance of family and work with flexible work hours and additional weeks leave; an increased minimum wage; regulation of employment agencies; and the cancellation of so-called 'orphan clauses', which set lower social benefits for employees hired after the date of the signing of the collective agreement or any specific agreement in place (Desjardins, 2014: 4). Changes in labour standards incorporated regulations for the harmonization of wages for temporary agency employees (Lévesque, 2018). Thus, employees of the same employer, including employment agency workers, receive the same salary while they perform the same tasks. Employment agencies, in particular those hiring temporary foreign workers, were required to hold an operating permit delivered by the CNESST to avoid any abuse of temporary foreign workers. In regard to the minimum wage, Coalition 5–10–15 demanded a minimum wage of $15 per hour, which was instead increased to $12 per hour. In all, the changes in labour laws demonstrate the ability of unions and social groups to defend workers' rights in a context of budgetary austerity. The progressive changes to labour standards followed widespread social mobilization of the Maple Spring (see Chapter 7).

In Spain, labour market reforms, in conjunction with the rollback and greater conditionality of social security provisions created an increasingly commodified and vulnerable labour force. After the onset of the crisis, Spain experienced a significant drop in employment, with 90 per cent of job losses in 2009 being associated with the dismissal of temporary workers or their non-renewal (Heyes and Lewis, 2014). By 2013, the unemployment rate hit 24 per cent, doubling since 2008 to reach almost six million people (Gialis and Leontidou, 2016). The first austerity measures were introduced in 2010, and included a reduction in dismissal costs for permanent contracts and smoothed the difference between temporary and permanent contracts. By 2012 reforms were extended to broaden the definition of fair causes for dismissals and simplify procedures. Measures also enabled employers to introduce internal flexibility without the need for trade unions or work councils consent; created a new form of employment contract with one year's probation without employment security; reduced compensation for dismissals; increased the priority of a company over multi-level employer agreements; and enabled, in certain cases, employers to reduce wages without union consent (Rodríguez et al, 2016a; Eichhorst et al, 2017; Doménech et al, 2018; Burroni et al, 2019). Similarly, with Spain experiencing drastic budgetary cuts, minimum income and social exclusion programmes expenditure decreased by 6.9 per cent and 8.8 per cent respectively, to levels dramatically lower than average expenditure in the EU-15 countries (Pavolini et al, 2015). Labour market reforms were intended not only to weaken employment protection legislation standards, but also to reshape the position of 'insiders', whereby all workers appear more and more like outsiders with low employment protections.[1]

Rodríguez et al (2016a, 2016b) reported the reforms had led to deterioration in working conditions, a weakening in collective regulation and greater trade union segmentation. However, there were also contradictory outcomes, including some employer disquiet and greater reliance on some state institutions.

According to the OECD (2014), these reforms: promoted the internal flexibility of employment; reduced firing costs for permanent jobs; moderated salaries, reduced collective and individual firing; and had the potential to increase productivity and competitiveness. An academic expert (interview, Spanish academic, Madrid, May, 2018) pointed out that much of the discourse about rigidity in the Spanish labour market is quite misleading. Reforms to increase flexibility had started under PSOE governments in the 1980s. The result was duality or, as some prefer, segmentation within the labour market. Part of the labour force enjoyed relatively secure conditions but a growing part experienced worse conditions, lower salaries, and a weaker position vis-à-vis employers. Initially this affected young people, women and migrants but increasingly came to affect the workforce as a whole (see also Rodríguez and Lucio, 2012).

Few measures addressed the social consequences of austerity or introduced structural changes in the Spanish production model (Bacaria et al, 2015). Between 2009 and 2016, various budgetary measures and 'stability programmes' were initiated in an attempt at fiscal consolidation. Spain's subsidies and social welfare benefits were scaled back by the Spanish government for 'the young, unqualified, long-term unemployed' and were replaced, at a lower spending level, by labour market activation schemes. Beneficiaries became subject to 'activation measures'. For example, the Extraordinary Activation Programme for the activation of long-term unemployed people with dependent relatives was implemented in 2015 and required recipients to 'regularly prove the commitment to activity and employment active search'. These policies have been shored up with the Spanish government's commitment to fight what it considered to be 'labour fraud'.

The direct impact of these in the labour market included freezing public sector employee compensation and a public sector hiring freeze, pension reform and social benefits contributions. However, implementation of new measures, including activation, has been impeded by a number of factors such as high unemployment and a lack of state capacity. Employment services are reported to be poor with overlap between national agencies, and those at the autonomous region level produce multiple undifferentiated programmes with complex bureaucracies – one interviewee claimed that employers had to submit as many as 34 documents to hire each worker under some programmes. In the case of an EU-funded youth job guarantee, funds had to be returned to the EU because state agencies were unable to utilize them, despite massive youth unemployment (interview, consultant, Barcelona, May, 2018).

Looking at labour and social policy reforms as a whole after the crisis, these were domestically driven and not formally part of the financial package that Spain received. Notwithstanding the Spanish narrative of the crisis, certainly EU pressures did serve to reinforce domestic elite preferences. Still, most of the changes were domestically triggered by the political and economic elites that favoured them: "Coming from socialists in the eighties and particularly the PP on the right, we see growing narrative of dysfunctional Spanish worker to the point it is automatic. The Troika pushed the idea that the labour market is dysfunctional" (interview, Spanish academic, Madrid, May, 2018). In addition, as another academic expert commented, there is significant deference to EU opinion and a desire to please:

> 'The 2012 labour market reform was probably the hardest reform in Europe, we didn't have an MOU like Portugal or Ireland where they had explicit guides. [It] went beyond what Europe was asking. Because the government wanted to send a message of compliance – we are still good students. We will do our best, will even go beyond what you are recommending because we want to.' (interview, Spanish academic, Madrid, May, 2018)

These reforms, along with the public sector wage cuts and deteriorating working conditions, longer hours, easier dismissals and declining public sector employment levels, contributed to significant wage moderation (Molina and Godino, 2020). The partial revival of social dialogue and collective bargaining since 2017 has produced some improvements in wages and conditions, including increases in permanent employment (Molina and Godino, 2020: 288). However, Spain still suffers from a much higher unemployment rate and lower employment rate, taken as a measure of international price competitiveness, despite unit labour costs being substantially lower than the OECD and euro area.

For Denmark, the 2008 financial crisis increased problems with the flexicurity model. Despite Denmark being flagged as having the lowest rate of unemployment in the EU before the crisis, by 2012 it had dropped to twelfth place (Madsen, 2013). The ability of the system to withstand economic downturn without breaking the consensual tradition of flexicurity was therefore placed in question, as not only did unemployment begin to rise, but Denmark also began to favour flexibility over security. Enlargement of the EU with its free movement of labour from low-wage areas has also raised complications for the Danish model. In Danish discourse, this mobility raises the possibility of 'social dumping' – in essence a deterioration in wages and working conditions due to an increased supply of labour. So far, this seems not to have altered the structures of collective bargaining, though increased competition among workers may have had a negative impact on outcomes (Lind, 2019: 168). However, the 'golden triangle' flexicurity compromises were affected by the economic cycle and responses to restructuring were more nuanced than is sometimes assumed. Within the public sector, New Public Management reforms including 'privatisation, contracting out, consumer choice, competitive tendering, performance related management and decentralisation (of wage setting and other issues)' all undermined previously established processes (Mailand and Larsen, 2020: 76; for more on public sector reforms, see Chapter 4).

Two major areas of this shift include the gradual erosion of security-related components, and increasing activation within active labour market policies (ALMPs). Within the security component, the post-crisis reaction included the introduction of an austerity programme in 2010. Welfare cuts were framed as an economic responsibility. The effect was that employers still benefited from greater flexibility in hiring and firing, while workers received less generous unemployment and social assistance benefits. The adjustments largely targeted the social protection of workers with high unemployment risk. Benefit duration was reduced from four to two years and the period for calculating benefit level was extended from 13 weeks to 12 months. Second, for those needing to requalify for unemployment insurance, the qualification period was doubled from 26 to 52 weeks of employment over the preceding three years. As well, adult education support for unskilled or poorly educated workers was halved from 80 to 40 weeks. Despite demonstrations against austerity, the government also phased out the early retirement scheme and increased the statutory retirement age from 65 to 67 (Madsen, 2013; Rathgeb, 2017). These changes left over one third of the workforce unentitled to income replacement in the event of unemployment (Rathgeb, 2017). Thus, despite the system still maintaining generous social supports in comparison to international standards, a growing portion of Danish society experienced income insecurity, exhibiting an overall disruption in the equilibrium between flexibility and security.

Similarly, the onset of the crisis began to highlight the increased emphasis placed on 'work first' or 'make work pay' philosophies within ALMP. After the crisis, there was a decrease in spending to the vocational system and a cutting of entitlements to training courses. Unskilled workers were not only facing rising unemployment and decreased assistance, but also faced competition due to technological displacement. The ALMP began focusing more on the motivation effects of employment policies rather than improving work qualifications. There were few opportunities to participate in education and training; instead, there was a stronger focus on short-term job training, job search assistance, early intervention and counselling, plus stronger sanctions for non-compliance. By 2013, only 6 per cent of those who were unemployed received access to training (Rathgeb, 2017; Hastings and Heyes, 2018). Unions have often argued that ALMP has focused on employability security rather than employment security, as the vague potential of holding a job in the economy was prioritized over defending jobs with particular employers. The power awarded to employers over employees therefore exhibits what has been coined flexploitation, and the disproportionate impacts of the post-crisis flexicurity model on workers. Thus, implicit within the flexicurity model is how governments have diluted employment protection while prioritizing flexibility over job and income security (Heyes, 2013). Alongside the cuts in social assistance and a work-first approach to ALMP, after the crisis the Danish government changed the tripartite agreement, whereby unions were no longer involved in drafting legislation, and social partners were excluded from the administration of labour market policy and placed solely in an advisory position (Bubak, 2018), with a negative impact on union density.

The 2008 financial crisis affected collective bargaining in Denmark by changing the relative bargaining power of social partners (Ibsen et al, 2011). The years following the economic crisis made it unclear what issues are to be handled by the state or by the collective bargaining system. The traditionally strong role of unions in influencing the regulation of the labour market was eroding, with the competences and decision-making power of unions changing. The ability of unions to ensure resources has been weakened and, as a result, the legitimacy of collective action has been questioned (Jørgensen and Schulze, 2011). Thus, key pillars of the Danish model – and the importance of social partners and collective trust in partnerships – have been damaged and this has weakened the collective bargaining ability of these institutions.

Ultimately, although the 2008 crisis may not be exclusively at fault for deteriorating collective bargaining within Denmark, the era does represent changing industrial relations in favour of employers occurring alongside reduction in welfare state social provisioning. While the Danish model highlights social dialogue and trust and the balance between flexibility and security, the changing relations between employees and employers demonstrates a move towards employer power and flexibility at the expense of employee job and income security. Despite the often-praised Danish model still retaining large union membership/collective bargaining capacities, the bottlenecks and structural problems within industrial relations demonstrates ongoing power asymmetries and the favouring of capital over labour.

A supply-side orientation was evident in all jurisdictions but with considerable variety in how it was applied. In Spain, apart from fiscal measures, systematic reforms to the labour relations system were introduced to expand the flexibility of employers, weaken employment protections for insider workers, and weaken labour. In Canada, a decentralized system with weak and poorly enforced employment standards protection, was already in place. Some progressive reforms were enacted in Quebec but there was little change elsewhere. In Denmark, the famous flexicurity system underwent adjustments that enhanced the flexibility side of the formula at the expense of the security side. And, in Ireland, protections for low-waged workers were diminished, and activation and conditionality principles were increasingly prominent in providing social benefits.

Attack on labour and collective bargaining

Reducing rigidities was an indirect route to constraining wages. In all four countries it was accompanied by more direct measures to weaken trade unions and weaken collective bargaining institutions and processes. To some extent, the processes were uneven and sometimes reversed either legislatively or through the judiciary. The role of the judiciary was itself contradictory, perhaps an indication that its traditional independence is not just an ideological cloak that masks class bias but may in some circumstances have a basis in reality. In Spain the labour courts served to modify the impacts of some of the worst reforms; in Canada (British

Columbia) courts ruled against government legislation; while, by way of contrast, in Ireland the Supreme Court struck down practices and institutions that had partially protected the interests of the lowest-paid and most insecure workers.

In Canada, the Conservative Harper government had included in its response to the crisis an Economic Action Plan including a temporary extension to employment insurance (EI) benefits and active labour market programmes. Previous reforms had already greatly reduced EI's coverage and benefits. Once the transition from stimulus to austerity was under way, further reductions were imposed in 2012 (Porter, 2015). Grounds for refusing job offers while receiving benefits were reduced, with the result that beneficiaries must accept jobs further outside their normal occupations and at lower rates of pay. The 2012 EI reform steers unemployed people into low-wage and low-skilled jobs, with the most severe impact on wages in already lower-wage jobs (Jackson, 2012). Based on these effects, '[i]t would appear,' notes Porter (2015: 37), 'that the government's austerity policy is also linked to an economic growth strategy involving the use of low-wage labour encouraged and enforced via EI policy.'

Two other pieces of federal legislation indicated the direction of the Canadian labour relations regime, had the Harper Conservative government been re-elected in 2015. Bill C-525, the Employees' Voting Rights Act 2014, made it more difficult for workers to join a union at the federal level and easier for employers to decertify one (Canadian Foundation for Labour Rights, 2015a). Bill C-377, an amendment to the Income Tax Act 2015 (Canadian Foundation for Labour Rights, 2015b) used the language of transparency and accountability to impose onerous accounting costs on unions. The effect would have been to further constrain trade union rights and capacity. In 2016 the Liberal government repealed both pieces of legislation (Press, 2016).

At the provincial level, and long before the crisis, BC had taken steps to privatize jobs and health services and to cut wages by 15 per cent, increase work hours for the lowest-paid workers, and placed very few limits on contracting out (Lee and Cohen, 2005: 7–8). As mentioned, this was part of a larger project of public sector restructuring taken on by the BC Liberals who came to power in 2001. In January 2002, the BC Liberals passed Bill 29, removing security protections, contracting out protections and allowing employers to avoid union succession rights by firing and rehiring workforces between contracts (Lee and Cohen, 2005: 9). Following a major strike by over 30,000 union members from across the public and private sector, the Hospital Employees' Union signed a memorandum with government limiting the severity of the collective agreement as it directed its members to stand down and return to work. The union won limits on contracting out, but had to accept the 15 per cent rollback on wages. Furthermore, existing contracts covering housekeeping, food and laundry services were retained by private health corporations (Isitt and Moroz, 2007: 91).

Sometimes court decisions produced victory for union resistance, but often at the cost of lengthy delays. A 2002 BC prohibition of teachers' collective bargaining on certain issues such as class size, staffing (contracting out) and integration of special needs students was rejected by the Supreme Court of Canada – 14 years later. As one unionist noted, "yes, the union won, but my daughter received her entire education under conditions subsequently ruled illegal" (interview, Canadian trade unionist, Vancouver, December, 2018).

Still earlier, in the 1990s, Ontario's Conservative Harris government had enacted cuts to the welfare state and amended labour legislation in a pro-management direction, provoking major opposition despite splits in the labour movement about the tactics (direct action or parliamentary-electoral) to be followed. The response was the Days of Action in Ontario, province-wide mobilizations involving tens of thousands, and eventually hundreds of thousands of workers. Despite these strong shows of solidarity, the movement eventually lost momentum. Whether they failed to reverse the government's policies or succeeded in preventing even more drastic cuts continues to be debated. When the Conservative government lost power to the Liberals in 2003, some labour reforms under Premier Dalton McGuinty did 'blunt the edges' of the preceding Conservative government's drastic measures (Smith, 2018: 291), but, more broadly, the new government embraced neoliberal austerity through budgetary and legislative measures designed to enhance the province's 'economic competitiveness' (Fanelli and Thomas, 2011: 142) including a wage freeze for public sector employees and reforms to employment standards legislation (Fanelli and Thomas, 2011: 153).

In Ireland, the end of central bargaining under the NESC social partnership arrangements led to decentralization of much Irish private sector bargaining to the company level though with some coordinated bargaining emerging since the depth of the crisis (Roche and Gormley, 2017a, 2017b). Decentralization of bargaining is generally favoured by employers since it allows them to adjust labour costs to a level commensurate with their degree of efficiency. The collapse of social partnership also meant that collective bargaining and wage-setting mechanisms effectively allowed employers to change rates of pay in unorganized sectors without recourse to any kind of employment contract, and therefore without the employees' consent. These sectors largely consist of peripheral workers. Close to 25 per cent of Ireland's employed labour force works part time, well above the OECD average of 17 per cent (OECD, 2018d). In certain sectors this has resulted in companies employing a small number of core employees central to firm functioning, casualizing the rest of their workers (Wickham and Bobek, 2016). We have seen that the ERO and REA systems were challenged by employers and ruled unconstitutional by the Supreme Court, reducing wage and conditions protection for many workers. A union representative (interview, Irish trade union official, Dublin, April, 2017) described the operation of Joint Labour Committees as follows:

> 'The advantage of them for workers was that there was a minimum wage system [...] at a time when there was no national minimum wage in Ireland. The workers in them got pay increases by the committees applying whatever was agreed under our national Social Partnership Agreements, to these workers. [...] they applied those pay increases as the minimum wage increase in those sectors [...] it was kind of a spill-over from the unionized sector into the non-unionized sector.'

Subsequent legislation in 2012 and 2015 did not fully restore the previous status quo (Maccarrone et al, 2019: 318–20). This means decentralization, though some viewed the collective bargaining system in Ireland as being already decentralized so renewed pressure on that score was redundant. As one Irish union official (Dublin, April, 2018) put it, "we are what the EU Commission would love every European country to be". Ireland's position with regard to labour market policy and collective bargaining, while already being weak to begin with, also deteriorated post-crisis. However, the European Commission has termed Ireland as the poster child for austerity, demonstrating approval of the overall shift towards rationalizing the system of flexibilization (Papadopoulos, 2016).

In Spain, unilateral reforms designed to increase flexibility for employers were enacted, ignoring social dialogue institutions and practices. The most significant of these reforms was in 2012 (though critics of the PSOE noted that the 2010 reform under that government had moved in the same direction). As a Eurofound report (2015a) noted, the stated intention of the 2012 reform was to promote flexicurity. In reality it was more about flexibility both within firms and by enabling greater external flexibility – that is, the increased ability to dismiss employees. This was positioned as a means of achieving a better balance in the use of open-ended and temporary contracts. The most significant changes were to give precedence to company-level agreements over industry-level ones in key areas including wages; increasing a company's internal flexibility through enabling unilateral changes to working conditions that exceeded the minimum levels established in a collective agreement. Subject to certain limitations, firms were given the possibility of opting out of sectoral-, regional- or national-level agreements. The automatic extension of collective agreements, *ultra actividad*, was limited to one year. Additionally, the reform allowed and defined the economic grounds for dismissal and termination of a contract and reduced the amount of compensation payable. These legislative changes and innovations were presented as a means of 'modernizing' collective agreements, by placing a greater focus on economic competitiveness. The number of collective agreements in force declined and reductions in collective bargaining encouraged the internal devaluation of wages, cutting the purchasing power of employees. Thus, the reforms favoured employer organizations, and, alongside external pressure of the EU institutions, allowed Spain to bypass well-established practices of social dialogue (Rodríguez et al, 2016b; López-Andreu, 2019). As a result, trade union legitimacy and the ability of workers to negotiate better working arrangements was drastically challenged post-crisis, adversely impacting workers' livelihoods.

Notwithstanding the clear intentions of reforms, their actual impact is disputed. At one level, the system looks much the same. There is a high degree of collective bargaining coverage and the major unions remain embedded in works councils and therefore have voice on issues covered by them. However, the reforms clearly tilted bargaining power towards the employers.

In Denmark, the 2008 crisis altered the relative bargaining power of social partners (Ibsen et al, 2011). The traditionally strong role of unions in influencing the regulation of the labour market had been eroding, with the competences and decision-making power of unions changing. Within the public sector, collective bargaining became more fractious. Employers locked out over 60,000 educators in 2013 and the dispute was ended by legislation that abolished collective agreements and prescribed new regulations governing teachers' work. These rules reflected employers' demands by transferring control over the distribution of working time from teachers to managers (Szabo, 2018). In broader public sector, concessions were made in the immediate aftermath of the crisis but partially recouped in subsequent rounds of negotiations.

In the private sector, the 'very restricted increase to minimum wage levels' in the 2010 agreement was compensated somewhat by certain welfare benefit agreements, most importantly the provision of 85 per cent of full wage for those newly unemployed up to three months after end of employment (Due and Madsen, 2010: 2, 12). This agreement was arguably a crisis agreement: employers successfully resisted wage growth, while trade unions focused on measures to increase job security, raising the costs of firing through the new unemployment benefit scheme. In the private sector 2017 agreements, Andersen and Ibsen (2017) noted some centralization of the framework for setting wage levels with more sectoral negotiations, a process led particularly by trade unions. At the same time, the negotiated welfare benefits were increasingly individualized. Minimum wage levels were agreed to grow faster than earlier in the crisis period, but did still not reach pre-crisis levels (Andersen and Ibsen, 2017). On the employers' side, there was satisfaction with the new, relaxed conditions for using systematic overtime. Employers could now enforce systematic overtime (with full compensation and other benefits) if they could not reach a local agreement with employees on variations to the weekly working time.

In sum, attacks on trade unions and collective bargaining proceeded in different ways. In Denmark, erosion and reduced reliance on existing institutions seemed prominent. In Spain, formal legislation and unilateral bypassing of social dialogue institutions were the main methods. Ireland's voluntarist system was easy to change. Social partnership through the National Economic Social Council ended, and with it collective bargaining activities became localized and decentralized. In the public sector, where this was less true, the government imposed outcomes (see the discussion in Chapter 4; also later in this chapter). In Canada, the heavy lifting of confronting public service unionism had been done provincially, prior to the crisis, and the legislative framework that made union organizing difficult and collective bargaining highly regulated and circumscribed, continued in place. In all the countries, of course, the economic and employment contract was a key factor shaping the behaviour of labour market actors.

Imposition of outcomes on bargaining

In Canada, where the factors described above failed to produce union acquiescence, stronger measures were sometimes employed. Since the crisis, the federal government has intervened to resolve labour disputes in favour of employers, enacting back-to-work legislation to end worker strikes. This is a continuation of long-standing practice (see Panitch and Swartz, 1988; McBride, 2017, chapter 9). Examples include postal workers and Air Canada unionized employees. The postal legislation allowed wage increases for four years (2011–14) and referred other issues to 'final offer selection' arbitration. The union challenged this and eventually reached a negotiated settlement with Canada Post in October 2012. The terms of the settlement included a two-tiered wage system and a hybrid pension plan combining defined contributions with defined benefits. A dispute between Air Canada and its employees triggered similar federal legislation to resolve the situation (Thomas and Tufts, 2016: 219–20).

Provincially, post-crisis developments featured wage freezes, efforts to legislatively diminish labour's organizations, and a mixed record on employment standards with some attention to improving minimum wages. Some of these developments had their origins in previous rounds of austerity politics. Ontario's 2010 budget included 'income freezes for non-unionized and management level workers in the public sector, and an attempt to secure a voluntary two-year wage freeze with the unions representing workers in Ontario's broader public sector' (Thomas and Tufts, 2016: 220; see also Fanelli and Thomas, 2011). In 2012, the government froze wages for the province's teachers, suspended the right to strike for two years, and empowered the government to impose contracts. Union resistance to the legislation was widespread and the government repealed the Act in 2013. But the legislation had succeeded in freezing wages and pension costs (Sweeney and Hickey, 2017).

The Irish government withdrew from existing agreements with unions, demolished bargaining institutions and imposed cuts unilaterally. The crisis resulted in the loss of central bargaining and social dialogue, two characteristics that had served as the main anchors moderating the voluntarism of Irish industrial relations. The immediate effect was wage freezes for public workers. In February 2009 the government also pushed through legislation titled Financial Emergency Measures in the Public Interest (FEMPI) that went further. FEMPI introduced a special pension levy, and a 7 per cent reduction in public sector wages. By March 2009, the government once again acted unilaterally when it passed an emergency budget to lower the salary of all public servants.

There was opposition in Ireland. In November 2009, all major public sector unions decided to mobilize for a national day of action, extending to all public sector workers. Eighty per cent of public sector workers (265,000 workers) were involved; however, substantive outcomes were limited.

Subsequent agreements between the government and the public sector unions (Croke Park I) traded further wage cuts and employment flexibility for a government commitment to abstain from compulsory redundancies. Later, after public sector unions rejected a second agreement (Croke Park II), the government drafted a new FEMPI bill punishing those employee groups not willing to sign up for bilateral agreements. The FEMPI bill became a decisive factor in the eventual acceptance of the

'Haddington Road deal', enacted in June 2013 (Hardiman and Regan, 2013; Szabo, 2018).

Through a series of negotiations that were essentially imposed on the public sector unions after the abandonment of social partnership, the Irish state managed, first, to freeze public sector wages and, second, to eliminate thousands of public sector positions and impose pay cuts. By 2014, public service numbers had been brought down by over 32,000 (around 10 per cent of the total) with commensurate savings for the public wage bill. It could be argued that the 'spirit' of former tripartite social partnership arrangements influenced the unions' willingness to engage in bipartite agreements, which enabled the government to implement its fiscal consolidation agenda (interviews, trade union officials and academics, Dublin, April, 2017).

No need for social dialogue in a crisis

Irish social partnership mechanisms (NESC) had once shaped the country's collective bargaining but collapsed under the impact of the crisis in 2008 and 2009. Renewal terms of an earlier agreement had been accepted by both the Irish Confederation of Trade Unions and the Irish Business and Employers Confederation (IBEC), but the Construction Industry Federation (CIF) withheld its support due to the deteriorating state of the construction industry (O'Kelly, 2010). As the crisis worsened in 2009, the government attempted to reduce wages, particularly in the public sector, while IBEC proposed that social partnership be suspended entirely. Little progress was made in the negotiations and the government unilaterally withdrew in March 2009, introducing an emergency budget the following month that included across the board pay cuts and pension levies for public sector workers (Doherty, 2011). This was followed by IBEC's formal withdrawal from social partnership in January 2010, which officially marked the end of Ireland's social pact.

NESC was not abolished but most of its staff were seconded to other government agencies and it became a pale shadow of its former self. In a series of interviews, the kindest description of post-crisis NESC was 'mothballed'; others preferred 'moribund' or 'dead'. Trilateral social partnership arguably did have a post-crisis legacy in the form of later bilateral agreements between the private sector and trade unions in the shape of the 'protocol governing collective bargaining – orderly conduct of industrial relations', and in the public sector the Croke Park, Haddington Road and Lansdowne Road agreements. Concessions were imposed by the Croke Park and Haddington Road agreements (wage cuts and freezes, staff reductions) on the public sector unions. Later, through the Lansdowne Road and Public Service Stability agreements in 2015 and 2018 respectively, gradual increases in pay were negotiated. Reflecting on the demise of social partnership one expert commented:

> 'The notion of kind of ongoing tripartite discussion backed up by a complex institutional architecture is just gone, I mean, it is extraordinary how quickly the whole thing just unravelled, because as you know it had become essentially the governance of Ireland was very much tied up in the nexus of these institutions. Effectively the whole edifice is gone with the exception of NESC, which is on life support.' (Irish academic, Dublin, February, 2013)

Some analyses have pointed to the increased influence of the foreign direct investment sectors, organized into the American Chamber of Commerce Ireland, and uninterested in social dialogue or collective bargaining (Regan, 2017).

In Spain, an immediate effect of the crisis was that social dialogue institutions were weakened and bypassed. In the early post-crisis years, a 2009 attempt by the social partners to negotiate an interconfederal agreement for collective bargaining (AENC) failed when the socialist government unilaterally imposed a labour reform in 2010. The reforms included rationalizing social security, freezing pensions, an increase in retirement age, tightened rules for early retirement and pension for survivors, and a reduction of public salaries (Natali and Stamati, 2014). These reforms provoked a general strike, though it did not change government's agenda (González et al, 2013); rather, another tripartite agreement embodied union concessions that legitimized the reform of social security, the increase of the age for retirement from 65 to 67 years, and the pension calculation basis from 25 to 35 years (González et al, 2013; Natali and Stamati, 2014). Later, the government also imposed changes to collective bargaining that gave priority to bilateral firm agreements over tripartite sectoral agreements, further weakening the power of unions. In the general elections of November 2011, the series of imposed and unpopular reforms resulted in the PSOE losing office (Pérez, 2014).

New attempts to negotiate the AENC failed and the PP government of Mariano Rajoy unilaterally implemented reforms that further advantaged employers in collective bargaining. Firms were given greater autonomy to take unilateral decisions. Company agreements were prioritized over multi-employer ones, enhancing individual firms' flexibility, and the period of *ultra actividad*, in which provisions of an agreement would continue after its expiration, was reduced (Cioffi and Dubin, 2016). This labour reform fuelled a general strike in March of 2012. It too failed to stop policy changes (González et al, 2013).

The slight economic recovery of 2014 somewhat reactivated social dialogue. The government, unions and employers signed an agreement on proposals for the tripartite bargaining to promote economic growth and employment. Also, a new AENC was achieved (Consejo Económico y Social, 2015). Yet, neither labour reforms nor changes in social dialogue were reversed (Bacaria et al, 2015). In general, social dialogue and collective bargaining deteriorated during the crisis due to unilateralism by the state, at both national and regional levels. As a result, there has been significant conflict and strikes (Molina and Godino, 2020: 318). In addition, bypassing social dialogue institutions and a narrower scope for consultations posed legitimacy problems for the unions, which were heavily invested in their ability to be consulted and have influence in those fora.

As mentioned earlier in the chapter, there was little by way of institutionalized social dialogue in Canada. What there was tended to be concentrated in Quebec and, even there, observers have noted that it is less robust than before (Graefe, 2012). And in Denmark there was evidence of significant pressure on the processes of social dialogue, as 'win–win' scenarios gave way to concession bargaining (Eurofound, 2013).

Social dialogue or partnership has not fared well during or since the crisis. It has been bypassed, effectively abolished or, where it remains, reduced in scope and significance. Whatever its limitations in the past, this avenue for expressing labour's voice on policy issues is even less effective now.

Controlling unit labour costs

We have noted how the dominant paradigm viewed rigidities – strong trade unions, state labour market measures (employment protection legislation, social supports and unemployment insurance), and centralized collective bargaining systems – as causing problems of competitiveness. In the name of achieving greater competitiveness, essentially through constraining wage levels, labour market and welfare state restructuring became focused on individual responsibility, flexibility and innovation, and on reducing individual rights and the collective power of trade unions. Fiscal austerity, public sector restructuring and labour restructuring all played a role in the narrative of achieving competitiveness.

The outcome of these negative labour market conditions was certainly consistent with the internal devaluation motif, shown by indicators of labour costs such as unit labour costs (ULCs). By no means an unproblematic statistic (see Buendia and Molero-Simarro, 2018), it is nevertheless widely used as a broad measure of (international) price competitiveness. ULCs are defined as the average cost of labour per unit of output produced. They can be expressed as the ratio of total labour compensation per hour worked to output per hour worked (labour productivity). As indicated in Chapter 1 (Figure 10), the post-crisis decline in ULC growth is evident after 2007–09.

Comparisons and conclusions

Moving to the next row in our Varieties of Austerity table from Chapter 1, labour market flexibility and restructuring involves several considerations underpinning these varieties. For institutionalization, differences are evident most notably through institutional starting points (pre-crisis), and given that the alignment of class power was different. Canada already had a legally regulated but highly decentralized collective bargaining system; Ireland and Denmark had voluntarist systems with a high degree of coordination through social partnership in Denmark, and there was an established if somewhat weaker coordination system in Ireland. Spain had a highly regulated system that enabled high collective bargaining coverage, despite low rates of unionization and institutionalized social partnership arrangements.

The degree of insulation is evident when the legal rights and protections for labour are extended, affirmed or rescinded. The strength of labour varied but had, in all cases, been in decline during the neoliberal period. Indeed, many of the attacks on labour had preceded the crisis. And in no case did a labour movement have a protective political ally. The general direction of policy change was consistent across cases, with specific details varying due to institutional inheritance and the balance of social forces.

Table 5: Varieties of austerity – dynamics or degrees of labour market flexibility

	Institutionalization	Insulation	Insinuation
Labour market flexibility	Bypassed or bolstered institutional starting points (pre-crisis): statutory or voluntarist collective bargaining systems, social dialogue procedures (or similar)	Extending, affirming, or rescinding: legal rights, protections, automatic stabilizers, addressing 'rigidities', impinging on trade union strength	Controlling unit labour costs: internal devaluation, supply-side low-wage competition

The general tone was reflected in the pronouncements of international organizations – flexibility in the labour market, decentralization of collective bargaining, erosion of social partnership or social dialogue institutions and so on. However, this international consensus on the need for labour market restructuring also reflected the preferences of national elites. The changes were at least as much domestically driven as they were shaped by international pressures.

Rather than showing any sign of thinking outside the box when faced with a major financial and economic crisis, national and international elites doubled down on ideas and policies that had long been part of the neoliberal arsenal. In the crisis context, these restructuring practices within the labour market fitted very well with states' self-imposed fiscal imperatives.

Demand stimulus was off the table after 2010. Insinuation and the rescinding of insulation thus proceeded largely through supply-side measures to reduce rigidities within the labour market that were intended to increase labour force participation through activation. As well as ideologically constructing this in a way that individualized responsibility for non-participation, and all its associated costs to the individual, activation and removal from social supports would also keep public expenditures low. Corresponding reductions or conditionalities attached to social support measures, as well as saving public expenditures, increased pressure on individuals to activate.

Institutionally, measures to decentralize collective bargaining (thus empowering firms) through labour reforms took advantage of the decline of union numbers and influence that was already apparent before the crisis. Throughout the crisis context, improving competitiveness through constraints on wages and living standards (internal devaluation) re-enforced the power of capital and denied voice to opponents in the great reallocation of blame that austerity embodied. Bypassing institutions of social dialogue had the same effect. Where these measures were insufficient the state stripped away insulating factors by increasing its coercive role, by imposing outcomes through unilateral pay cuts and freezes, normally in the public sector, or by back-to-work legislation – a favourite device within the decentralized but regulated Canadian system. Various forms of privatization including the ubiquitous public-private partnerships served to weaken the still strong public sector unions and to reduce wage costs.

In all cases there were measures on the supply side to activate the unemployed to reattach themselves to the labour market, a classic case of insinuation by transferring blame for labour market non-participation to the individual. Other measures aimed to control labour costs by increasing the power of business vis-à-vis labour, and to use fiscal policy and privatization to change the calculations of labour market actors. There was some variety among the instruments used. The Canadian system, being already highly decentralized, saw little action in terms of institutional reform of the structures of labour relations. In Spain and Ireland however, such reforms were made to weaken labour. These reforms were central to Spain's response because of its highly regulated inheritance, though perhaps less effective than proponents had anticipated. The Spanish reforms were intended to enhance the position of companies or firms and to reduce the costs of dismissals. Ireland's voluntarist system lent itself to unilateralism without the need for extensive state reform. Social dialogue was bypassed for a considerable period, weakening labour's influence, and the operation of social dialogue produced much the same result in Denmark. That country's much vaunted flexicurity system eroded as the flexibility part of the system became much more prominent. In Canada, federal back-to-work legislation imposed outcomes on collective bargaining processes and, at the provincial level, there were significant instances of contracts being rolled-back, and unilateral cuts, as well as privatization of formerly union protected public service jobs, with negative impacts on wages and conditions.

Taken together, class struggle from above (deleterious best practices) and the thematic unfolding of the 2010 austerity response – creating insecurity, attacking labour and collective bargaining, imposing outcomes on bargaining, hampering or bypassing social dialogue, and controlling unit labour costs in a race to the bottom-style effort for low-wage competitiveness – amounts to complex but unidirectional varieties of austerity for labour. As the next chapter will show, this climate was harsh for precarious workers, those who were poor, marginalized and vulnerable, and indebted households.

6

Insecurity and Poverty

The neoliberal era has been one of increased inequality in both income and wealth distribution. The trend started in the 1970s in the US and has been most dramatic in the North Atlantic world but is also apparent in most of Europe. An OECD report (2017) noted that income inequality in Europe had grown over several decades. In Canada, gains in income were similarly concentrated at the top of the spectrum. Between 1982 and 2015, 'The average real pre-tax income of the top 1 per cent of tax filers more than doubled, increasing by $320,000 – but the bottom 50 per cent of tax filers did not even keep up with inflation – their real income fell by an average of $1,546' (Osberg, 2017: 28).

More generally, various scholars have made the case that the neoliberal period has been characterized by the rapid growth of transnational firms and finance, and the ongoing transfer of income and wealth to the wealthy few (see Piketty, 2014; Atkinson, 2015; Peters, 2020). As Faroohar (2016: 15) summarizes, 'the share of financiers within the top 1 per cent of the income distribution nearly doubled between 1979 and 2005'. By this calculation, an unprecedented level of inequality was already in place when the crisis struck. While income inequality earned through bonuses, super-salaries and a dismantling of progressive income tax systems is one part of the story, wealth (and finance) is particularly implicated because, again quoting Faroohar (2016: 15):

> [e]ven when you consider the salaries of the modern economy's supermanagers – the CEOs, bankers, accountants, agents, consultants, and lawyers that groups like Occupy Wall Street rail against – it's important to remember that somewhere between 30 and 80 percent of their income is awarded not in cash but in incentive stock options and stock shares.

This type of income often escapes even quasi-progressive payroll-based income tax systems. Thus, in the US, 'the top twenty-five hedge fund managers in America make more than all the country's kindergarten teachers combined' (Faroohar, 2016: 15–16).

Austerity itself is not the whole cause of inequality. Processes of financialization and wealth inequality began well before the 2008 crisis and subsequent austerity measures. Austerity does, however, greatly exacerbate market (income and wealth) inequalities, and frustrates the economic growth necessarily for a rising tide to actually lift all boats. Austerity measures also indicate the preferential treatment (insulation) of particular groups in society when such efforts exacerbate vulnerabilities created by market dynamics. There is a huge disconnect between the treatment, through buy-outs and socialization of debt, of those responsible for the crisis (finance, business, and capital – see Chapter 2) and those who were the victims of it (insinuation). Given the pattern of austerity (institutionalization) – public sector cutbacks, social services reductions and conditionality (curbing the social wage), the weakening of labour's representative institutions and bargaining power legislatively, as well as by recessionary unemployment (see Chapters 3, 4, 5) – life has become much harder and more insecure outside the elite circles driving austerity policies. Writing of Canada, Heather Scoffield (2019) argued that Canada's relatively mild income inequality data do not mirror the lived experiences of those who struggle with poverty on a daily basis, and who bear witness to its entrenchment. This chapter concerns itself with the victims who bear no responsibility for the crisis and its aftermath, but have born its costs.

If the working class is the general target of the austerity project, it remains the case that particular groups are especially hard-hit, often through the mechanism of an insecure and precarious labour market, accompanied by diminished social provision. We survey the situation as it affects young people, women and migrants, and outline how poverty manifests in housing and food insecurity. In many countries, including the four that are our focus, commodification, individualization and privatization were intensified over the crisis period in the name of reducing the budget deficit (see Chapters 2–5). For significant sectors of the population, this has engendered various forms of often overlapping and mutually reinforcing poverty. These include insufficient income to meet basic needs such as housing and food costs. Just as the social dialogue institutions and other class-based processes designed to give labour a voice were unilaterally bypassed by governments (see Chapter 5), so too were governments cutting funding to organizations that had given voice to disadvantaged or underrepresented groups. This chapter examines some of these dynamics through two major themes: manufacturing insecurity (through labour market precarity – especially for youth, women, immigrants and low-pay workers – thereby creating more debt for many households) and vulnerabilities (through food and housing insecurity).

Manufacturing insecurity: precarity in the labour market

Central to the lived experience of austerity is an insecure, precarious and often hostile labour market, with states' promotion of labour market flexibilization and wage constraint being two main adjustment mechanisms (see Chapter 5) compounding the already-deleterious attributes of capitalist compulsions. The rationale has been to improve national competitiveness through internal devaluation; in fact, these measures are better at slashing wages than at promoting growth (see Uxo et al, 2016). As noted in previous chapters, labour market flexibilization has been part of a reform agenda centred on market-driven structural adjustment through downward wage pressures, erosion of workers' rights and erosion of public services (Bengtsson et al, 2017; Picot and Tassinari, 2017). Thus, the austerity era has involved incursions on social and legal protections for workers, which effectively deepened precarity by empowering employers' control over their own labour forces through deregulation of the labour market, through the loss and individualization of workers' rights, and through a narrowing of labour union-based collective protection. By shifting the balance of power toward employers, austerity has meant working lives more greatly characterized by vulnerability, uncertainty and insecurity (Russell and Dufour, 2016; López Andreu, 2017).

Conditionalities attached to benefits, often referred to as 'activation' (see Chapter 5), can push people into the poverty trap of accepting part-time work in order to avoid losing eligibility for much needed social security (Bone, 2014; O'Hara, 2015; O'Brien and Kyprianou, 2017). Austerity rhetoric has been combined with pre-austerity neoliberal imperatives to individualize and responsibilize both the workforce and the workless population. Similarly, in a context of increasing unemployment as well as long-term unemployment, changes in unemployment insurance systems that make it tougher to qualify, reduced payments, and impose limits on the duration of benefits eligibility, have had an impact on living standards. Precarious workers or those working with intermittent employment – overrepresented among women and youth – are worse off because they are often not covered by the unemployment insurance or welfare systems (Addabbo et al, 2015). More generally, a culture of 'low-wage dependency' has been established. Workers are trapped in jobs that do not pay them adequate wages to properly support themselves and their families. They are therefore forced to accept more and more precarious work, including zero-hour contracts, and work in unsafe and unhealthy conditions just to make ends meet (O'Brien and Kyprianou, 2017).

Precarity is widespread in the labour force but, as we will now explore, it is especially concentrated in certain groups: youth, women, migrants, low-wage workers and those experiencing housing and food insecurity. Illustrated later in the chapter through various quantitative and qualitative measures, in sum, these groups generally have higher unemployment rates than the average, are harder hit by austerity measures and/or during times of crisis, and are offered the fewest state protections. They are least responsible for crises and austerity but are made to experience its most dramatic effects through the insulation and insinuation features of austerity.

Youth

Youth unemployment in Canada is higher than the national average but relatively low in comparison to other OECD countries.[1] However, quality jobs among youth appeared on a downward trend, with temporary, contract and fixed-term employment increasing more quickly among youth than older workers. Since 2010, 60 per cent of jobs acquired by young people have been part time (France, 2016). For First Nations youth, the situation was worse; in 2009 only 41 per cent were employed at all, 10 per cent lower than non-First Nation youth, with this trend worsening since the crisis (France, 2016). Youth not in education, employment or training (NEETs) are of particular concern since this status has been associated with increased risk of social isolation, crime, mental health issues, violence and drugs, alongside long-lasting 'scarring' effects related to part-time work, temporary contracts, limited labour rights and loss of career hopes. The Canadian NEET figure was 13 per cent of young people in 2015, below that of Spain and Ireland but higher than in Denmark.

Although young people in Denmark were disproportionately affected by the crisis, their circumstances were in some ways better in comparison to our other cases. The NEET rate in Denmark remained relatively low: 7 per cent in 2017 (European Commission, 2020). Denmark experienced a decrease in labour force participation in the 20 to 29 age group as many moved out of the labour force and into education. After the crisis, youth under the age of 30 without a qualifying education became ineligible for social assistance, and instead there was a shift towards 'education activation' (Andersen, 2017).

Young people in Ireland were particularly hard-hit by the crisis. Men between the age of 20 and 24 saw their employment rates fall from 70 per cent in 2008 to 48 per cent in 2010, and it remained at 44 per cent in 2014. Young women's employment rate dropped consistently, from 66 per cent in 2008 to 54 per cent in 2010, and to 46 per cent in 2014 (Barry, 2014). Unemployment rates for youth more than doubled between 2008 and 2012, from 13 per cent to 30 per cent. The number of NEETs also doubled in Ireland between 2007 and 2012, reaching 19 per cent. This number would have been much higher had it not been for the emigration of many young people between 2008 and 2013 (Papadopoulos, 2016). Clearly the unemployment effects were significant and, in some cases, remained at peak levels for some time, whereas in others a hesitant recovery began after the easing of the crisis. A particularly disturbing implication of the escalation in youth unemployment rates is talk of a 'lost generation' in countries like Ireland. Emigration increase, while producing of a statistical decline in youth unemployment, also means the loss of human capital resources.[2] Despite these figures, spending on Irish youth projects was cut by 44 per cent between 2008 and 2014 (Mercille and Murphy, 2015). Austerity was also imposed on active labour market policies (ALMP) at the same time as funding limits impeded the ability to tackle youth unemployment. Ireland's training agency cut the duration of training programmes to compensate for an increased number of beneficiaries (Papadopoulos, 2016). Fiscal austerity also produced new forms of entry-level statutory jobs for young teachers, nurses and state employees, creating lower wages and poorer working standards than those experienced by their peers (Murphy, 2017).

Spain has traditionally had the highest youth unemployment rates and the weakest links between education and work. NEET rates increased by 10 per cent from 2007 to 2012, and the 2017 NEET rate exceeded that of pre-crisis 2007. Between 2009 and 2015, the male youth unemployment rate was higher than the female one; however, the proportion of well-educated NEETs has increased, particularly for women. The percentage of youth in long-term unemployment increased from 1.5 per cent in 2007 to 18 per cent in 2013, and by 2016, Spain was third in the EU with 11 per cent long-term unemployed youth (Rodríguez-Modroño, 2019). The share of temporary employees is the highest among youth under the age of 25, as this age cohort represented 59 per cent in 2008, increasing to 73 per cent in 2016 (Felgueroso et al, 2018). Thus, alongside high rates of NEETs, the rise in atypical and precarious jobs is especially high among youth in Spain. Youth policy is largely administered by local governments in Spain, while the central government has only a minimal presence. The 2012 budget from the National Youth Institute of Spain went back to its 2002 amount. Similarly, many youth services in the regional local governments were shut down, and activities and programmes have been eliminated and staff numbers decreased. As a result, austerity cuts impacted the structures and services dedicated to youth policies, contributing to the deterioration and erasure of youth policy in Spain.

Women

In Canada, women's employment rate stayed relatively constant between 2007 and 2017, fluctuating between 68 and 70 per cent. While men experienced a steeper decline in their employment rate during the onset of the crisis (77 per cent in 2008 to 74 per cent in 2009), their employment rate remained above that of women (OECD, 2018a). Before the recession, 30 per cent of men were in non-standard work arrangements, while among women it was 40 per cent (O'Manique, 2015).

Denmark has the highest employment rates in the EU-28, with 79 per cent for men and 72 per cent of women in 2013. However, there is an adverse gender gap for women, where part-time employment (2013 figures) represented 35 per cent of female employment, compared to 16 per cent of men (Agustín, 2015). As well, the child benefit was reduced in Denmark as the ceiling limit on the maximum amount of the universal child allowance was reduced by €4,600 per family per year, regardless of the number of children, ultimately affecting women with care responsibilities (Elomaki, 2012). Women's employment rate fell from a peak of 61 per cent in 2007 to 55 per cent in 2011.

In Ireland, due to high rates of employment loss among men (particularly in the construction sector), the gender gap in employment narrowed significantly (Barry and Conroy, 2012). Ireland also experienced the largest growth in women's part-time employment rate out of all four case studies, increasing from an already significantly higher 35 per cent in 2007, to a peak of 39 per cent in 2011. This number has decreased to around a third in 2017, but still remains between 7 and 11 per cent higher than the other countries (OECD, 2018d). Public sector job cuts (see Chapter 4) disproportionately affected the women who filled 65 per cent of those jobs, and over 80 per cent in areas such as education and health care (Cullen and Murphy, 2017). Reductions in public sector pay levels had an impact on large numbers of women, and when combined with cutbacks in employment levels and freezes on recruitment, there were larger job losses and fewer job opportunities for women (Barry, 2014).

In Spain, women are three times more likely than men to be in part-time jobs, and also had the largest gender wage gap for part-time employment in the EU-28 at 31 per cent in 2014. Increased female part-time employment may help explain the rise of the at-risk-of-poverty rate from 25 per cent in 2007 to 29 per cent in 2014 (Gálvez and Rodríguez-Modroño, 2016). The risk for wage cuts during the recession was comparatively high, but women's risk slightly exceeded men's, alongside a much lower chance of women transitioning from temporary to permanent jobs (López-Andreu and Rubery, 2018). Austerity policies also effectively caused increases in unpaid care work as cuts in public spending on social services, care, and decreased family income resulted in a larger share of the unpaid work burden (Gálvez and Rodríguez-Modroño, 2016). Spain's female unemployment rate surged from 13 per cent in 2008 to 18 per cent in 2009, peaking at 27 per cent in 2013. Spain experienced the highest female unemployment rate out of the four case studies (OECD, 2018b). However, like Ireland, the significant loss of employment in male-dominated sectors due to the crisis and recession meant that the gender gap in unemployment rates almost closed during the recession. Austerity took its toll too: by targeting sectors overrepresented by women (public services, social security, health care, education and the like), by 2011 female unemployment picked up speed.

Immigrants

Immigrants felt the full force of the initial crisis period. Between 2008 and 2009, immigrants in Canada with five years or less residence, representing a mere 3 per cent of those employed, absorbed almost a quarter of the country's job losses (Barass and Shields, 2017). In recent years, eligibility criteria for dependents of economic-class migrants have been tightened (to help minimize state dependency), shifting toward a more restrictive and market-oriented policy. Changes to family sponsorship have also occurred alongside reduced state-funded settlement services and welfare-state programmes for newcomers. A heavy contractual burden is placed on adult immigrant sponsors instead of the state. The imposition of austerity in 2010 also represented decreased levels and quality of settlement supports available to migrants, with funding increases cut and/or precarious, short-term, and contract-based financing provided for settlement agencies. Thus, since the crisis, integration and welfare for immigrants has been increasingly hollowed out, despite average or elevated levels of immigrants coming into Canada (Barass and Shields, 2017).

Denmark has one of the smallest immigrant populations in the OECD, accounting for only 8 per cent of the total population in 2013. Immigrants were nonetheless disproportionately affected by the crisis. Denmark had one of the highest gaps in employment and activity rates between immigrants and native peers in the OECD, with unemployment of migrants being roughly twice as high as native-born Danes. In 2013, one third of unemployed migrants had been unemployed for more than one year, 8 percentage points above Danish nationals. Immigrants were also overrepresented in low-skilled jobs (representing over a quarter of low-skilled employment, but only 11 per cent of total employment). Similarly, the in-work poverty rate is three times higher for immigrants (OECD, 2016). Migrants were less eligible for various social benefits. Attitudes towards migrants' right to unemployment benefits is linked to economic contribution, and for the first five years of living in Denmark immigrants must pay for their own mandatory health insurance and enjoy no access to social benefits (Jørgensen and Thomsen, 2016). Integration policy in Denmark did increase between 2008 and 2011, particularly focused on the introduction of language programmes. Despite this, integration conditions have become stricter through demonstrating 'active citizenship', language proficiency requirements, and not being a recipient of social assistance for three years before application for permanent residence (Collett, 2011).

Immigrants played a key role in the Irish boom pre-crisis, with non-Irish nationals increasing from 9 per cent to 16 per cent of total employment between 2004 and 2007. After 2007, immigrants experienced declining opportunities in the Irish labour market as sectors employing high rates of migrants (construction and hospitality especially) were affected. Significant gaps in employment and unemployment rates existed between immigrants and the native-born (O'Connell, 2017). Migrants have experienced issues accessing social assistance and Child Benefit payments due to the 'habitual residence condition' (assessing connection to Ireland), and as claiming welfare has an impact on applications for citizenship, many non-EEA migrants avoid it (Doorley et al, 2013). Ireland has also been condemned by UN rapporteurs for breaches in international human rights law regarding the treatment of migrants within the migrant fishing workers scheme. Under the atypical workers scheme, migrants from outside the EU are extremely vulnerable to modern slavery and serious abuses on Irish fishing vessels, where laws on minimum wage and maximum hours have been regularly ignored (Lawrence and McSweeney, 2019).

In Spain, while overall unemployment figures were around 26 per cent in 2012, the migrant unemployment rate was a whopping 37 per cent (IFRC, 2013). The proportion of paid employees among first generation immigrants from the Middle East or North Africa (MENA) dropped from 69 per cent to 41 per cent in 2014, and only 22 per cent of female immigrants from MENA had paid jobs in 2014. The crisis facilitated the suspension or restraining of pathways for low- and middle-skill migrants. Spanish funding for immigrant integration increased between 2005 and 2009, but was reduced drastically thereafter. Funds dispersed to municipalities and regions through the Spanish integration fund were also reduced, and by 2012 the national government suspended its fund for immigrant integration, forcing autonomous communities, provinces and municipalities to accommodate the shortfall (Collett, 2011).

Low pay and precarity

As part of a precarious labour market, Canada has experienced job polarization as the gap between low- and high-paying jobs has widened. The rate of low-paying full-time jobs has risen twice as fast as the number of high-paying jobs. Similarly, wages in high-paying sectors have growth twice as fast as in low-paying sectors (Tal, 2015). The gap in hourly wages is high – temporary workers and part-time workers earn less than 60 per cent of the hourly wage of standard workers. Similarly, more than two thirds of employees in the lowest decile of earnings are non-standard workers, with poverty rates for non-standard workers accounting for 30 per cent or more (OECD, 2015a). Part-time and temporary employment has stayed relatively constant, encompassing roughly one third of all workers (ILO, 2016). While not all temporary and part-time workers are employed in the gig economy, that model has become more accepted: 2017 statistics showed that non-traditional workers (as in independent contractors, on-demand workers and remote workers) made up 20 to 30 per cent of the workforce in Canada (Randstad, 2017). The number of temporary workers in Canada has increased by 50 per cent in the last 20 years, rising faster than the number of permanent jobs, with temporary workers earning 20 per cent less an hour compared to permanent employees (Naidu-Ghelani, 2019). Non-standard work is becoming a big issue in sectors that are more precarious, namely information, culture and recreation, educational services, and accommodation and food services. The federal government does not have a formal definition of non-traditional/precarious work arrangements and therefore no formal data is collected on it (Fong, 2018).

From the 1990s to 2007, the level of part-time employment, fixed-term contracts and self-employment remained steady in Denmark. Total atypical employment (including self-employed, part-time workers, fixed-term workers, agency workers or a combination of these) accounted for 35 per cent of the Danish workforce in 2015 (Mailand and Larsen, 2018). Due to Danish flexicurity measures, atypical workers are often covered under the same collective agreements and legislation as permanent employees, making them less precarious relative to atypical workers in other countries (Bredgaard et al, 2009), but there was some deterioration as a result of post-crisis 2010 austerity reforms. Deterioration included halving the duration of benefits from four to two years, and tightening re-eligibility criteria by requiring those who have lost their right to unemployment insurance benefits to work 52 weeks (previously 26 weeks) within three years in order to be re-eligible (Svarer, 2015). Additionally, reforms to the disability pension scheme and flex-job scheme in 2012 included altering marginal part-time workers' salary entitlements from reflecting full-time hours, to only hours worked (Mailand and Larsen, 2018). Changes in active labour market policy (ALMP) have left those in temporary, part-time and agency contracts with increased activation obligations, stricter availability rules, and sanctions for those who do not perform their activation activities (Nielsen et al, 2019). As a result, almost 34,000 unemployed were prevented from accessing unemployment insurance benefits, and, when combined with declining membership rates of voluntary benefit funds (meaning one third of the workforce in 2012 was not entitled to income replacements), this resulted in a de-universalization of Danish unemployment protection (Rathgeb, 2018). Those working in marginal part-time employment, especially those in contracts with few hours, now have more difficulty in amassing enough hours to secure the right to unemployment insurance (Mailand and Larsen, 2018). Temporary employees who lose their job have coverage rates 10 percentage points below those of unemployed workers who previously had permanent contracts (ILO, 2016).

The Irish Congress of Trade Unions has accused employers in the accommodation, retail and hospitality sectors of seeking out low-paid employees and working them for as long as possible for little reward (Miley, 2019). Employment protection legislation (EPL) standards slightly worsened between 2008 and 2013, and employers actively took advantage of weak or absent EPL to advance precarious labour practices. This included weak enforcement against bogus self-employment, poor regulation of internships and traineeships, and the bypassing of legislation through the use of 'if and when' contracts (Murphy, 2017). In an interview (Dublin, June 2017) an academic and social activist noted that the deprivation index, based on 11 measures, increased for as many as half the population. In that context, some groups in particular, such as lone parents, experienced severe deprivation – the deprivation rate for that group was 62 per cent. Disabled people were among others affected.

Even for relatively well-protected groups in Ireland, such as pensioners, there were costs. A Sinn Féin legislator pointed out:

> 'it looks like they were relatively untouched. But that's only if you look at it from the point of view of income, whereas, of course, people on the state pension would be heavily dependent on the public health system, heavily dependent on the public transport system, heavily dependent on their local authority for maintenance of their public housing, and therefore they would have been disproportionately affected by all of those [...] you know, so we've, we've had this debate where income inequality was the big measure[...] [but] unequal access to public services becomes as important a determinant of people's quality of life.' (Irish legislator, Dublin, June, 2017)

The passing of the Social Welfare Act 2010 and reforms of ALMPs in Ireland included an increase in conditionalities and compliance in order to receive unemployment benefits. Increased sanctions and conditionalities force workers to accept lower wages and enhanced workplace monitoring as a precondition for employment. Those who cannot engage in the labour market in the first place, the most marginalized, are often excluded altogether (Murphy and Mercille, 2019). Between 2011 and 2014, Ireland experienced polarizing employment shifts, with employment growth between 2013 and 2014 mostly in low-paid jobs (Eurofound, 2015b). According to the Nevin Economic Research Institute, work in 2016 was more precarious than in the years leading up to the crisis, with higher deprivation rates and shares of workers experiencing in-work poverty, and the report estimated that between one third to one half of all Irish employees are in employment with medium to high risk of precariousness (Nugent, 2017).

In Spain, too, the link between austerity measures and the various forms of insecurity is absolutely clear. Labour market reforms in Spain, including greater flexibility in the organization of the workforce, changes to collective bargaining, wage suppression, and the unequal impact of dismissals and wage adjustments on precarious work (temporary contracts), have increased the number of people living in disadvantaged positions. The pursuit of internal devaluation also reduced purchasing power and increased vulnerability to material deprivation. For migrants this was especially damaging. A BBC reporter (Hedgecoe, 2020a) quoted a representative of the Association for Domestic Workers and Carers in Zaragoza, in north-eastern Spain, as saying that the unregulated nature of the sector makes it difficult for workers to have a contract and a job for three years, both of which are required in order to gain residency papers. She went on to say that the lack of regulation also means wages can be woefully low: "Often [employers] are not even paying the minimum wage, which is €950 [£830; USD$1,060] per month as of 2020. There are people earning €500, €600 or €700."

The use of fixed-term contracts in Spain was prominent before the crisis. From the mid-1990s until 2008, these covered over 30 per cent workforce. In 2007, 32 per cent of all employees in Spain were employed in temporary contracts, compared to the EU-28 average of 15 per cent. Following the onset of the crisis, an astounding 90 per cent of all job losses in Spain were due to the dismissal of temporary contract workers, or non-renewal of their contracts (Heyes and Lewis, 2014). This improved the statistics on the ratio of permanent to non-permanent jobs temporarily, but did not really involve a restructuring of the labour market in favour of permanent jobs. One CCOO (Comisiones Obreras) Spanish union official (Madrid, May, 2018) commented that, "temporary employment was now lower because of depression. Obviously the first that are fired are temporary, which is cheaper. But when the recovery started, that rate of temporary employment started rising again."

Austerity meant public sector budget cuts, severe changes in employment regulations, and enhanced employer power in dismissing and modifying working conditions (López-Andreu, 2017). The reforms introduced more internal flexibility mechanisms, including amendments to employment contracts (via reduced wages), and removal of the requirement for administrative authorization for suspending contracts or reducing work-days. The aim of these reforms was to address employment decline and labour market segmentation through changing employment protection legislation (EPL) to stimulate the use of open-ended contracts over temporary ones. While reforms such as employment promotion contracts were supposed to favour labour market entry for disadvantaged workers, it left them unprotected during the first year (Picot and Tassinari, 2017). New contracts signed in 2015 showed a daily wage reduction of nearly 12 per cent. According to the CCOO Economic Department (n.d.), the effect on wages and incomes was significant: between 2008 and 2015, average monthly wages fell by 2 per cent, hourly wages for doing the same job by 8 per cent, and annual wage income by 9 per cent. The logic of the reform was explained by a consultant interviewed in Barcelona (September, 2018):

> 'The idea was that making it easier for employers to lay off workers, whatever kind of worker, would promote employers to recruit permanent rather than temporary contracts. Permanents would be less protected, employers exposed to less risk than before, this was idea. From point of view of reducing

> duality one cannot say that the reforms have worked. Attitude of employers continues to be about same, usually preferring to recruit short term.'

The reforms led to a significant reduction in the (de jure) stringency of employment protection, and while EPL is close to the average of OECD strictness for regular jobs and above the average for temporary jobs, implementation was a problem. The lack of enforcement and sanctions has not reduced the use of temporary jobs, and while the share of people in temporary jobs is below the pre-crisis peak, the flow of temporary contracts is larger than ever (Felgueroso et al, 2018). Bentolila et al (2017) demonstrate the dominance of temporary jobs vis-à-vis permanent jobs, given that a larger share of new jobs created are both temporary and shorter than before the crisis. Workers employed in temporary contracts bounced back to 27 per cent of the entire labour force in 2017 (the highest since 2008), with contracts lasting less than six months accounting for half of all temporary contracts (ILO, 2019).

Housing and food insecurity

The effect of labour market precarity is widespread insecurity, which for many leads to an inability to meet basic needs such as decent, affordable housing and the provision of food. Evidence in all our case countries suggests that in austere times, significant proportions of the population find it difficult or impossible to adequately meet these needs.

Harvey (2005) identified a number of key practices that could lead to the threat of eviction: privatization of state-provided housing; financialization of social housing as a primary commodity in the global capitalist economy; the manipulation of austerity to justify a withdrawal of government housing subsidies; and state redistribution of wealth to private landlords through rent paid through government subsidies, effectively rerouting public monies into private hands. To these might be added permitting the conversion of existing stocks of housing, or the building of new units, for short-term rental purposes tied to tourism rather than residents. The state therefore plays a crucial role in intensifying the risks faced by low-income groups in relation to housing insecurity (Cooper and Paton, 2019). In contrast, states could offset or eliminate housing insecurity by providing adequate stocks of social housing. However, social housing, tied to state funding, is extremely vulnerable to austerity policies.

In 2011, an estimated 50 per cent of Canada's lowest quintile were in core housing need. Core housing need includes those who live in housing deemed inadequate, unsuitable (overcrowded) or unaffordable (costing more than 30 per cent of before-tax income) (Pakeman, 2015). This has occurred alongside the ongoing reduction of social housing in Canada since 1993, and downloading onto provinces and municipalities (HSC, 2014).

Housing affordability, for both buyers and renters, has deteriorated since the crisis. Canada's affordability measure (meaning the median home sales price divided by the median annual household income) was at 4.9 in 2008, judged to be 'seriously unaffordable'. By 2018 however, the figure was at 6.7 or 'severely unaffordable'. Canadians now need 56 per cent more money to buy a home, and 25 per cent more money to rent a home compared to 2008, while income only increased on average by 15 per cent over that decade (Point2 Homes, 2018). Similarly, a study by the Canadian Centre for Policy Alternatives demonstrates that there were no neighbourhoods in two of Canada's biggest cities (metro Toronto and Vancouver), where a full-time minimum wage worker could afford a one- or two-bedroom apartment without spending more than 30 per cent of their earnings. They would have had to work, per week, 112 hours (Toronto) or 96 hours (Vancouver) to afford a modest two-bedroom apartment (MacDonald, 2019). Statistics Canada only began tracking evictions, another measure of housing insecurity, in 2018. To date, British Columbia reigns as Canada's eviction capital, with 4 per cent of households forced to move in 2018, followed by 2 per cent of households in Ontario (Wong, 2019).

The situation in Denmark was somewhat better as social housing in Denmark remains comparatively high, with public housing accounting for approximately 21 per cent of housing stock. Municipalities are required to allocate 20 per cent of housing to those in acute housing need, and this increases to one third in Copenhagen. Still, there were problems. Despite the housing allocations system and housing benefits, demand often exceeded supply in larger cities, with vulnerable groups (for example lone mothers and people with disabilities) particularly affected. The rent in newer public housing is often too expensive for those on cash benefits to afford (Benjaminsen and Andrade, 2015). Affordability of housing became increasing problematic for poorer households between 2007 and 2017, with 84 per cent of youth living under the poverty line overburdened by the cost of housing (Council of Europe, 2020). For potential buyers, real house prices increased 19 per cent between 2012 and 2016; housing prices in Copenhagen increased by 43 per cent during the same period (Gaál, 2017).

In Ireland, decreasing social housing availability due to reduced state spending has resulted in an increased reliance on subsidized private rented accommodation, subjecting low-income renters to rent inflation and resulting in a rise in homelessness (Norris and Byrne, 2017). The private rented sector is, historically and currently, marked by low quality in comparison to other forms of tenure, as the absence of regulation allows some landlords to deliver poor service, especially in areas of scarce supply (Bone, 2014). All in all, reduced public expenditure on supporting affordable housing leads to greater housing insecurity. With the rising cost of living in Ireland, homelessness increased every month since the first count in 2014, including a 93 per cent rise among young people (Nugent, 2018). For buyers, housing prices initially fell following the crisis in 2009, but the trend reversed in 2013 and was followed by year-on-year increases of over 8 per cent annually (Thomas, 2018). By 2013, Ireland was the fifth most expensive country in the EU, with prices 17 per cent above the European average (Oxfam, 2013).

Average household income in Spain dropped by 13 per cent between 2009 and 2015, and approximately 4 per cent of households (700,000) are said to have no income (Mayores UDP, 2017). Only 2 per cent of Spain's housing stock (rented and owned) is social housing, and the central state budget was significantly reduced by 40 per cent between 2008 and 2013, while central government transfers to municipalities were reduced by 12 per cent in 2013 and 14 per cent in 2014. Similar to the other countries analyzed here, the state housing plan increasingly focused on subsidies for rental housing for low-income families (HRW, 2014).

Spain's rental prices have increased by 50 per cent between 2014 and 2019 (Valdivia, 2019). In 2016, 43 per cent of Spaniards who rented private housing spent over 40 per cent of their earnings on rent, representing 12 per cent more than the EU average (AFP, 2018). The combination of low labour income and risk of unemployment in Spain has made it difficult for a large number of households to rent adequate housing, let alone access a loan to purchase a home. Young households (aged 30 to 44) – who have already felt disproportionate impacts from the crisis – have experienced rising rent-to-income ratios from 19 per cent in 2010 to 30 per cent in 2018 (Valdivia, 2019). As a result, coupled with decreased access to social housing, vulnerable households are becoming priced out of housing, and are suffering from reduced disposable income.

Between 2008 and 2010, homelessness increased by 16 per cent. Night counts done in Spanish cities in 2011 revealed that migrants made up 50 to 75 per cent of people living rough, with 63 per cent of those registered with homeless networks being migrants. For example, homeless shelters in Catalonia reported a 20 per cent increase from 2008 to 2010 in the number of migrants using their services (Fondeville and Ward, 2011).

The number of evictions in Barcelona in 2008 increased 16 per cent due to financial difficulties caused by the onset of the recession. Around

200,000 families were under threat of eviction by 2010, including a large number of migrants (Fondeville and Ward, 2011). From 2009 to 2017, Spanish courts ordered between 400,000 and 600,000 home repossessions (Edwards, 2017). An imbalanced housing market has led to many homeless across the country (re)claiming homes and buildings, with 45,000 buildings nationwide having squatters between 2012 and 2017. Spanish courts took on average two years to remove squatters, making it a viable option for many. This has, however, spurred increases in private security services and the creation of companies such as Desokupa (meaning 'unsquat') in Barcelona to guard or 'negotiate' with squatters (Edwards, 2017). Some estimates put the number of homeless people in Spain as high as 35,000. A United Nations special rapporteur pointed out that 26 per cent of Spaniards, and 30 per cent of Spanish children, were at risk of poverty or social exclusion, and 30 per cent of young people out of work. Among minority communities, such as the Roma, as many as 92 per cent were at risk of extreme poverty, and 52 per cent were unemployed (Hedgecoe, 2020a)

Inability to put food on the table is another symptom of poverty and is measured in part by the growth of food banks. Food bank usage can be connected to various pressures, including mounting pressures on household finances due to job cuts, wage stagnation, higher personal or household indebtedness, increasing utility and shopping bills, austerity-driven benefit changes and the application of sanctions. Food banks, sometimes working alongside transnational food companies interested in decreasing food waste and exhibiting corporate social responsibility, are sometimes depicted as a solution to poverty. Poor people are fed while creating a social role for churches and voluntary groups. Critics point out that this effectively depoliticizes and erases the structural factors leading to food insecurity, such as austerity (Strong, 2019).

Food bank usage has grown substantially over the past few decades in order to fill the gaps left by a declining social safety net. Usage in Canada increased by 28 per cent between 2008 and 2016 (Food Banks Canada, 2016), but gradually decreased after that. It was estimated that at the height of the crisis in 2011, just over 12 per cent of Canadian households (1.6 million households) experienced some level of food insecurity, amounting to 3.9 million people. Two thirds of households whose major source of income was social assistance were food insecure, and 37 per cent of those on employment insurance or workers' compensation benefits were as well (Tarasuk et al, 2011).

Although there are few comprehensive studies of food insecurity in Denmark, a study done by Holm et al (2018) estimates that approximately 200,000 households cannot afford enough food, with 4 to 5 per cent of

Danish households experiencing insecure access to food. This figure, while still significant, was lower than our other cases, an indication of the residual effects of a more comprehensive type of welfare state. Food insecurity is more evident in low-income and lone parent families, and between 31 and 48 per cent of households receiving social assistance, disability pension or unemployment benefits. Whether or not this has changed drastically in the recent decade is unknown, but the reintroduction of the social assistance ceiling and scaling back of social services after 2015 is projected to increase food insecurity if employment does not increase (Holm et al, 2018; Hornbek-Copenhagen, 2018).

In 2010, approximately 10 per cent of the Irish population were experiencing food poverty, with the most at-risk groups including: people under 40 (single or divorced, widowed or separated), those living in social housing, those living with children under the age of 18, those who were unemployed, ill/disabled, or those in the lowest-income quintile. The number of people experiencing 'official' food poverty (according to the Department of Social Protection) in 2015 was one in nine (550,000 people). When factoring in those experiencing food poverty due to social exclusion (that is, they cannot afford to socialize with family or friends with food or drink once a month), the incidence increases to over 20 per cent (Healy, 2019). Food bank usage in Ireland increased in the years following the recession, with food initiatives expanding across the greater Dublin area in particular (Baker, 2015).

Similarly, Spanish food banks' food volume grew by approximately 20 per cent in the years following the crisis. Caritas (a Catholic charity for social relief) reported attending to over a million people in 2011, tripling from about 370,000 in 2007. The main recipients were immigrants (28 per cent), older people (21 per cent), people with drug dependence (12 per cent), homeless people (10 per cent), long-term unemployed people (9 per cent), children and teenagers (7 per cent), and terminally ill people and their relatives (6 per cent) (Perez de Armino, 2014). Food insecurity in Spain (alongside other areas of insecurity discussed) prompted thousands of people (many of them immigrants – possibly illegal – and without welfare benefits) to search dumpsters, scavenge and seek out black-market trade for recycled materials. There were an estimated 2,000 people searching dumpsters in Barcelona, every night during the recession (Frayer, 2012).

More debt

Resort to personal debt served as a coping mechanism in times of labour market insecurity and precarity. While the risks of financial markets were socialized (see Chapter 2), families (especially low-income ones) remain individually responsible for indebtedness they incur associated with welfare spending retrenchment. The institutionalization of austerity positions personal and household debt as a primary mechanism through which households can meet the costs of social reproduction, given that many costs have been offloaded by the state (through welfare retrenchment, for example) and capital (through low wages and precarious employment). Alongside debt is an increase in unpaid labour, performed mostly by women. Thus, changes in the labour market, and changes in the burden of social reproduction, have sometimes incentivized families to rely on unsecured debt (credit cards) and secured forms of credit (mortgages).

In some cases, notably Canada, private household debt has been as a means of compensating for declining public services and stagnant real incomes. Canada's debt-to-income ratio increased during and after the recession, with the 2019 debt-to-disposable income ratio levels remaining at approximately 180 per cent of disposable income, some 20 per cent higher than in late 2007.[3] Much of this debt accumulation post-recession is due to mortgage liabilities. The rise in debt-to-income is most pronounced among lower-income families in metropolitan areas such as Toronto and Vancouver, where families in the lowest quintile carry rates of, respectively, 420 and 400 per cent of debt-to-disposable income (Gellatly and Richards, 2019). Thus, the expansion of personal debt may have ameliorated some impacts of austerity in Canada by substituting longer-term liabilities for immediate ones. However, in our other cases, where household debt as a percentage of GDP declined after 2007, this was different.[4] Even so, debt took a toll and many suffered through extortionate interest rates charged by same-day outlets and other vehicles of instant, unsecured, loans, which increased in all four of our cases.

According to the Financial Consumer Agency of Canada, the use of short-term, high-cost loans more than doubled in Canada from 2009 to 2014 with over 2 million Canadians resorting to using payday loans each year. A survey of 1,500 payday loan users showed that only 50 per cent of users lived in households with annual incomes under $55,000, meaning that usage was not confined to low-income earners. Forty-five per cent of respondents stated that they used payday loans to cover unexpected costs (such as car repairs). However, 41 per cent reported they use them for recurring and expected expenses such as rent or utilities (FCAC, 2016).

Three out of ten Spanish families regularly run out of money at the end of each month, with nearly half of all households facing serious financial difficulty at some period and 3.5 million of the country's unemployed receiving no social security. Meeting short-term needs has resulted in increased use of payday lenders, which can charge annualized interest rates of between 3,500 per cent and 4,500 per cent (De Barron, 2016). Once in debt the situation can become much worse; debtors are registered on credit agencies' debtor lists, accessible to retailers, real estate agencies and landlords. It becomes increasingly difficult for debtors to sign apartment leases, buy anything on credit, or even purchase a mobile phone contract. As a result, debt exacerbates poverty. Some of those categorized as in serious debt lived in fear that their employment earnings could be subject to a court order to garnishee their wages to service their debt.

In Ireland, housing costs and associated debt played a prominent role. The Irish Bank Resolution Corporation and National Asset Management Agency were the largest vendors of distressed real estate loans in Europe in 2014, demonstrating the dominance of vulture funds in Irish real estate and the state's culpability in crisis management schemes. With over 100,000 mortgages in serious arrears, initial projections were that 20,000 to 30,000 homes would be repossessed (DDCI, 2016). In the event, between 2008 and 2019, repossession orders were granted on only 2,721 private dwellings, encompassing 0.4 per cent of total stock of residential mortgages. An additional 5,474 were surrendered voluntarily (Fahy, 2018). While not insignificant, these figures are testimony to continued legal protection for those in arrears, and a lack of public or even judicial sympathy for the banks and their agents.

One of the main manifestations of individual or household debt in Denmark is the payday loan industry, 'the instant cash loan market is a growing market. In 2010, 20,384 instant cash loans were taken out totalling DKK 37 million. The Danish Competition and Consumer Authority estimates that in 2014 a total of 136,000 instant cash loans were taken out totalling approximately DKK 430 million' (DCCA, 2015). The majority of payday loans were issued to people outside the labour market, including sickness benefit recipients, retirees, or those without a steady income. Existing outside the labour market also complicates their ability to pay back the loans (Dwan et al, 2018).

The examples provided in this section are typical of countries experiencing austerity. It has been argued that debt serves as a means of social control. In the UK, for example, the rate of unsecured debt, such as consumer credit with home credit stores, payday lenders and pawnbrokers, has grown four times faster than secured lending. Often efforts to avoid housing insecurity lead borrowers expose themselves to food insecurity. As Alexandri and Janoschka (2017) point out with respect to the similar if more extreme developments in Greece, increased household debt where people are unable to meet bank, tax and social security obligations, serves as an effective mechanism of control of the impoverished population.

Comparisons and conclusions

We have previously noted declines in union density and the ideological merger of governments with different political party affiliations under neoliberalism and New Public Management. The institutionalization of austerity weakened the organizations that speak for people who are disadvantaged, and created voice and organizational challenges for a fragmented precariat (those living in poverty, households with high debt, women, migrants, youth and so on). The state also moved to undermine other organizations that once played an advocacy role, representing women, migrants and Indigenous peoples. The Irish National Women's Council of Ireland experienced a 35 per cent spending cut in 2012, ostensibly to prioritize front-line service over advocacy. Women's shelters and childcare services also experienced up to 40 per cent cuts to their funding. This left many community development groups unable to meet their core objectives. Social expenditure reductions to income supports and social services show a gender bias (being targeted on such items as lone parent/childcare benefits). As a result, in 2013, 63 per cent of lone parents, predominantly women, experienced deprivation. It has been estimated that reduced childcare and lone parent benefits prevented up to 25 per cent of parents from accessing paid employment due to high childcare costs (Barry, 2014).

Alongside this, state bodies such as the Equality Authority, the Irish Human Rights Commission, and the National Consultative Committee on Racism and Interculturalism faced large funding cuts or closed down altogether, greatly affecting the ability of migrants to have a voice. Austerity also hampered integration efforts by removing resources and dedicating less effort towards representation or advocacy (Gross, 2014). Thus, while migrants experienced disproportionate impacts regarding their employment status, they also face declining institutional support, hindering the capacity to interrogate and investigate inequality and racism in Ireland. Further, the Status of Women Canada's budget was cut by 37 per cent, and more than 30 women's organizations lost 100 per cent of their funding, National Indigenous peoples' organizations (including women's organizations) were cut by 40 per cent, and some were removed completely. By 2015, Canada was 35th on the World Economic Forum's gender gap index, whereas it had ranked 14th in 2006 (WEF, 2017; GENC, 2018). In Denmark, women's interests were also adversely affected by austerity measures such as the closure of Equality Unit within the National Labour Market Authority (NLMA). Equality tasks were supposed to be taken over by the NLMA, but after it was absorbed by the Danish Agency of Labour Market and Recruitment, as of 2015, no explicit gender objectives were carried out (Agustín, 2015).

The dull grind of neoliberal austerity has not only failed to revive the economies of the states in which it has been imposed; it has also imposed a heavy cost on these societies, particularly the indebted working class and other social groups – youth, women and migrants among them. The costs can be observed in general labour force statistics and in the accounts of various forms of associated poverty, including in housing and food. The four countries we have used for illustration vary in the degree of austerity they have experienced, and in the way austerity policies have been targeted and implemented. Here a national frame reveals certain varieties of austerity and the varieties of capitalism and welfare state literatures may help explain the superior performance of Denmark with respect to vulnerable groups (but not immigrants, where its performance was little different from the other cases.) But when looking through a social lens, we also can see much cross-national variation in this age of austerity – experiences differ dramatically according to class, gender, race, age and citizenship. Regardless of its specific expression, the common thread of austerity is nevertheless the constraint and suppression of working-class living standards, the empowerment of capital and the wealth and incomes of those representing it.

Moving to the next row in our Varieties of Austerity table from Chapter 1, varieties of austerity with respect to precarity, poverty and household or individual debt, can be identified in three ways. First, the impact of the economic crisis combined with the effects of austerity policies – fiscal through budget cuts and conditionalities; privatization that eliminated many well-paid jobs and through the imposition of user fees on consumers; and labour reforms that created insecurity and suppressed earnings – has been to both insulate and expose certain groups in society, creating a large pool of disaffected citizens. There are crosscutting dynamics at play here given that not all are necessarily low paid. Housing insecurity, for example, is an issue for many with higher incomes. Precarity and youth unemployment affects students who are not themselves high income, but may well come from families who are, and who had higher aspirations for their children. Second, given that many who suffer overlapping types of poverty are marginalized and hard to

Table 6: Varieties of austerity – dynamics or degrees of precarity

	Institutionalization	Insulation	Insinuation
Precarity	Voice and organizing predicaments for those who are poor, in precarious, low-wage jobs and have high debt	Impact of crisis and austerity measures on particular sectors, occupations, households, individuals	Causalities of austerity: poor, precarious and vulnerable people

organize, processes of institutionalization have instead involved the reversal or erosion of voice for these groups in policy discussions. Third, by manufacturing degrees of insecurity through labour market precarity and producing more debt for many households, casualties of the austerity era mount. The global financial crisis may not be the responsibility of youth, women, immigrants and low-pay workers, but the collateral damage of austerity measures insinuates their culpability.

While those who are poor and/or lead precarious lives may have been largely muted in policy discussions (at least to the extent that austerity measures represent a frontal assault on their particular interests and needs through deleterious institutionalization, insulation and insinuation), there have been many anti-austerity protests by labour and through broader social campaigns and protests. In some cases, outlined in the next chapter, campaigns and protests that began with specific aspects of austerity became generalized and contributed to the formation of new movements and parties, or shifts in support away from more established ones. Often this is discussed in terms of right-wing populism – and Spain and Denmark provide examples of these. But other developments could serve as examples of left populism and its connection to the theme of diffuse precariousness explored in this chapter; exemplified by protests against mortgage foreclosures and evictions in Spain that led to the foundation of Unidas Podemos, protests against water charges that helped Sinn Fein emerge as a major player in Irish politics, and protests against tuition fee increases in Quebec, Canada, which altered the policy landscape. And the generalized malaise surrounding the social effects of austerity for multiple social groups surely contributed to a steady decline in popular support for the parties most associated with austerity in Spain and Ireland, again discussed in the next chapter.

7

Limits and Possibilities of Resistance

Austerity, in one form or another, coloured the politics of the past decade (2008–18). As the previous chapters have demonstrated, austerity comes in varieties: fiscal consolidation by means of balanced budgets and expenditure cuts or restraint, plus multiple modes of public sector restructuring and privatization, and labour restructuring by flexibility and internal devaluation. Having, in previous chapters, tracked the impact of austerity, both as a general programme and in its specific forms, we now turn to the issue of how much and what kind of resistance there has been and its effectiveness in halting or reversing these policies. Reactions to austerity vary enormously from enthusiastic support, to various levels of acceptance and consent (ranging from enthusiasm, to resigned – there is no alternative), to disaffection (Clarke, 2017). Resistance, too, comes in many forms (Dean, 2014; Horvat, 2014). Some actions may be highly individualized, such as refusing to accept responsibility and making the tough choices required by the justificatory rhetoric of austerity (Mitrea, 2017). Others might involve efforts to mitigate the effects through self-sacrificing behaviour (Baines, 2017). Often these responses will barely register on a scale seeking to measure resistance yet they do indicate, where detected, non-acceptance of austerian policies and practices on the part of individuals or spontaneously formed collectivities. Other forms of resistance are more visible and can be compared according to a number of criteria. One might be the scale on which they develop – from highly localized, to regional, national or international. Another is whether resistance is primarily defensive, directed against some specific instance of austerity, such as reductions in a social service, or the eviction of an occupant from housing, or resistance that escalates into a protest against austerity in general. More interesting, from our perspective, is whether they achieve some transformative potential to not only undo some or all austerity measures, but also/instead to construct an alternative that goes beyond it (Pineault, 2014; Graefe and Rioux, 2017).

We see the institutionalization of routes for austerity-related dissent as having emerged through either formal or informal channels via unions, protests and political campaigns or policies. The impact of these resistances (and their relative degree of institutionalization) involved not only winning or losing a specific struggle or campaign, but also shifting the insinuation of burden and blame – often prompting later success through the rise of right and left populism within the political system. Explicit or implicit recognition that austerity involves the insulation or exposure of particular segments of society (whether class-based or pertaining to other social groups like immigrants, women and youth) suggests some forms of resistance were more systemic in nature (focused on structural transformation), and some were more opposed to one-off aspects of austerity reforms (like service deterioration or cuts to specific programmes). For large movements and organizations (like the 15-M Movement in Spain and the Maple Spring in Quebec, Canada), the perceived targets of resistance were often multiple. In all of the country cases presented here we find expressions of populism from both the left and right. Some, such as Unidos Podemos (Spain), the Red Green Alliance (Denmark), Sinn Féin (Ireland) and Quebec Solidaire (Quebec, Canada) are politically situated to the left of mainstream social democracy. Others, specifically the Danish People's Party (Denmark), Vox (Spain) and the Coalition Avenir Québec (Canada) are of the radical right.

The broader context is one of neoliberal globalization in which the organized working class has been weakened, partly by structural changes associated with economic globalization, but also, and equally importantly, by policy-driven flexibilization in the name of achieving greater competitiveness (see Chapter 5). Political alliances with social democratic parties were of decreasing value as those parties became increasing subject to neoliberal ideology and, when in office, tended to be complicit in austerity policies and New Public Management. If the organized portion of the working class is weaker and subject to precarity, insecurity and fragmentation, then the unorganized portion (see Chapter 6) suffers these characteristics to an even greater degree.

We turn now to survey two types of resistance: defensive activities, carried out primarily by trade unions; and campaigns, often including unions but also a range of broader social movements. Campaigns focused frequently on quite specific aspects of austerity but later evolved into general challenges to austerity, the consequences of which were the destabilization of political systems in Spain and Ireland, and greater political space, however confined, for alternatives to austerity. The final section of the chapter examines the impacts of austerity and resistance within the formal political realm of left and right populist parties.

Defensive resistance

Under conditions of deep recession, high unemployment and legislative attack, and with unreliable political allies, organized labour was in a weak position in all four countries across the post-crisis austerity period. Apart from protesting austerity measures, the main activity was damage limitation, either through conducting defensive collective bargaining to minimize losses, or through trying to use social dialogue institutions – or, where these had been abandoned by governments and capital, pushing for their restoration.

In Spain, large general strikes were called in 2010, 2011 and 2012 to protest the government's anti-labour legislation and general austerity measures (see Campos Lima and Artiles, 2011). Governments of social democratic persuasion, the Spanish Socialist Workers' Party (the PSOE), and of the right People's Party (PP), were both targets. The first general strike occurred in 2010 in response to austerity measures being rolled out by the PSOE. The strikes were successful in shutting down many of the major cities as well as international travel. The second major post-crisis Spanish strike was in response to the PSOE's move to raise the retirement age to 67 from 65 (Clendenning, 2011). The 2012 strikes, which were met with riot police violence, were directed against the new PP government's deepening of the austerity agenda – a new round of spending cuts, tax increases and labour legislation aimed at increasing labour flexibility. Though impressive in size and solidarity, the strikes had little immediate political impact.

Workers in specific public services also organized marches against privatization policies. They were called tides (*mareas* in Spanish), with different colours assigned to different sector marches. The 15-M Movement of anti-austerity activists had been involved in the tides, with the support of various networks (more on 15-M later in the chapter). The most significant of these were the green tide (education) and the white tide (health care). Social media were utilized to mobilize efforts including local assemblies and strikes. Mass demonstrations and petitions were organized, and in five days a million signatures against privatization in the health sector was collected. Legal action was also taken in courts where judgments sometimes blocked the government's plans (Romanos, 2017: 141).

Outside Spain, labour resistance to post-crises austerity was present but quite limited in scope and impact. The Irish Congress of Trade

Unions (ICTU) responded to austerity programmes by demanding that the burden of the crisis should not be felt by those who could not bear it, nor caused it. It asked for a strategic investment initiative in job creation schemes and education and training, and an increase in taxation of the business sector and high-income earners. ICTU's proposals, however, received little attention from the government and Troika, and they were sidelined in favour of fiscal consolidation policies (Geary, 2016). A series of national demonstrations involving up to 100,000 protesters in 2009 and a one-day strike involving 250,000 public sector workers failed to change government policy. A planned follow-up strike was cancelled to allow for the return of social partnership negotiations though those ultimately concluded with the state abandoning the system (O'Connor, 2017).

Increasingly, the unions preferred social dialogue to mass action. As the leader of ICTU David Begg put it, 'the time-honoured option of protest is not, of itself, a sufficient response because nowhere has it made a real difference' (cited in Geary, 2016: 134–5). Similarly, another union leader noted that 'political strikes are not part of our DNA' (cited in Geary, 2016: 134–5). Realistic as these assessments may have been, renewed social dialogue was not particularly successful either. The partial success of negotiations between public sector unions and the government involved major union concessions (in the Croke Park and Haddington Road agreements, see Geary 2016; see also Chapters 4 and 5) but also sowed divisions between the private and public sectors and divided an already weak trade union movement.

In Denmark, there were some large public sector strikes early in the crisis and some major protests organized by the largest Danish union federation LO (Landsorganisationen i Danmark – Danish Confederation of Trade Unions) and a number of its member organizations. However, demonstrations and other forms of resistance were limited, and there were no general strikes (Mailand, 2014: 422; Scheuer et al, 2016).

In Canada, there were protests, and unions certainly tried to mitigate the impact of austerity by various means (see Thomas and Tufts, 2016; McBride, 2017, Chapter 9; Sweeney and Hickey, 2017). However, in English Canada at least, there was nothing on the scale of Ontario's 1990s 'Days of Action' that had greeted an earlier round of austerity measures. Back then, hundreds of thousands of people had participated in a mixture of rotating political strikes and mass demonstrations. After 2008, Quebec labour federations prepared a major mobilization effort for the round of public sector bargaining that began in 2009–10 (Collombat, 2014). However, the Finance Minister, Raymond Bachand, aimed to impose or raise user fees for public services through privatization in three main sectors: hydroelectricity, health services and higher education.

The attack immediately led to strong responses. Movements against user fees included a number of unions, organizations and groups, but rival coalitions represented different and at times divergent responses (Collombat, 2014: 147).

Challenging austerity

The lived experience of austerity has taken multiple forms and affected a wide variety of social groups (see Chapter 6). As a result, there has been lots of low-level, often localized or issue-specific, resistance to aspects of austerity. Frequently protests have taken the form of demonstrations, marches, sit-ins, petitions and so forth. In some cases, this type of resistance has escalated into much larger expressions of protest, often using innovative tactics, and with broader consequences for the political system. Among the broader consequences have been counter-mobilizations from the right.

Protests are exemplified by the so-called Maple Spring in Quebec (Canada), a movement triggered by tuition fee increases in post-secondary education; in Ireland, by the Right2Water protests over the imposition of water charges and water meters; and in Spain by housing issues connected to mortgages and evictions. Each of these issues and their protest movements had significant, if somewhat time-lagged, impacts on their political systems. Different issues – tuition fees, water charges, mortgages and evictions – served as sparks which ignited populist protests that had some immediate impact in alleviating the effects of austerity but also contributed to longer-term changes in the political system.

In the Canadian province of Quebec, the biggest and longest student protest in history eventually transformed into a wider social struggle. This protest emerged from the 2010–11 Quebec budget under the Liberal party, which not only was characterized by regressive funding of public services, but also aimed to raise post-secondary tuition fees by 75 per cent over five years (Collombat, 2014; Bonin, 2016; Spiegel, 2016). The initial phase of the movement focused primarily on higher educational reform, staging protests against tuition rises and critiquing the government's continual underfunding of post-secondary education (Giroux, 2013). Three major student unions became important vehicles in the movement eventually named the Maple Spring (Pineault, 2012). One of these, CLASSE (Coalition of the Association for a Student Syndical Solidarity) directly rejected the regime of neoliberal capitalism and aimed to abolish tuition fees rather than limit their increase (Bonin, 2016; Spiegel, 2016). The movement gained momentum once the students situated their fight within the broader discourse of neoliberal austerity measures, and associated the tuition hikes with the growing burden of individual debt and the privileging of corporate interests. A growing number of groups, such as Quebec sovereigntists and feminist collectives joined anti-capitalist coalitions (Giroux, 2013). By 22 March 2012 more than 300,000 students, or 75 per cent of the post-secondary student population in Quebec, were involved. Strikes, picket-line protests and nightly demonstrations continued for nearly six months (Begin-Caouette and Jones, 2014).

Grassroots opposition to austerity in Ireland did produce concessions. Examples include successful opposition to a government attempt to restrict eligibility for free medical care for those over seventy. However, that movement did not question austerity as an approach so much as it implied austerity should not be applied to one subgroup of society – senior citizens. Royall (2017) attributed the lack of coordinated resistance to the 'long-established relations of dependency with respect to the state and to the trade union movement that contributed strongly to reduce its militancy in general and facilitated its caution and ambiguous responses to austerity in the post-2008 period in particular' (Royall, 2017).

The Irish state used the economic crisis and Troika bailout to initiate domestic water reform. Ireland had never had domestic water charges, but the 2010 budget and the National Recovery Plan of 2011–14 introduced them, for fiscal rather than environmental reasons (Power et al, 2016; Quinn et al, 2016). However, unlike welfare reform, water reform required active participation from society for registration and installation of water meters, thereby making disruption an effective tool of resistance. By 2015 only half of Irish households had registered their details (Trommer, 2019). Protest techniques ranged from marches, to lobbying or burning registration kits, and returning unopened packages with 'no consent–no contract' written on it (Power et al, 2016). Physical disruption of meter installation was also prevalent, with social media acting as a key site of organization whereby large groups of people would block the utilities from accessing houses. 'Water meter fairies' began removing meters (Trommer, 2019). Regional-based organizations and larger organizations such as Right2Water developed networks to wage a larger campaign at the national level (Fletcher et al, 2018). The anti-water charges protest was led by the Right2Water campaign and included a number of political parties, such as Sinn Féin, as well as some independent representatives, trade unions and community groups. Some unions including UNITE, Mandate, CPSU and OPATSI funded the campaign, although ICTU did not endorse it (O'Connor, 2017: 85).

Mass resistance to Irish neoliberal reforms eventually emerged against water taxation where meters would be installed and user charges levied (see

Chapter 6). The context was one where austerity had produced significant social costs: '30.5 percent of Irish people lived in deprivation, 13.2 percent suffered food poverty, male suicides had increased by 57 percent, while emigration, homelessness and unemployment rates soared' (Royall, 2017). It was the largest popular mobilization in modern Irish history. Demonstrations were widely dispersed in towns and neighbourhoods throughout the country. Almost 60 per cent of participants in the campaign linked the issue to anti-austerity sentiment more generally, agreeing that austerity had gone too far (cited in O'Connor, 2017: 84). The survey also established that the majority of protesters were between 30 and 50 years of age, that almost 55 per cent had never participated in a protest and a significant number hailed from working-class areas (O'Connor, 2017: 84). Broad public opposition, large-scale Right2Water protests and sustained local disruptions eventually forced changes in the position of the main opposition party, Fianna Fáil. In the 2016 general election they, and a number of smaller parties, campaigned to end water charges. In June 2016, the new Dáil Éireann suspended water charges, and an Irish parliamentary committee made a series of recommendations in 2017 about continuing tax-based funding for water provision, refunding paid water charges and abandoning the meter programme (Trommer, 2019).

Aside from the labour responses, Spain also saw the emergence of significant social movements contesting the implementation of austerity. On 15 May 2011, protests erupted across Spain taking the form of street marches, prevention of evictions, online petitions, and encampments in the squares of more than 53 cities, with Madrid as the epicentre (Casero-Ripolles and Feenstra, 2012). It was here that 15-M Movement was born. And it was these '*indignados*' as the media characterized the activists, who 'provided the kick-off for a permanent mobilisation' (Fresmillo, 2013). Most notably, the 15-M Movement utilized large protests and occupations and combined these tactics with a collective focus on the role of citizenship (Gerbaudo, 2017). The Movement's demands included the right to housing, elimination of special privileges from politics, improving labour market options, high quality public services, tighter controls on banks, criticism of the two-party system, and demands for greater opportunities for participatory democracy. The demand for decent housing had the most traction, as the housing crisis hit Spain hard, with over 400,000 Spaniards evicted between 2008 and 2011 (Vilaseca, 2014), and over 3.4 million empty properties in 2011 (Blanco and León, 2017).

The scope of the 15-M Movement expanded to include 'dissatisfaction with the two-party political system, the venality of political and economic elites [and] widespread corruption' (Hughes, 2011). It was successful in generating counter-hegemonic narratives to neoliberal austerity and mobilizing large groups of citizens for protest, and together with other organizations and movements, aiding the formation of new political parties at national (Podemos) and municipal levels (Barcelona En Comú and Ahora Madrid). In addition to political mobilization, 15-M was the foundation for a range of mutual aid activities and their encampments 'turned into local assemblies, supporting or leading local demands and protests. Joining or building from scratch consumer cooperatives, providing advice to those losing their jobs, or organising popular education events' (Fresmillo, 2013). Their mission in practice was to find collective solutions to the problems of daily life people were confronting.

Springing directly from the 15-M Movement local and workplace assemblies were the human *mareas* (tides) opposed, as mentioned earlier, to privatization in the health and education sectors. These *mareas* protests sought to 'ally with broad sectors of society for the defence of a public or common sphere' and in so doing moved beyond the standard workplace demands for better wages and working conditions (Mendez de Andes, 2014). In Madrid, the health care *marea* initiated not only protests and occupations, but also a 'popular consultation' that gathered nearly one million signatures in opposition to the privatization of local hospitals. And these efforts met with some success as a Madrid court suspended privatization plans that had been put in place for six public hospitals, forcing the regional health minister to resign, and ultimately causing the local government to simply abandon the privatization agenda (Mendez de Andes, 2014).

Within the 15-M Movement, the Platform for People Affected by Mortgages (PAH) emerged as an example of the new politics being created from below. As a key player, with hundreds of local assemblies across the county, PAH employed a broad array of campaign methods toward an equally broad range of venues including 'mutual aid, popular campaigns, legislative pressure, court appeals, direct action, squatting, popular media, and militant activism' which took its struggles to 'the national parliament and the European Court of Human Rights' (Mendez de Andes, 2014). Following a number of eviction-related suicides in 2014, PAH collected 1.4 million signatures in a citizen's legislative initiative in an attempt to push the government to change the mortgage laws. The law governing citizen-led initiatives required only 500,000 signatures so this was a major success. However, parliament did not accept the initiative. In response, PAH organized a shaming campaign expressed in demonstrations taking place at the private homes of parliamentary representatives and government ministers who had opposed this initiative (Mendez de Andes, 2014).

As the foregoing suggests, a key element of the 15-M Movement was its horizontal, non-elitist grassroots approach, which imbued the movement with a type of mobility while allowing it to address the multifaceted nature of the crisis affecting Spain (Cameron, 2014). Such popular initiatives expressed an emerging new politics that sought to 'restructure the conditions of our life in common from a radically democratic point of view' (Mendez de Andes, 2014). The social movement(s) developed an explicitly electoral arm with Podemos – Unidos Podemos in 2016 – as a multi-party left electoral alliance. This was not just a new party of the left but intended to be a party of a new kind of left as 'these movements', from which Podemos emerged, 'opened up discussions about the reorganization and reorientation of left strategy; they basically brought "the party" and the question of how to govern back onto centre-stage' (Venizelos and Stavrakakis, 2020). Electoral success soon followed; in 2015, at the local/regional level, left-wing coalitions won control of municipal governments in Madrid, Barcelona, Corona, Cadiz and Zaragoza. The victories were fragile, however, as subsequent elections have either reversed these results, as in Madrid, or rendered their continuation much more problematic, as in Barcelona.

As the cases presented demonstrate, austerity, at least in part, either gave rise to new social movements and/or set in motion a new electoral dynamic populated by new actors and older political entities that were re-energized by the crisis.

Austerity, populism and elections

The 2008 crisis and subsequent austerity created the conditions for political change, a possibility which was partially realized. A new politics emerged, in some cases with electoral realignments, which had its origins in the pre-crisis years as the neoliberal counter-revolution reached its zenith in the 1990s. Of particular significance was the increasing delegitimization of liberal representative democracy that followed on three decades of economic and institutional restructuring, and the resulting integration of social democracy (once the political home of the Western European working class) into neoliberalism. Peter Mair (2013) termed the result of political, institutional and even cultural disorganization, 'the void'. His book was concerned with understanding the 'hollowing out' of liberal democracies after decades of neoliberal assault. Hollowing out is observed through various metrics including lower voter participation, electoral volatility, declining party identification and membership,[1] and rising vote shares for populist parties. Mair's conclusion was that the mainstream parties of the centre left and right, but particularly those of the centre left, lost legitimacy as they embraced neoliberal policies (Mair, 2013).

Increasingly indistinguishable from the centre right (Crouch, 2011: 162), social democratic parties became electorally threatened. In many places, including Denmark, the electoral squeeze came from the radical right. In others, such as Spain, both right and left populist formations emerged.

On the material and political sources of populist movements, Baier (2016: 76) finds that

> populism draws on the contradiction between the promise and the reality of democracy, it expresses a much deeper structural antagonism in capitalist societies, that is, between the alleged equality that democracy professes and the actual inequality that the hierarchical economic order continually reproduces [...] Its growth is therefore a sign of a serious crisis of democracy.

What differentiates populism of the right and left is that 'right populism conflates "the people" with an embattled nation confronting its external enemies [...] The left, in marked contrast, defines "the people" in relation to the social structures and institutions – for example, state and capital [...]' (Gandesha, 2018). The populism of both left and right, 'indicates a discursive practice that aims at creating links between the excluded and suffering in order to empower them in their struggle to redress this exclusion. These discourses are articulated around "the people" as the central political subject demanding incorporation into the political community' (Venizelos and Stavrakakis, 2020).

As governments moved to implement austerity measures it was common, though not universal, for incumbents to be punished in subsequent elections. However, replacement governments tended to be as committed to austerity as the ones displaced. So, expressions of public anger, a manifestation of resistance, did occur. But alternative political vehicles were either not available or, where parties advocating an alternative to austerity did exist, failed to attract significant support. That said, in several of our cases – Ireland, Spain and Quebec in particular – the established 'centre' political parties did lose ground in terms of their share of the vote. Typically, these were either two more or less indistinguishable right-of-centre parties, as in Ireland; or some version of neoliberalized social democracy, and a conservative party on the right, as in Spain and Quebec.

In Canada, the minority Conservative government that was in office when the crisis struck managed to avoid blame and achieved majority status in the 2011 election. Four years later, however, it lost office to the Liberals, who conveyed the message that the time for austerity was over. The Liberals campaigned on modest budget deficits to stimulate growth, largely through infrastructure spending (tethered to public-private partnerships). Provincially, despite changes of government, and episodes of minority versus majority governments in some provinces, there seemed little deviation from fiscal restraint and other components of austerity. However, it was significant that federally one of the two main parties, the Liberals, departed from the fiscal austerity script in the 2015 election, and won. This was not done under pressure from the quasi-social democratic New Democratic Party, which remained committed to balanced budgets.

During the 2019 Canadian federal election, balancing the budget or reducing the deficit was no longer a hot button issue. The importance of deficit politics appeared to be changing, with only 13 per cent of survey respondents stating it was among the three most important election issues, and only 3 per cent of uncommitted voters believing it to be a top issue in Canada (Wherry, 2019). A third of respondents appeared interested in more spending on government programmes, even if that meant no tax cuts or continued budget deficits (Russell, 2019). The orthodoxy of a balanced budget appeared to be dwindling, with more pressing Canadian issues coming to the forefront. However, due to their austerian policy stance in previous elections, the social democrats were unable to take advantage of this shift.

Among Canada's ten provinces, Quebec presents the most interesting case of party realignment. For decades the dominant backdrop to Quebec politics had been the question of Quebec independence. Its main electoral options were the pro-federalist Liberals or the sovereigntist Parti Quebecois (PQ). But the 2008 crisis, and the politics of severe austerity, engendered a shift in the nature of Quebec elections and the available electoral options.

Responding to protests against post-secondary tuition fee increases, the incumbent Liberal government had in May 2012 attempted an aggressive and repressive response through Bill 78, legislation that suspended all post-secondary classes until August, imposed heavy fines on those who blocked classes when they resumed, and restricted the right to demonstrate by making it easier for the police to declare demonstrations illegal (Collombat, 2014). These violations of free speech, association and assembly caused the eruption of various mass protests, including the pots-and-pans movement and resistance against the larger social order (Giroux, 2013). In the subsequent September 2012 election, the Liberal party under Premier Jean Charest lost its majority and was replaced by a minority PQ government. The next day, the premier designate Pauline Marois declared the party's intention to cancel the tuition increases and repeal Bill 78. Once in power the PQ redefined its tuition freeze as a policy of indexing fees to inflation but the protests by this time had died down and did not resume.

The PQ government remained committed to fiscal austerity although it did not entirely deliver on that pledge, and made some other cautious reforms (Graefe and Rioux, 2017: 284–6). However, it was defeated in the 2014 election and the decidedly pro-austerity Liberal Party resumed office, ran budget surpluses, but lost office to the Coalition for Quebec's Future (CAQ) in 2018, a right-wing party with a right populist cultural agenda of banning public servants from wearing religious symbols. During its first election campaign in 2012, CAQ focused on populist measures like cutting income taxes, ensuring accessibility to family physicians, creating space for for-profit health care, reducing public expenditures and the deficit, and attacking the influence of special interest groups (code for trade unions) in government decision making (Bélanger and Falk Pedersen, 2014: 145–6). Perhaps reflecting this populist base, and the fact that austerity under the PQ and the Liberals had proved electorally unpopular, the CAQ's first budget loosened fiscal constraints and significant increases in public expenditures were announced. Certainly, the Maple Spring protests contributed to the defeat of the pro-austerity Liberal government in 2012, and later to the rise and increased success of the anti-austerity and leftist party Quebec Solidaire (QS) in subsequent elections. Austerity had become damaged goods in Quebec by the time of the 2018 elections. By early 2020 the CAQ government had passed two full budgets, both of which included increases in spending for health/social services and education. Fiscal austerity in Quebec, as at the federal level, seemed increasingly passé.

The shift to the right in Quebec, with both the PQ and CAQ, created space for the emergence of political formations on the left. In 2006, several small leftist parties merged to form Quebec Solidaire (QS). QS does not identify as explicitly socialist, but defines itself as 'resolutely of the left, ecologist, altermondialiste, pacifist, democratic, and sovereigntist' (Fidler, 2012: 147–8). Its initial electoral success was limited to downtown Montreal. However, in the 2018 election, QS more than doubled its share of the popular vote in winning 16 per cent and in the process increased its share of seats from three to ten, matching the PQ's seat count.

The Danish electoral landscape has seen shifts between 'blue bloc' conservative and 'red bloc' social democratic coalition governments. From 2008 to 2019, there were three changes in government (with elections in 2011, 2015 and 2019). The 2011 Danish elections saw the incumbent blue-bloc coalition led by centre-right Venstre (Liberals) lose power to a red-bloc coalition led by the social democrats. When the social democrat-led red bloc was in office in Denmark, the radical left Red–Green Alliance (RGA), for a time, played a strategically important role in maintaining a left majority in parliament but did not join the government by taking up cabinet positions. The RGA is a political party with strong links to social movements. For example, they were supportive participants in struggles including the environmental movement, defending teachers against increased work flexibility and contributing to protests against the sale of a state-owned company to Goldman Sachs (Betzien and Voss, 2012). However, as the RGA achieved electoral success it had to grapple internally with how to appeal to a wider range of voters, how to stay connected to grassroots organizations, how to navigate between ideals and pragmatism, and how to remain activist oriented without becoming bureaucratically cumbersome (Betzien and Voss, 2012). In 2015, the centre-right bloc returned to government and then, in a 2019 reversal of electoral fortunes, a social democrat-led red-bloc coalition returned to government. It is noteworthy that Denmark's post-crisis electoral alterations between centre-left and centre-right blocs had little effect on austerity policies.

A right populist party, the Danish People's Party (DF – Dansk Folkeparti) had been founded in 1995. It had a left counterpart in the shape of the RGA, which emerged from the margins to win a consistent 6 to 8 per cent of the votes in national elections in 2011, 2015 and 2019. Like the DF, the RGA was an alternative for voters who had become 'disaffected with the Social Democratic-led government's austerity policies and attacks on the welfare state' (Johansen, 2015: 194). However, the combined challenges to the established order did not change the dominance of the traditional coalitions and their leading parties.

The failure of alternatives to emerge might be considered in light of the now long-standing institutionalization of austerity as budget restraint, public sector restructuring and labour market flexibilization, not to mention the diffused impacts of austerity on vulnerable groups and generalized precarity (particularly for women, youth, migrants and indebted households). Another more general, though connected, reason was the ideological vacuum represented by social democracy (Evans, 2017). Social democratic parties had long adapted to the contours of what was ideologically acceptable under various renditions of capitalist political economy (McBride, 2005). As Keynesianism gave way to neoliberalism, the room for social democratic manoeuvre narrowed and frequently social democratic governments, where they existed, acted in ways that undermined their working-class base by failing to not only address the '3Is' of austerity, but also themselves enacted austerity measures. In the period of austerity following the global financial crisis, these tendencies were clearly apparent in all our cases.

In Ireland, the share of the vote going to the dominant parties, Fianna Fáil and Fine Gael, fell from around 69 per cent in 2007 to 43 per cent in 2020; in Spain the share going to the PP and PSOE fell from 84 per cent in 2008 to under 50 per cent in 2019; and in Quebec the Liberal and Parti Quebecois portion declined from 75 per cent in 2007 to around 42 per cent in 2018. The loss of vote share does not necessarily imply political transformation but, as detailed below, there is evidence that in Spain and Ireland at least, the impact of austerity, combined with other powerful factors in those societies, did result in the erosion or decay of existing political arrangements. Erosion offers both opportunities and challenges for the future that could include either the reversal of austerity and dismantling of neoliberalism, or its reimposition by ever more authoritarian means.

During the onset of the crisis, the PSOE in Spain was able to retain its minority government status in the 2008 election, before recording in 2011 its worst return for the party since 1977. Having made anti-austerity promises in its 2008 election platform, including plans for full employment (*The Economist*, 2008), the PSOE, in line with a brief period of internationally approved stimulus spending, seemed to want to spend its way out of the crisis. Later, due to concerns over the deficit and national debt, the government turned to neoliberal policy solutions, thus undermining its electoral base. Between 2008 and 2011 Zapatero's PSOE embraced numerous austerity measures, including massive cuts to spending and the 2010 regressive labour reforms. The crisis hit hard, and a combination of soaring unemployment and restricted social benefits combined to make the Zapatero government extremely unpopular. The party spent the rest of the decade in opposition and not until the two 2019 elections did it manage to articulate policies that countered the dominant austerity narrative.

However, the right-wing PP that succeeded it in 2011 was even more committed to austerity, and it retained office until April 2019, when the PSOE achieved minority government status. Austerity seems to have played a role in elections that led to a changeover in governing party; however, although Podemos emerged in 2014 as an anti-austerity alternative, governments remained broadly committed to the austerity package that the PSOE had initiated. And it must be noted that responsibility for austerity did not impede the PP's retention of power for an eight-year period.

The most significant instance of resistance to austerity in Spain (in electoral terms) came with the rise of Podemos. A new party, formed out of the social movement of the '*indignados*' and 15-M anti-austerity protests, Podemos[2] made a breakthrough in the 2014 European elections when it gained 8 per cent of the popular vote. In the 2015 and 2016 national elections, both figures were at roughly 20 per cent. By April 2019, the total had declined to 14 per cent and fell one point further in

November to 13 per cent. The decline can be partly attributed to internal factionalism within Podemos, which discredited its pledge to move beyond the machinations of the traditional political parties (Sola and Rendueles, 2018). Another was the complication caused by the national question, in the current context of Catalan nationalism. In the rest of Spain this led to an assertive Spanish nationalism including the development of a far right, anti-immigrant, anti-Catalan independence party, Vox, which gained 15 per cent of the vote in November 2019. All the establishment parties were also opposed to holding referenda on Catalan independence, and the Podemos position – support for Catalonia's right to hold such a referendum while hoping for a result in favour of remaining in Spain – proved a difficult sell. Miley (2017) argued the Catalan authorities' defection from the constitutional order was instigated in part by the dynamics of austerity, and that it has rendered the country's constitutional framework – but not the austerity regime – susceptible to collapse. Clearly, these national/regional factors, and therefore austerity indirectly, played a role in the complicated and finely balanced parliamentary situation that followed the November 2019 election.

During its rise, Podemos articulated two main themes: the need to make Spanish politics more democratic and to do things differently. The first theme tapped into the widespread disaffection and anti-establishment sentiments within the Spanish population that were exacerbated by the deep economic crisis (Lancaster, 2017: 923; Sola and Rendueles, 2018). The second theme was opposition to the austerity policies pursued by both establishment parties in the wake of the crisis.

With the crisis ongoing during the majority People's Party (PP) government, austerity measures continued and contributed to its losses in the 2015 elections when it lost 64 seats and was forced into minority status. However, the Socialist Workers' Party (PSOE), with its own track record of austerity measures and inability to develop an alternative also lost 20 seats. Anti-austerity newcomers Podemos were able to capture 69 seats – only 21 seats behind Pedro Sánchez's PSOE. The other big winner was the right-wing Citizens Party that gained 40 seats and ran on the key area of Spanish (unified) nationalism (Jones, 2015). After months of unsuccessful negotiations to form government, new elections were held in 2016. Those results, too, were inconclusive and ultimately resulted in the continuation of the minority PP government. The rise of Podemos and a right-wing party, Ciudadanos, which remained committed to neoliberal policies, but advanced its own anti-establishment message focused on corruption, had created 'electoral instability' and 'party-system change' (Lancaster, 2017: 920). Podemos initially tried to position itself in a new, non-ideological political space going beyond traditional notions of left and right. In reality, though, its programme and political base were left wing and rooted in the unorganized working class. Thus, the party draws disproportionate support from workers, compared to owners and supervisors, outsiders (unemployed, temporary workers and students) compared to senior citizens, and low-income rather than high-income individuals (Sola and Rendueles, 2018).

Spain had two elections in 2019, an indicator of the extent of electoral and parliamentary volatility. The PSOE became the largest party in April and retained that position in November, with 28 per cent of the vote, despite losing seats and a small decline in its share of the vote. Podemos also saw its share of the popular vote decline from 14 per cent in April to 13 per cent in November, and lost seven seats between the two elections. On the right, the PP achieved 17 per cent in April and increased that to 21 per cent in November; the Ciudadanos were decimated in November having declined from 16 per cent in April to 7 per cent in November (and losing 47 seats of the 57 they had held), while the extreme right-wing Vox improved its position from 10 to 15 per cent.

Vox was formed in 2013 with the objective of rallying right-wing voters disillusioned by PP's policies. Its surge in the 2019 elections was linked to the exploitation of Spanish nationalism as a response to the Catalonian independence movement (Jannessari, 2019; Maestre, 2019; Rosenbach, 2019). Positioning itself as the party of 'sovereignty and the nation-state' (Rosenbach, 2019), the only force capable of dealing with the Catalonia crisis, Vox stole Ciudadanos' 'anti-independence thunder' (Jannessari, 2019). As Vox's popularity rose, PP and Ciudadanos tried to mimic its harsh anti-Catalan rhetoric, but this tactic failed to stem the rush of voters toward Vox and its appeal to Spanish nationalism (Jannessari, 2019). Vox's other signature issue is its anti-immigrant line, which includes popularizing misinformation about the number of illegal immigrants, their propensity to criminality, and exaggerating their welfare benefits (Maestre, 2019). On balance, the right improved its position, yet a left coalition including PSOE and Podemos, committed to reversing some of the austerity policies of the preceding ten years, was able to win parliamentary approval and form a government with the support of the Catalan Left Republicans and the Basque Nationalist Party.

The 2019 coalition agreement contains significant proposals to reverse important aspects of austerity. These include: repealing the 2012 labour reforms that weakened collective bargaining and enabled easier dismissal of workers in the name of flexibility; introducing a 22 per cent increase in the minimum wage and better terms for precarious workers; rent controls; reductions in university fees; more money for the health system and establishing an oversight commission that includes experts, doctors, nurses, labour leaders, patients and advocacy groups; progressive tax reforms; and a free and universal new childcare programme for pre-schoolers. On the other hand, the PSOE insisted on no repeal of its own 2010 labour reform (which had also strengthened capital's hand in dealing with labour) and acceptance of the EU's fiscal rules. Podemos also had to abandon proposals to nationalize and then convert Bankia into a public investment bank, proposed taxes on banking profits, and the establishment of a new public energy company (Greene and Gilmartin, 2020). For Podemos, participation in related coalitions pose considerable actual or perceived risks of co-optation. Notwithstanding major challenges for the new government (including determined opposition from business, media elites and the political forces representing them; a thin and fragile parliamentary majority; the national question in Catalonia and the exploitation of Spanish nationalism by forces such as Vox; and stringent EU budget rules), for the first time since the crisis, the political space to reverse a decade of extreme austerity had emerged.

Anti-austerity space also opened up in Ireland. In 2011, the Irish Labour Party joined a coalition with Fine Gael. Participation in a coalition government arguably constrains the policy preferences of minority partners (Labour, in this case); however, the participation of the social democrats in severe austerity measures does not appear to have been ideationally problematic for them. Perhaps the calculation was that the effects of austerity might be mitigated by participation, rather than opposition and resistance. If so, it was not a politically successful strategy. The party achieved its best ever election result in 2011 with 37 seats in the Dáil. It then fell to its lowest ever tally (seven seats) in the 2016 election, and continued its decline in both popular vote and seats (six) in the 2020 election. The 2011 election of a large Labour parliamentary contingent, and to a lesser extent Fine Gael, where both had campaigned for the renegotiation of the memorandum of understanding, was one instance where protest among the Irish electorate occurred without producing change. Labour rejected the offer to try to forge a broad left-wing opposition, which would have put pressure on a Fine Gael minority government. Instead, it chose to join a coalition with the Fine Gael party. The Fine Gael election programme, while critical of the deal concluded between the Irish Fianna Fáil government and the Troika, focused on prototypical austerity measures. The manifesto pledged to create growth and jobs through 'budget cuts rather than job-destroying tax increases', while investments in infrastructure were to be 'funded in significant part through the sale of non-strategic state assets'.[3] In a similar vein, the government promised not to raise income taxes, corporate taxes or employer taxes and to reduce a growing deficit to 3 per cent of GDP by 2014. Labour preferred to support a right-wing government rather than try to create a critical leftist alternative to austerity. The previous government had agreed to the Troika's memorandum of understanding, thereby compromising the country's economic sovereignty. And because neither Fine Gael nor Labour were willing to renegotiate the agreement, the election merely rearranged the players of the austerity game rather than upsetting the austerity regime itself (O'Connor, 2017: 72).

In the 2016 Irish election, both coalition partners suffered big losses and the anti-austerity Sinn Féin made some gains. Fine Gael was able to form a minority government and continue its austerity policies with limited support from Fianna Fáil and some independents. With the Labour Party discredited as a result of its participation in the pro-austerity coalition, anti-austerity political formations did benefit in the 2016 general election. Most notably, Sinn Féin, primarily a nationalist party aiming at a united Ireland, which between 1997 and 2011 had never secured more than five seats in the Dáil Éireann, increased its number of seats to 14 in 2011 and further to 23 in 2016, increasing its share of the vote to 14 per cent. Sinn Féin's economic proposals represent Keynesian-style interventions that call for ending austerity through adequate government investment and revenue-raising measures based on wealth and progressive taxation (Sinn Féin, 2010). There was also some limited success for left-wing parties such as the Solidarity–People Before Profit electoral alliance, which was able to secure six seats in the Dáil with 4 per cent of the vote. Solidarity (initially the Anti-Austerity Alliance) and People Before Profit are both socialist parties that secured three seats each in the Dáil. Their platforms were highly critical of austerity measures in Ireland as well as neoliberal policies more generally. The alliance aimed to end Ireland's status as a tax haven, introduce a financial transaction tax, abolish indirect taxation, increase corporate taxes and wealth taxes, and invest revenues in housing, public services and sustainable growth.[4] Despite a big loss in local council elections in 2019, dropping from 157 councillors (out of a total of 949) to 81 with a corresponding fall in its share of the popular vote, Sinn Féin recovered and emerged as a leading force in Irish politics after the 2020 election. It has been the leading parliamentary opponent to austerity since 2011 and had now won the most votes, 25 per cent, and an equal number of seats (37) compared with Fianna Fáil, its nearest rival (with 37 seats and 22 per cent of the vote).

The significance of Sinn Féin outdistancing its centrist rivals, who had dominated the Irish state since its inception, has been referred to by Irish commentators as an 'earthquake', and as a 'seismic shift'. One analyst commented that 'It took nine years and three elections, but the economic crash of 2008 has demolished the Irish party system' (Finn, 2020). Sinn Féin campaigned on working-class issues like housing affordability and health issues. Exit polls showed these were most important in voters' minds and also that two thirds wanted public services investment to be prioritized over tax cuts (Finn, 2020) – a clear rejection of the conventional wisdom of the austerity politics pursued since the crisis. The party was the overwhelming first choice of voters under 35 (Dolan, 2020). The exit polls also showed a class divide. Among upper- and middle-class voters Sinn Féin scored only 14 per cent; among skilled workers and the working class and non-working categories the party polled 33 to 35 per cent, an amount almost equivalent to the combined Fine Gael/Fianna Fáil total of 39 per cent (Burtenshaw, 2020). At the time of writing, numerous permutations of possible coalition governments remain on the table and it is by no means certain that Sinn Féin will be willing or able either to form a government or participate in one. However, the election does seem to have produced a verdict on austerity and those who implemented it, creating a space at least for alternative politics to prosper at some point down the line.

Comparisons and conclusions

Resistance to austerity has been varied and uneven yet seemed unable to prevail against determined governments locked into an austerity discourse representing the interests of banking and finance, and business and elites generally. The austerity policy package was also reinforced by the conventional wisdom and pressures exerted by international organizations like the EU. Yet the anti-austerity movements do seem to have contributed to the erosion of established political systems in Spain and Ireland such that anti-austerity measures, and a new sense of a public purpose as an alternative to the private and individual self-interests of neoliberalism, may have some chance of being implemented. Denmark and Canada were remarkably stable post-2008, in terms of political party alignments. In Denmark, it remained a matter of whether the centre-left or centre-right blocs would govern. In Canada, at the national level, the alteration in government between the centrist Liberals and the right-wing Conservatives remains unchanged. In the Canadian provinces, a version of this rotation between centrists and conservatives tended to dominate save for Quebec. Even in Canada, despite continued provincial enthusiasm for the mantras of neoliberalism and austerity, the federal government seemed by 2015 to have reached the conclusion that the obsession with fiscal austerity had become more of a liability than an asset. However, while the fiscal aspects of austerity may have been relaxed, the drive to privatize via public-private partnerships and to keep labour and public sector compensation under control remained as strong as ever.

Table 7: Varieties of austerity – dynamics or degrees of resistance

	Institutionalization	Insulation	Insinuation
Resistance	Routes for dissent: unions, protests, political campaigns (formal to informal, legal to illegal)	Roots of austerity: one-offs, systemic	Triggers and victims: political parties and political system

Having now outlined a full spectrum of austerity-related assaults and incursions – debt and finance, public money, public sector restructuring, labour market flexibilization, precarity and poverty – we are in a position to fill in the final row of our Varieties of Austerity table from Chapter 1, this line capturing varieties of resistance to austerity. Resistance comes in many forms; thus, we may speak of resistances (plural) not just for their national or temporal differences, but also for their characteristics and how they fit within the schema imposed by austerity itself. In this chapter we detailed three categories of resistance: labour, social movements and political parties; these categories fit into two types of reactions to austerity: defensive reactions by organized labour, and campaigns that capture a wider swath of actors and interests. Institutionalization is thus indicated through the extent to which routes for dissent exist within formal or informal channels (whether unions, protests, political campaigns or the like). The routes challenging austerity tend to vary, based on whether the roots of austerity – its impact, insulation and exposure – are perceived to be more systemic in nature (like trenchant capitalist class struggle and opposition to deleterious structures of financialization or privatization), or related to one-off aspects of austerity reforms (like water pricing, service disruption, user fees or other specific measures), though the perceived targets of resistance can also vary within organizations and movements (like the Maple Spring). A multitude of targets might imply a murky yardstick for success. In any case, challenges to austerity in various guises also brought (potentially) unforeseen consequences. The political systems of Spain and Ireland, for example, have been destabilized over time, and new political space has opened up for alternatives to austerity. The consequence of these resistances is therefore not only the winning or losing of particular struggles and campaigns, but also shifts in the insinuation of burden and blame through the rise of right and left populism, and anti-austerity scapegoating. Next, in the concluding chapter of this book, we move beyond austerity to capture some aspects of the contemporary period not covered earlier (roughly 2018 to 2020) and to suggest alternatives beyond austerity that centre on rebuilding the public purpose.

8

Conclusion: Beyond Austerity

When the global financial crisis hit in 2008, its immediate policy aftermath destabilized several decades of neoliberal spending restraint through widespread banking sector support and economic stimulus. More familiar elements of the neoliberal policy package would not be suppressed for long, and austerity soon followed through a number of measures affecting public sector spending and discourse, staff and agencies, labour market flexibilization and programme restructuring. Necessary to the needs of capital as a bout of state activism had been, its continuation was to be avoided. The resumption of austerity was painful for many, creating vulnerabilities and exacerbating problems for already precarious communities. A crisis of capital soon transformed into more debt for households, less generous social programmes, enhanced precarity for women, youth and immigrants, and discipline for labour generally. There is an undeniable class component to austerity in its many guises, interwoven with social disparities of all sorts.

Austerity is multi-faceted, as are national experiences. For some countries, like Ireland and Spain, restraint and retrenchment emerged in 2010 in the context of serious structural issues for budgets and labour markets; they too, along with Denmark, had equally to deal with banking sector collapse. Elsewhere, countries like Canada escaped the worst of the initial crisis only to face deep cyclical downturn owing to an international credit crunch and export market-induced recession. Whatever the combination, the 2008 crisis is an important origin story for the past decade of austerity. It is not the only origin story, however. Often austerity was launched where the crisis was comparatively mild (Canada), or where similar plans had been in place for some time (Ireland, Denmark), and austerity reforms were incongruent with the actual experience or cause of the crisis (Canada, Ireland, Denmark, Spain). And in all cases, labour market and public sector restructuring were located in decades-old neoliberal reforms, institutional inheritances, exposure to international organizations, and related to structural positions in the global economy. The international pressures to implement austerity measures were apparent in all cases, though they varied from moral suasion to conditionalities in exchange for financial assistance. In no case, however, did we conclude that international pressure compelled national states to adopt the measures. As far as we could determine, national elites were of similar mind to those in international organizations. They might insinuate that, for example, 'the Troika made us do it', but in reality, international pressure was a welcome reinforcement for measures already desired, contemplated or planned. Whether any of these states could have resisted international pressures is an untested proposition, since none of them showed any inclination to do so.

To analyze austerity (in long- and short-run forms) there is, on the one hand, the comparative political economy literature dealing with national varieties of capitalism and welfare state; on the other hand, there is the critical political economy literature offering theories of capitalist crises, class struggle, economic pressures and recovery, and forms of state restructuring. Together these literatures can tell us a lot about austerity for its continuities and differences. In this spirit, the varieties of austerity framework grapples with how austerity involves commonalities and cross-cutting national differences; it is class-based but not always neoliberal in the sense that sometimes contradictory legacy institutions and state forms exist; austerity is harsh for many but also rewarding for some, with distinct winners and losers relating to new or resilient patterns.

Thus, austerity exists in degrees – it is not just less; and it exists as a dynamic process, which includes new and often contradictory arrangements. Austerity involves the '3Is' identified in Chapter 1 and applied throughout the book: institutions, insulations and insinuations. Institutionalization insofar as agencies and organizations are bolstered or torn down, and an air of permanence for austerity-related approaches and customs is created. Extending economic and political protection for some, and creating exposure and forced adjustment for others, implicates austerity-driven changes through insulation. Burden and blame shifting also make insinuation a big part of the austerity story. The 3Is can be considered separately but are in fact intertwined transformations across and within national jurisdictions through intensive and extensive reforms, reallocations and redistributions.

It could be argued that the varieties of austerity, in emphasizing dynamics or degrees of 3Is, represents a typology without stable categories. However, the object mirrors its subject: austerity itself is an unstable category. Austerity is no single thing, like solely achieving balanced budgets, because a range of processes, tempos and relations are at play to accomplish this transformation. The varieties of austerity framework in table form, presented in each chapter of the book, tries to capture, as best as a static table can, dynamism and degrees of change.

A flaw of the varieties of capitalism and welfare state literatures is that they obscure as much as they reveal: there is at least as much variety within types as between them. Similarly, their national-scale orientation ignores or confuses actually existing and interrelated developments, to say nothing of international forces. Taking these observations to heart, to the extent possible in a single book, the varieties of austerity framework attempts to highlight crosscutting, multi-level developments while still addressing the national differences and commonalities so important to the lived experience of austerity. This analysis focuses mainly on the state, and not, say, private sector practices, because the state is the agent of austerity, a point we return to shortly on state theory and the social relations that compose state agency. The state is simultaneously an ally and foe of alternatives to austerity.

While the varieties of austerity framework is important to our analysis, it must contend with numerous chapter themes revealed through four country cases. The obvious implication is that there is a lot going on here, with many moving parts and considerations. To which we suggest that this is as indeed it should be given the complications involved with a decade (or multiple decades) of restructuring affecting public budgets, public sectors, labour across occupations and sectors, and economic scales from the local to global. The thematic chapter treatment is merged with the varieties of austerity framework in the table below to summarize each chapter's themes and 3Is. The themes lay out the specific nature of the dynamics or degrees of austerity, illustrated through examples in our four country cases; and the 3Is indicate how the varieties of austerity manifest in each chapter, in the book as a whole, as well as across the book for each of the three.

Austerity has been an economic failure and a moral disaster. From a moral perspective, those responsible for the crisis have profited, while others, who had little if anything to do with creating it, have paid a significant price, and continue to pay through austerity policies. In terms of the categories used in this book, we have described this as a strategy of insinuation, or blame shifting. The private sector, seeking capital accumulation through complicated financial flows, was central to the crisis. States were complicit in this process through regulatory failure in the first place, and then by rewarding those responsible through state largesse in the form of various bailouts and buyouts, with the bill being ultimately picked up by the population at large. In so doing, states encouraged future moral hazard – why should financial elites behave

Table 8: Varieties of austerity – summary of dynamics and degrees

	Themes	Institutionalization	Insulation	Insinuation
Chapter 2: debt and finance	Stimulus and guarantees; bailouts; write-offs and taxpayer-borne risks; partnerships and privatization; international pressures	Exceptionalism: mobilizing new or existing government or public-private agencies for private sector debt relief and the socialization of toxic assets by the state	Bailouts and guarantees: size of contribution, 'haircuts', terms and conditions	Return on bailout
Chapter 3: public money	Fiscal narratives and budget framing; characterizing the nation; justifying crisis management via austerity; priorities of crisis era governance, rationalizations of reform beyond merely cuts; European citizenship	Decision-making agencies: empowering particular agencies or departments and actors to make crucial decisions about who gets what, when and how (fiscal allocation)	Degree of autonomy from centralized or supranational decree; budgetary ring fencing	Target of debt/deficit: responsibility and repayment
Chapter 4: public sector restructuring	Changes in public sector employment; increased centralization of political decision making; privatization and marketization	Scope of changes in public spending and decision making: public-private partnerships (PPPs), devolution, downloading and centralization	Nature of the contribution of public services and public sector; nature of budget imbalance; contribution to income support	PPPs and value for money; New Public Management and efficiency, effectiveness

(continued)

Table 8: Varieties of austerity – summary of dynamics and degrees (continued)

	Themes	Institutionalization	Insulation	Insinuation
Chapter 5: labour market flexibility	Supply side measures to reduce 'rigidities' within the labour market; measures to weaken collective bargaining institutions; imposition of outcomes on bargaining; reducing or bypassing the influence of social dialogue institutions	Bypassed or bolstered institutional starting points (pre-crisis): statutory or voluntarist collective bargaining systems, social dialogue procedures (or similar)	Extending, affirming or rescinding: legal rights, protections, automatic stabilizers, addressing 'rigidities', impinging on trade union strength	Controlling unit labour costs: internal devaluation, supply-side low-wage competition
Chapter 6: precarity	Household poverty and insecurity (personal debt); labour market precarity (workers' rights, youth workers' rights, youth, women, migrants); housing and food insecurity; voice (advocacy)	Voice and organizing predicaments for those who are poor, precarious, low-waged and have high debt	Impact of crisis and austerity measures on particular sectors, occupations, households, individuals	Causalities of austerity: poor, precarious and vulnerable people
Chapter 7: resistance	Labour, social movements, political parties	Routes for dissent: unions, protests, political campaigns (formal to informal, legal to illegal)	Roots of austerity: one-offs, systemic	Triggers and victims: political parties and political system

responsibly when others will assume the consequences of their actions? Moreover, in facilitating this blame-shifting exercise through dishonest and cynical messaging, state officials and politicians have further undermined trust in public authorities. This is consistent with long-standing neoliberal tropes that the state is not the solution, it is the problem; and to the extent that the exercise is successful, it disempowers those who would develop alternatives to austerity.

Infringing on the nature of the capitalist state, engineered to reflect a private rather than a public purpose, has to be part of the solution. Notably, austerity imposes fiscal limits on the state's range of actions by privileging the goal of balanced budgets and public debt ceilings. The doctrine of neoliberalism gives priority to restraining, retrenching or redirecting state action given the possibility that public authorities could become infused with the notion of popular sovereignty and use the powers of the state to constrain the power of capital. Second, as we have amply demonstrated in the book, austerity also disempowers labour, another potential threat to the power of capital. Through reduced and conditional social and labour market policies (in which benefits are based on the activation of recipients), a labour market characterized by flexibility, and associated pressures on collective bargaining, labour's potential power is weakened.

Economically, austerity has failed to work as proponents stated it would. It has produced a deep and prolonged recession, high unemployment, continued income inequality and social inequity. The impact of the crisis varied by country, often dependent upon a country's location in the international political economy, its pre-crisis situation, and whether austerity was imposed (albeit with the willing compliance of national elites) or adopted voluntarily. The dual scourge of crisis and austerity also varied in its impact by social class (with the biggest impact on the working class), age (young people most affected), gender (women often more affected than men), and migrant status (greater impact on migrants than on native-born). Existing inequalities were deepened. Unemployment increased, dramatically in certain countries and especially so for the young. In many countries, workers experienced direct wage cuts, or lost income through loss of hours. The effects of greater inequality, higher unemployment and insecurity were exacerbated by austerity measures such as cuts in social and health care spending. These factors imposed human and social costs on both individuals and communities, and carried additional economic costs including increased health care spending, policing, lost production, and unused skills and human capacity. Inequality contributes to diminished trust in institutions and the political system, and lower levels of social capital are matters of increasing concern.

The burden of carrying and/or repaying debts assumed by banking sector investors and financialized firms (for example the automobile sector) is significant. Looking at the relationship of deed versus onus through the lens of insulation, the class nature of austerity and its private and public backers is clear. Some have been insulated – banks, financiers; some have not – the working class, and those marginalized in various ways by the operation of neoliberal capitalism.

Austerity's actual record has demolished the intellectual argument advanced by prominent mainstream economists, international organizations and political leaders. Who can still seriously claim that public debt hinders growth at a definite threshold, that investor confidence is boosted by trenchant austerity, that privatization and public-private partnerships enhance public benefit, or that flexibility in labour markets benefits employment and competitiveness? The answer should be 'no one'. But the reality is different.

This austerity-era discrepancy between myth and reality points to the salience of the theories of the state reviewed in Chapter 1. The state has acted as the instrument of predominant capitalist interests, especially those concentrated in the financial sector, and as a structural expression of how states crucially support capital accumulation. However plausible the critics of austerity have been, they have not made practical headway against the entrenched ideological orthodoxy that supports the distribution of class power and shapes state roles and priorities. So, theories of policy change reviewed in Chapter 1 might have some descriptive validity insofar as they posited continuity was more likely than change. However, by neglecting what we called the elephant in the room – power and interests – they would be quite inadequate as explanations of what occurred after 2008. Parties and movements opposed to austerity and wishing to develop alternatives have not so far achieved success. But given the unpopularity of austerity and the rise of other social forces, they have contributed to destabilizing existing arrangements in some locations (Spain and Ireland especially). It is not possible to predict in what direction these unstable situations will evolve. All we can say is that ten years of austerity have undermined the legitimacy of some political systems or political configurations within them.

Democratic theory has always included the idea that people should be able to use their political power to choose the ends and means they decide on. In this book, our focus on institutionalization has revealed the way institutions, national and international, have deprived people of real choice. Important issues have been 'depoliticized' by removal to remote and unaccountable venues, institutions that formerly provided voice to elements of society outside the top elites have been bypassed, marginalized or reconfigured in the name of implementing austerity.

Alternatives to austerity range from very specific demands to reverse some budget reduction or to restore some social programme, to broader projects that challenge the existing economic order by integrating economic, social and environmental priorities. There is no shortage of policy agendas. Most implicitly involve something that, in our view, should be far more prominent – a new public purpose based on democratic popular sovereignty rather than narrow private interest, and a set of institutions capable of delivering a fair and sustainable society. The three varieties of austerity suggest a target and a path forward in developing alternatives.

Viewed in class terms, workers have lost much of their previous insulation from the impact of a private, market-based economy (however meagre this may have been). As a result, they have confronted enhanced unemployment, underemployment, precarious employment, reduced social mobility, a declining social wage, restructured public sectors, reformed labour markets and heightened insecurity. These experiences stand in stark contrast to the benefits enjoyed by the top 10 per cent of income earners, and in particular the top 1 per cent who are insulated from the fallout, both social and economic, for which they are largely responsible. An immediate priority would be to reverse this pattern of insulation; next would be to replace the structural determinants of such outcomes by bringing the market under strict control, along with subsequent incursions on the very institutions of the crisis-ridden market system enabled by the state (unfettered private property, unbridled profiteering and price-determined social wellbeing). An early stage in this would be to win the battle of insinuation and assign blame and responsibility where it belongs. Those favouring alternatives to austerity do not need to insinuate who caused the problem that austerity has demonstrably failed to cure. The evidence is clear and so must be the responsibility.

With the old institutions having failed so miserably, new ones will be needed. Clearly, they must in some way be *public* institutions and reverse the depoliticizing trends of the old ones. This would entail a degree of deglobalization and increasing the role of nation-states, not because they are homelands of nations, but because they are the largest vehicle conceivable at present in which something like popular or public sovereignty might be exercised. There are, of course, no guarantees what a repoliticized environment would produce. Some warn that authoritarianism is a possible outcome, and this should certainly be taken seriously (see Chapter 7 on right-wing populist parties that have emerged as of late). However, we already have a situation in which policy instruments that could be used to control or regulate capitalism are increasingly insulated from the means of democratic accountability. States often show far more deference to the concerns of global creditors than to the happiness of their own citizens. Many have termed this a version of undemocratic or authoritarian liberalism.

Notwithstanding the risks, correcting insinuation through an accurate attribution of blame requires new policies to restore the protection or insulation of working-class people from the impact of unregulated markets, and the construction of new institutions for different purposes, embedded in and accountable to the society. These routes can offer a pathway to a better future than austerity and neoliberalism can or have delivered.

Throughout our cases, the workings of the state are observed to be critical to outcomes. Theorizations of the capitalist state, some quite sophisticated, were reviewed in Chapter 1. However, in reviewing the experience with austerity at least, it seems the neoliberal state demonstrates a crude instrumentality that gives a contemporary expression to the *Communist Manifesto*'s framing of the state as a committee for managing the affairs of the ruling class. In other words, the capitalist state is a class-constructed state that may, as the varieties of austerity surveyed here suggest, manage those affairs differently, but within a common framework. Structural interpretations of the state's role in legitimation, accumulation and coercion are equally supported given the systemic compulsion to crisis-response, without the need for obvious (or, in any case, necessary) demands by particular capitalists.

The 2020 COVID-19 crisis of reproduction and accumulation is in itself not easily comparable to 2008 given that the latter was largely concerned with credit, banking and international trade. However, both crises reveal the failures of the neoliberal and austerity models of public provision and labour practices. The virus may be a health issue but the failure of global supply chains, privatized institutions (particularly health services) and precarious low-paid but 'essential' frontline workers are wrapped up in the neoliberal governance system. The breadth and depth of 2020 may also provide more openings for the construction of alternatives than the previous crisis.

As this next section details, the 2020 pandemic has been associated with significant emergency spending by government, but a long-run downturn in economic prospects means austerity is far from vanquished.

COVID-19 crisis and the ongoing legacy of austerity

From its resurgence after 2008, austerity remained largely dominant (as an institutionalized narrative if not full-fledged budgeting practice in many jurisdictions) until the global COVID-19 pandemic hit. The shock of the pandemic, the lockdowns, loss of life, panic buying, and the government-mandated closure of large parts of economic and social life, led many to reflect on social/individual values and desires, and thus began something of a wide-scale contemplation of the normal which had been left behind. Reflections such as these were fuelled at least in part by the sudden and necessary large-scale infusions of cash and credit into the economy as governments reacted in emergency mode to the economic implications of the pandemic – measures which had been declared impossible during the austerity period after 2008.

The ensuing economic meltdown in mid-2020 has also starkly revealed the legacy of austerity and neoliberal capitalism. Austerity agendas generated structural wage and productivity stagnation, cuts to public services and declining capacity of the state itself. People resorted to low-paid, precarious work in order to cope (Mitchell, 2020). The poverty and vulnerability exacerbated by austerity policies and their 3Is implications thus amplified the effects of the virus. Housing insecurity generated through budget cuts and privatization, combined with increasingly punitive cuts to benefits, forced many communities into unnecessary precariousness and poverty. Not only did the austerity legacy create social conditions in which health problems multiply, it also reduced the capacity of public health and social systems to respond. Austerity left health and welfare state systems in many countries overburdened, understaffed and lacking necessary resources (that is, personal protective equipment, ventilators, hospital beds). Privatization undermined sectoral capacity by reducing health care access for the most vulnerable due to lack of coverage, and permitted overcrowding as a means of profit-generation in long-term care facilities where, in Canada for example, death rates in the for-profit sector greatly exceeded death rates in not-for-profit facilities. Labour practices in such residences prompted disease transmission due to many low-paid, limited-hours employees supplementing their incomes by working in multiple facilities (Hedgecoe, 2020b; Malek, 2020). While austerity did not cause the pandemic, it led to a lack of preparedness, increased spread, and had a disproportionate impact on vulnerable (precarious, racialized) communities.

The ultimate direction and substance of the post-coronavirus recovery – what the pandemic recovery will look like, and what the contours of a new normal will be – are unclear. The international experience of the pandemic has given rise to a questioning of the neoliberal era and led to proposals for a new social contract and recognition of the value of public programmes and state spending to mitigate contagion and stabilize economic and social disruption. As mentioned, before the significance of the COVID-19 virus was understood, austerity was still the rule. Once the threat was grasped, however, governments 'magically found a way to pay for all kinds of programmes and supports written off as impossible before. The sky, it seems, is the limit' (Gindin, 2020). On the other hand, there are those who warn 'sustainable' spending and debt will have to be restored once the health emergency is over, indicating austerity may have been temporarily suspended, but is far from dead. In terms of the 3I categories we have applied in this book, the institutional structures implemented to shore up austerity have not been fundamentally challenged, the scope of insulation from the effects of the crisis has broadened to include many workers whose continued spending is crucial to the economy but cannot be regarded as permanent, and the debate over the insinuation of who will bear the burden of possible future economic remedies is just beginning. Here we briefly review discussions and debates in the cases of Canada, Ireland, Spain, and Denmark.

Canada

Canada's initial response to the pandemic was to provide employers with a 10 per cent subsidy on workers' wages, reflecting the Canadian finance department's fiscal conservatism and failure to grasp the magnitude of the unfolding pandemic, which was widely depicted as inadequate and thus later increased to 75 per cent (Department of Finance Canada, 2020). The government's fiscal response expanded along with the size of the deficit (this growing ten-fold larger than that incurred to battle the 2008 crisis). A more existential debate soon emerged with regard to immediate interventions versus the structural changes needed to support long-run future recovery. In broad terms, one vision seeks a return to public finance orthodoxy (austerity) and the other the rebuilding of the public sector and social programmes.

The Conservative Party characterized the Liberal government's expenditures as having 'abandoned their fiscal anchors' and 'lost control over the federal debt' (Conservative Party of Canada, 2020). The quasi-social democratic New Democratic Party (NDP), in contrast, made calls for wealth and progressive income tax reform, and an expansion of the unemployment insurance programme. The government introduced a monthly $2,000 per person Canada Emergency Response benefit with few eligibility criteria, until September 2020, when those who are unemployed will shift over to the less generous employment insurance (EI) programme. In response, the NDP called for a revitalization of EI: 'This is the perfect opportunity to finally right those wrongs, restore funding that has been cut in the last twenty years, and expand EI for all workers in need' (NDP, 2020).

Think tanks and interest associations have been active in imagining the substance and direction of a post-pandemic recovery programme. The left-leaning Canadian Centre for Policy Alternatives issued a detailed policy programme that was decidedly anti-austerian. Its Alternative Federal Budget Recovery Plan proposed several areas for greater public expenditure including measures to 'implement universal public child care so people can get back to work, reform employment insurance, strengthen safeguards for public health, decarbonize the economy, and tackle the gender, racial, and income inequality that COVID-19 has further exposed' (CCPA, 2020). Conversely, the conservative Fraser Institute warned that Canada is on the path toward 'fiscal crisis' and that 'government must develop a credible plan to return to a balanced budget within a three-to-four-year period once the COVID recession has ended' (Hill and Palacios, 2020).

Peak labour and business organizations expressed their different agendas and perspectives on pandemic policy and economic directions. The Canadian Labour Congress (CLC), the umbrella organization for trade unions at the national level, characterized the Canadian government's approach to the crisis as 'measured and proportionate' and that 'calls for austerity and cuts are misguided, cruel and out of step with what most Canadians expect from our governments' (CLC, 2020). CLC President Hassan Yussuff also called for a recovery that includes a national childcare programme and for social dialogue through a multi-actor national task force for post-crisis recovery (CLC, 2020). The Canadian Chamber of Commerce, representing business interests, also proposed a road map for recovery. The plan centred on a recognition that the recovery will be laden with both public and private debt. Not only has government debt been ratcheted up through lost revenue and higher expenditures, private sector debt is on the rise as businesses, banks and landlords confront the reality of economic hardships and take on additional debt to survive. Consequently, the plan calls for increased government spending and support, but with fewer regulations in order to promote competitiveness and productivity: 'Canada will have to walk a fiscal tightrope between reducing debt and deficits and maintaining a competitive tax system that encourages business investment and economic growth' (CCC, 2020).

In general, Canadian recovery debates inside and outside government mirror more familiar fiscal conservative and progressive positions. Interestingly, few called for an explicit turn to austerity at any point. Even the business-oriented newspaper of record, *The Globe and Mail*, renounced a turn to austerity with an editorial board opinion, which stated clearly that 'austerity wasn't the right path before the pandemic, and it can't be the road chosen after it' (*The Globe and Mail*, 2020). That said, Canadian governments at all levels often cast pandemic-era spending as being facilitated by previous (righteous) fiscal discipline.

Inside government, former Bank of England governor Mark Carney was recruited to advise Prime Minister Justin Trudeau on the economic recovery plan. Some suggested that Trudeau and his allies were 'pushing for a transformational social and economic agenda' (Argitis and Bolongaro, 2020a). While details were scant, media reports indicated that the broad strokes of the recovery plan included reforming some aspects of the 3Is, particularly the effects of austerity institutionalization, by addressing deficiencies in the social safety net, infrastructure spending targeting industries facing long-term damage, new spending for sectors deemed strategically important, immigration, and a national day care programme for young children (Argitis and Bolongaro, 2020b). Tension resulted between Finance Minister Bill Morneau and the prime minister over this direction. Morneau and the finance department's 'concerns about cost or lack of analysis were ignored' and they found themselves at 'the losing end of many policy arguments' (Argitis and Bolongaro, 2020a). Clearly this was one factor in Morneau's subsequent resignation as finance minister (Curry, 2020). This fault line between fiscal conservatives and those social and political forces wanting to use the pandemic as a platform for a much more ambitious era of social and economic intervention has run throughout the Canadian debates since the inception of the crisis.

Ireland

Ireland's key economic policy responses to the COVID-19 crisis involved fiscal expansionary measures amounting to about 4 per cent of GDP. One package included income support measures such as the COVID-19 wage subsidy scheme which covered up to 70 per cent of wages, the COVID-19 enhanced illness benefit, which provided €350/week in benefits, and the COVID-19 pandemic unemployment payment, which paid a flat benefit of €350/week. Also included was €1 billion in liquidity support for affected businesses, and €2 billion in health expenditure to expand capacity in public hospitals, to develop community-based responses for vulnerable populations, and to procure essential equipment to deal with the pandemic. A second package included a €2 billion pandemic stabilization and recovery fund for small- and medium-sized enterprises (SMEs), a €2 billion COVID-19 credit guarantee scheme, and provisions to warehouse tax liabilities for 12 months during which time no debt enforcement action would be taken by Ireland's Revenue Commission

(IMF, 2020). Other measures to assist SMEs during the pandemic included tax deferrals in affected sectors (retail, hospitality, leisure and childcare); suspending interests on certain late payments along with debt enforcement until further notice and a contract tax rate review; and the removal of customs charges on critical pharmaceutical and medical products.

In monetary policy, the Central Bank of Ireland made payment holidays available for mortgages, personal and business loans (IMF, 2020). The European Central Bank (ECB) pledged to increase lending and to step up purchases of government debt. ECB commitments for asset purchases (quantitative easing) expanded significantly as the ECB launched the €750 billion Pandemic Emergency Purchase Programme (which also included the purchasing of private, non-financial corporate debt) and later increased the maximum size of its purchases of government bonds to €1.35 trillion (Belz et al, 2020). On 21 July 2020, EU leaders agreed to the details of an economic recovery fund with €750 billion (£677 billion; USD$859 billion) in loans and grants (BBC, 2020). The package allows the European Commission to distribute €390 billion in grants to the hardest-hit countries, with the rest of the funds being available for low-interest loans. Several 'frugal' member states including the Netherlands, Denmark, Austria and Finland all opposed the initial proposed figure of €500 billion in grants and the figure was revised downwards to reach agreement (Togoh, 2020), which could indicate that the institutional architecture of austerity remains in place and effective.

Much like the fiscally conservative voices in Canada, the Central Bank of Ireland governor has called for a 'credible' path to cut debt after the COVID-19 crisis has been resolved (Brennan, 2020). Put in context, Ireland's debt-to-GDP ratio was at 59 per cent in mid-2020, a point below the EU average and the 60 per cent threshold set by the Stability and Growth Pact (Parliamentary Budget Office, 2020). The Irish Fiscal Advisory Council, an independent statutory body and fiscal watchdog, released a long-term sustainability report in July, stating that in the post-COVID-19 climate, there will likely be need for 'some fiscal adjustment once the economy has recovered' which 'should play a key role in returning the debt ratio to a safe downward path' (IFAC, 2020). Conversely, the Irish Congress of Trade Unions released a policy paper titled 'No Going Back', which lays out the policy alternatives centred around a 'New Deal for workers and households' including universal basic services, fiscal reform around taxation and social expenditures, and an expansion of social protections, claiming that 'now is the time to consider the type of economy we want in the long run' (ICTU, 2020: 17).

Ireland's COVID-19 fiscal debate was coloured by the country's dramatic experience with the 2008 crisis, which in part shaped the historic results of the 8 February 2020 election that saw the anti-austerity Sinn Féin surpass both Fianna Fáil and Fine Gael in the popular vote (see the discussion in Chapter 7). By mid-April, Fianna Fáil and Fine Gael agreed to a 'full and equal partnership', the very grand coalition they had renounced, for five years (Bray and McCarthaigh, 2020). Still, the parliamentary arithmetic left them short of a majority: a third, and perhaps even a fourth, party coalition partner was necessary. The agreement between the two parties was dubbed a 'plan to recover, rebuild and renew Ireland after the COVID-19 Emergency' and most importantly proposed a programme which offered a vision for greater public investment and the building of a more comprehensive social safety net (Fianna Fáil and Fine Gael, 2020). The Green Party stated unequivocally that they 'would not be involved in talks with any of the three larger parties' unless these would lead towards an all-party national unity government (McGee and Bray, 2020).

However, in May, 2020, the Green Party began formal discussions with Fianna Fáil and Fine Gael on government formation. Negotiations progressed slowly due to policy differences over public finance and social protections – and specifically how to manage the growing deficit, the carbon tax and pension eligibility age. With respect to public finance, the Green Party clashed with Fianna Fáil and Fine Gael negotiators, arguing that the deficit should increase as needed until the pandemic crisis had subsided. In contrast, Fianna Fáil and Fine Gael contended that the deficit would have to be addressed by 2023 (McGee and Horgan-Jones, 2020). Moreover, the Green Party countered the deficit hawks, noting that such a commitment would 'lead to a repeat of the austerity measures of a decade ago' (McGee, 2020). Even the president of Ireland, a non-partisan but elected role, weighed in, saying 'The price paid for austerity is a situation that must not come up again […] It is time for a paradigm shift […]' (Leahy, 2020).

Notwithstanding their differences, by mid-June, the three parties had an agreement in principle subject to ratification by each party's rank and file members. The progressive tone of the agreement pointed to a shift away from previous policies. The main points included a Green New Deal with an annual 7 per cent reduction in carbon emissions; a new social contract including the provision of an income safety net for those whose employment was dislocated by the pandemic; striking the Low Pay Commission to research and set an appropriate minimum wage; a commitment to progress towards a living wage; the construction of 50,000 social housing units; and commitments to broaden access to childcare (Kelly et al, 2020). The programme was criticized from within the Green Party, whose finance spokesperson, Neasa Hourigan, warned that the new coalition might prove to be 'the most fiscally conservative government in a generation' (Clancy, 2020; Reynolds and Coulter, 2020).

Sinn Féin and other left-wing forces, depicted the deal as 'the road back to austerity, either now or later' (Taylor, 2020). Such assessments rested on distrust of the two main parties, whose austerity credentials have been amply displayed in the post-2008 period, the vagueness of the agreement's commitment to public investment and stimulus, and suspicions that the EU would tighten fiscal rules once the pandemic crisis was over (Reynolds and Coulter, 2020). Thus, it may be the case that institutionalization of austerity endures even if some aspects of insinuation and insulation have been shunted (temporarily).

Denmark

Danish fiscal interventions during the COVID-19 pandemic included measures for workers and businesses, countercyclical supports, a postponement of tax payments, and government guarantees (ILO, 2020). Counter-cyclical spending combined increased spending for higher social benefits as well as public investment in municipal projects (for example, buildings, road and infrastructure updates, and so on), a recapitalization of Scandinavian Airlines, and a DKK 10 billion fund for large, export-oriented companies in key industries to secure loans (DMF, 2020a; KPMG, 2020). The Denmark Ministry of Finance (Finansministeriet) also announced a stimulus package totalling DKK 76 billion over the next two years. The package included plans for green renovations of public housing, provisions for green transition investments in energy, industry and waste, as well as investments in an education and retraining programme for future labour market needs.

Denmark strengthened its relatively robust safety net by introducing a number of new subsidies and social spending policies, under the guise of pandemic stabilization programmes, and by providing liquidity support. The programmes aimed to increase economic support throughout the pandemic, ranging from the suspension of social assistance eligibility requirements, to the provision of temporary compensation, the postponement of payments and extension of tax periods, and supplying unemployment and sickness benefits reimbursements. Each programme varied in cost, with the Ministry of Finance 2020 budget deficit projections ranging from best-case scenario equal to 7.25 per cent of GDP, to a worst case of 9 per cent of GDP (DMF, 2020a).

New programmes, including the temporary compensation for fixed costs of business, were created to assist businesses meet inflexible costs.

Interestingly, in terms of insulation (of business) this programme is the most expensive in Denmark, at DKK 65.3 billion. The temporary wage compensation scheme, worth DKK 6.2 billion (DMF, 2020b), entitles businesses that have laid off more than 50 employees, or at least 30 per cent of their workforce, to a subsidy equal to 75 per cent of their payroll cost with a maximum of DKK 30,000 per employee. Hourly employees may receive 90 per cent compensation, or a maximum of DKK 30,000 per month. Other schemes provided all media (print, radio, television, film) compensation for revenue losses (DMF, 2020b), infrastructure assistance to Danish municipalities and regions to move forward with investments in roads, buildings and other infrastructure (KPMG, 2020a; DMF, 2020b). The Danish government also provided liquidity support through various programmes on top of these subsidies and social spending programmes. The government assisted with payment postponement, new loan schemes, and supporting Scandinavian Airlines and the broader travel industry. In the area of monetary policy, the Danmarks Nationalbank increased interest rates by 15 basis points to –0.6 per cent and announced an extraordinary lending programme that would make one-week, collateralized loans available to banks at –0.5 per cent interest rate (ILO, 2020).

Debates over the way forward in Denmark were relatively subdued. By early August 2020, five months into the pandemic, few substantial debates had occurred among government and opposition parties, non-governmental organizations and business interests regarding government response to the pandemic. Minor critiques on both the left and the right focused primarily on the need for increased assistance to specific groups, such as older people (Dahl, 2020; *Jyllands-Posten*, 2020). What this silence or agreement over new emergency spending means in the longer run for the 3Is of austerity in that country, however, remains to be seen.

Spain

The Spanish coalition government under Prime Minister Pedro Sánchez introduced multiple economic supports to mitigate the effects of the COVID-19 pandemic. As cases began to curve sharply upward in March 2020, the national government announced €100 billion in financial support for workers and businesses. According to Economic Affairs Minister Nadia Calviño (2020), this was the country's largest single spending initiative in its history; it sought to flatten the virus curve, minimize the economic impact of social isolation measures for workers and their families, and support companies and SMEs by providing liquidity in the face of looming bankruptcies. Following a significant contraction of GDP from April to July 2020, the EU stepped in with an additional and historic €140 billion package comprising grants and loans to mitigate the economic impacts of COVID-19 in Spain (Ordiz, 2020). Though the state's economic interventions follow many other countries in terms of their approach to mitigating the crisis, their magnitude raises important questions surrounding what future fiscal policies might be employed to cover the emergency measures, particularly after over a decade of austerity in response to the 2008 crisis.

The most important support mechanism is Spain is the ERTE (Expediente de Regulación Temporal de Empleo) or action of temporary employment regulation, which allowed companies to furlough employees for a limited period of time while government provided those employees with 70 per cent of their income. Set to expire in September 2020 and now extended until 31 January 2021, companies are tasked only with paying social security contributions and reinstating worker contracts after ERTE coverage ends.

Funcas (Fundación de las Cajas de Ahorros), a Madrid-based economic and social research think tank, forecast significant problems for fiscal capacity and growth as a result of these historic economic interventions. The National Statistical Institute (Institutional Nacional de Estadística) concluded that the Spanish economy shrank by 18.5 per cent from April to June 2020 and that full-time employment fell 17.7 per cent. On the whole, the Spanish government expects that GDP will shrink by 9.2 per cent in 2020 followed by a rebound of 6.8 per cent in 2021, thus anticipating significant GDP contraction overall. Some estimates suggest that GDP will not return to pre-pandemic levels until 2023, at which point public debt could be 116 per cent of GDP (Funcas, 2020). There are, however, indications that some sectors of the economy will fare better than others, like agriculture, chemicals, pharmaceuticals and businesses that can work remotely, while hospitality, tourism, service industries and transportation will likely suffer for some time.

Spanish workers have been particularly hard hit by COVID-19, especially those in precarious circumstances – that is, those already exposed to, rather than insulated from, economic volatility and austerity. Family savings are projected to shrink by 16 per cent by the end of 2020 due to low wages, unemployment and lost savings from stock and bond market volatility (Funcas, 2020). Personal consumption spending is estimated to decline by 12 per cent, further eroding the prospects of the labour market and long-term employment security (Funcas, 2020). Several cite the 2012 labour reforms previously discussed in this book as creating long-run problems that have only been exacerbated during the pandemic, given that most of the unemployed were already precarious, temporary contract workers (Manchon, 2020; Torres, 2020). Prior to the pandemic, the governing coalition of the PSOE and Unidas Podemos sought to repeal the austerity-driven 2012 labour reforms (COPE, 2020); however, the European Council's release of €140 billion in 2020 comes with strings attached. In part, the EU's Spanish support package deal involves shelving the recently drafted 21st-century reform of subcontracting, dismissals and labour market development (la reforma de la subcontratación, del despido y el desarrollo del Estatuto de los Trabajadores del Siglo XXI), in what would have been a significant reform of 2012 austerity institutionalization, until at least 2022 (Ortega Socorro, 2020). Thus, the EU's funding package not only raises issues of national jurisdiction over matters of domestic social policy, but indicates continuity in the institutional and insinuation apparatuses of austerity.

Like in other countries, the impact of austerity in Spain is clearly evident in the health care system. While Spain is sometimes lauded for its effectively managed and decentralized health care system, a series of hospital privatizations and health sector budget cuts under former Prime Minister Mariano Rajoy between 2011 and 2018 have exacerbated the pressures of COVID-19 (Fernández, 2020). Madrid's health care system, for example, the centre of the country's COVID-19 outbreak, was under considerable strain due to funding cuts in the wake of the 2008 crisis (España, Amnistía Internacional, 2020). In May 2020, WHO-Europe head Hans Kluge warned against further austerity measures in health care (*La Vanguardia*, 2020). At the height of COVID-19 infections, 97 per cent of hospital staff were working into the last week of their temporary contracts; once notified of renewal these often came with new terms and required relocation to different facilities (Valdés, 2020a, 2020b), a shocking indicator of how many precarious workers are far from insulated from crises even when they are essential to a country's physical and economic health.

Spain's political elite, like those in most other EU member states and OECD countries, share in a broad consensus that emergency spending measures are necessary, but temporary. For some, the COVID-19 crisis proves that austerity measures have left critical health and social infrastructure vulnerable to emergencies, but for others the way forward involves relying on market forces with minimal help from the ECB. Torres (2020) believes so far that EU support has been targeted unfairly at specific companies, creating market distortions, unfair advantages, and constraining the autonomy of the Spanish government to manage its fiscal affairs. At the other end of the spectrum, Pablo Hernández de Cos, the governor of the Bank of Spain, has advocated for the expansion of labour flexibilization as part of the economic policy response to the pandemic

(Lafraya, 2020). Thus while an extension of post-2008 austerity measures may be currently stalled, their institutionalization and related effects of insulation and insinuation endure; likewise, domestic efforts to reverse 2012 austerity initiatives have been effectively thwarted by the conditions attached to EU-provided pandemic support.

Beyond austerity

As of August, 2020, it remains likely that the worst economic downturn in several generations awaits. In seeking to cope with the pandemic, governments across the wealthy Global North have increased public debt to unprecedented levels. Once the public health crisis has passed, advocates of Austerity 2.0 can be expected to emerge (as indeed stimulus is often cast as temporary, extraordinary, and facilitated through prior austerity). As in 2008, the rationale will be the fiscal stress created by state expenditures and the resolution, predictably, will be through balancing state budgets in which public services and labour compensation will be the primary targets.

However, history is not preordained; it is cyclical but not repetitive. The COVID-19 crisis has demonstrated the public value of universally accessible, state-provided or funded health care, and of low-wage workers employed in all manner of services and production – from food to long-term care. Given widespread public recognition and celebration of the crucial social roles played by many workers, if the clock is turned back to a setting where their work is considered important but unworthy of protection, we will know that 2020+ shares much in common with 2008+. It is also possible that an alternative future could emerge in which rebuilding the public purpose would be at the centre of a new normal. The contours of a post-austerity state are unclear given the impact of the latest crisis and the deep-seated nature of austerity within neoliberal capitalism. The earlier financial crisis had already demonstrated that the central neoliberal axioms – that capitalism cannot fail, and that the state should practise limited intervention in the economy – were subject to challenge. The latest crisis dramatically reinforces those conclusions and adds challenges to other neoliberal postulates such as the viability of global supply chains and the superiority of private provision (one need look no further than for-profit care homes!).

The remedy to readily apparent social and political fragmentation and disorder must lie in a rediscovery and redefinition of public and collective purpose. New institutions, policies and practices must be built to create a new public space supportive of sustaining and advancing democratic practice. Political and ideational space has opened in 2020 to enable a serious reconsideration of the past four decades and its obstacles to wellbeing. Obstacles are not simply economic; they deeply implicate politics and political institutions. Actual alternatives cannot merely *bring the state back in* but rather must bring in *a new kind of state* and fundamentally challenge capitalist social relations. The 3Is of austerity – its institutions, insulations and insinuations – can be overcome, though this will have to involve much more than a narrow focus on budgets and their funding cycles. At its core, reformulations would need to involve a radical politics and a democratic state with wide representation, including popular democratic public administration and institutions embedded in and accountable to civil society, made functional through a new ethos of collective decision making, planning and ownership.

Notes

Chapter 1

1 Unless otherwise noted, all $ are in CAD.

2 See McBride (1992) for a distinction between forms of legitimation: concrete and material benefits on one hand, ideological or persuasive activities on the other. McBride makes it clear that these categories are to be seen as a way of classifying state activities and policies, and not, as some would maintain, as 'functions' that capitalist states must carry out. See also Jessop (2003) on state power and the state as a social relation.

3 This theoretical framework has evolved since the 1990s, as the theoretical implications of including gender and family in the model have been explored.

Chapter 2

1 Interview quotes and translated documents lightly edited for meaning.

Chapter 4

1 https://concordia.net/index/Concordia_Index_September_2013.pdf

2 In this regard, and on the influence of large corporate advisers on the recent privatization processes in Europe, see the report by the Transnational Institute (Vila and Peters, 2016).

Chapter 5

1 Further, while permanent contracts have increased, Spanish workers experience very high rates of part-time and temporary employment (OECD, 2018d).

Chapter 6

1 'Youth' is understood to be those aged 15 to 24 by statistics-gathering bodies like the OECD. To be unemployed, one has to be actively seeking employment. While being a student complicates this dynamic, to be unemployed and recently graduated with significant debt can be especially deleterious.

2 www.bbc.co.uk/news/uk-northern-ireland-22689189; www.bbc.co.uk/news/business-22702003

3 https://data.oecd.org/hha/household-debt.htm

4 https://data.oecd.org/hha/household-debt.htm

Chapter 7

1 Near-universal declines in party membership supported this view. For example, between 1980 and 2009, party membership declined by 44 per cent in Ireland, and 37 per cent in Denmark (Mair, 2013: 41).

2 'We can', in Spanish. The party was later renamed Unidos Podemos and then Unidas Podemos – 'United we can'.

3 Fine Gael (2011) 'Fine Gael Manifesto', web.archive.org/web/20111014163110/http:/www.finegael2011.com/pdf/Fine%20Gael%20Manifesto%20low-res.pdf

4 Solidarity: 'What We Stand For', www.solidarity.ie/principles

References

Addabbo, T., Amelia, B., Casaca, S.F., Duvvury, N. and Ni, A. (2015) 'Gender and Labour in Times of Austerity: Ireland, Italy and Portugal in Comparative Perspective', *International Labour Review*, 154(4), https://doi.org/10.1111/j.1564-913X.2015.00250.x

Abildgren, K. (2007) *Financial Liberalisation and Credit Dynamics in Denmark in the Post- World War II Period*, Working Paper no. 47, Copenhagen: Danmarks Nationalbank, www.nationalbanken.dk/en/publications/

AFP (2018) 'Why Rising Rents across Spain are Causing a New Crisis', *The Locals*, 26 September, www.thelocal.es/20180926/why-rising-rents-across-spain-are-causing-a-new-crisis

Agustín, R. (2015) *The Policy on Gender Equality in Denmark – Update*, Policy Department Citizens' Rights and Constitutional Affairs, Brussels: European Union, www.europarl.europa.eu/RegData/etudes/IDAN/2015/510026/IPOL_IDA(2015)510026_EN.pdf

Albo, G. (2012) 'The Crisis and Economic Alternatives', In L. Panitch, G. Albo and V. Chibber (eds) *Socialist Register 2013: The Question of Strategy*, Pontypool: Merlin Press.

Alesina, A. and Ardagna, S. (1998) 'Tales of Fiscal Adjustment', *Economic Policy*, 13(12): 489–545.

Alesina, A., Favero, C. and Giavazzi, F. (2015) 'The Output Effect of Fiscal Consolidation Plans', *Journal of International Economics*, 96(S1): S19–42.

Alexandri, G. and Janoschka, M. (2017) 'Who Loses and Who Wins in a Housing Crisis? Lessons from Spain and Greece for a Nuanced Understanding of Dispossession', *Housing Policy Debate*, 28(1): 117–34.

Allard, G. and Trabant, A. (2008) 'Public-Private Partnerships in Spain: Lessons and Opportunities', *International Business & Economics Research Journal*, 7(2): 1–24.

Alonso, J. M. and Clifton, J. (2013) *Public Sector Reform in Spain: Views and Experiences from Senior Executives*, prepared by Coordination for Cohesion in the Public Sector of the Future (COCOPS) Research Project, https://repositorio.unican.es/xmlui/handle/10902/8106

Álvarez, J.A. (2008) *La Banca Española ante la Actual Crisis Financiera* [Spanish Banking in the Face of the Current Financial Crisis], Estabilidad Financiera no. 15, Banco de España.

Amable, B. (2004) *The Diversity of Modern Capitalism* (1st edn), New York: Oxford University Press.

Andersen, H.T. (2008) 'The Emerging Danish Government Reform: Centralised Decentralisation', *Urban Research & Practice* 1(1), 3–17, http://dx.doi.org/10.1080/17535060701795298

Andersen, S.E. (2011) *The Evolution of Nordic Finance*, Basingstoke: Palgrave Macmillan.

Andersen, S.J. and Ibsen, C.L. (2017) *Større Valmulighed for den Enkelte* [*Greater Choice for the Individual*], Copenhagen: Employment Relations Research Centre (FAOS), https://faos.ku.dk/temasider/ok-forhandlinger/2017/analyser/ok-2017-stoerre-valgmuligheder-for-den-enkelte/Artikel_OK17_marts.pdf_copy

Andersen, T.B. (2017) 'Youth Education and Employment – Recent Danish Reform Experiences', *CEifo Forum*, 18(2): 47–51.

Andersen, T.B. and Malchow-Møller, N. (2015) 'Innovations in Mortgage Finance and the Onset of the Great Recession in a Small Open Economy with a Euro Peg', *Comparative Economic Studies*, 57(4): 711–34.

Andreosso-O'Callaghan, B., Lenihan, H. and McDonough, T. (2014) 'The Evolving Model of Capitalism in Ireland: An Insight into Enterprise Development and Policy', *Economic and Industrial Democracy*, 37(2): 319–44.

Argitis, T. and Bolongaro, K. (2020a) 'Relationships Strain Between Trudeau and Morneau over COVID Recovery Plan', *National Post*, 15 August, https://nationalpost.com/news/canada/relationships-strain-between-trudeau-and-morneau-over-covid-recovery-plan

Argitis, T. and Bolongaro, K. (2020b) 'Mark Carney Helping Justin Trudeau Craft Economic Recovery Plan to Pull Canada Out of Recession', *Financial Post*, 10 August, https://financialpost.com/news/economy/trudeau-taps-carney-for-help-in-crafting-covid-19-recovery-plan

ASTI (Association of Secondary Teachers, Ireland) (2013) 'ASTI Members Reject Haddington Road Agreement and Vote for Industrial Action', *ASTI News*, 20 September, www.asti.ie/news/latest-news/news-article/article/asti-members-reject-haddington-road-agreement-and-vote-for-industrial-action-1/

Atkinson, A. (2015) *Inequality – What Can Be Done?* Cambridge: Harvard University Press.

Azmanova, A. (2012) 'Social Justice and Varieties of Capitalism: An Immanent Critique', *New Political Economy*, 17(4): 445–63.

Bacaria, J., Coll, J.M. and Sánchez-Montijano, E. (2015) *The Labour Market in Spain: Problems, Challenges and Future Trends, Policy Brief*, Sim Europe, Gutersloh: Bertelsmann Stiftung, www.social-inclusion-monitor.eu/uploads/tx_itao_download/EZ_Policy_Brief_SIM_Europe_ENG_2015_03.pdf

Baier, W. (2016) 'Europe at the Crossroads: Right Populism and Reactionary Rebellion', In L. Panitch and G. Albo (eds) *The Politics of the Right: Socialist Register 2016*, London: Merlin Press.

Baines, D. (2017) 'Care and Control in Long-Term Care Work', In B. Evans and S. McBride (eds) *Austerity: The Lived Experience*, Toronto: University of Toronto Press, pp. 125–44.

Baker, N. (2015) 'Soaring Demand for Food Banks', *Irish Examiner*, 5 May, www.irishexaminer.com/ireland/soaring-demand-for-food-banks-328680.html

Banting, K. (1987) *Welfare State and Canadian Federalism* (2nd edn), McGill-Queen's Press.

Baragar, F. (2015) 'Crisis and Canada's Macroeconomic Policy: 2008-2012', *Studies in Political Economy*, (96): 93–122.

Barass, S. and Shields, J. (2017) 'Immigration in an Age of Austerity: Morality, the Welfare State and the Shaping of the Ideal Migrant', In B. Evans and S. McBride (eds) *Austerity: The Lived Experience*, Toronto: University of Toronto.

Barrett, S.D. (1998) 'The Importance of State Enterprises in the Irish Economy and the Future for Privatisation', In D. Parker (ed.) *Privatisation in the European Union: Theory and Policy Perspectives*, London: Routledge, pp. 136–49.

Barrett, S.D. (2006) 'Privatisation in Ireland', In M. Kothenberger, H.-W. Sinn and J. Whalley (eds) *Privatization Experiences in the European Union*, Cambridge, MA: MIT Press, pp. 265–88.

Barrow, C. (1993) *Critical Theories of the State: Marxist, Neomarxist, Postmarxist*, Madison: University of Wisconsin Press.

Barrow, W. and Keck, M. (2017) 'Globalization Theory and State Theory: The False Antinomy', *Studies in Political Economy*, 98(2): 177–96.

Barry, U. (2014) 'Gender Perspective on the Economic Crisis: Ireland in an EU Context', *Gender, Sexuality and Feminism*, 1(2): 82–103.

Barry, U. and Conroy, P. (2012) *Ireland 2008–2012: Untold Story of the Crisis – Gender, Equality and Inequalities*, Dublin: TASC Think series, https://issuu.com/tascpublications/docs/barryconroymay12final

BBC (2011) 'Greek Government Austerity Measures', BBC News, October 19, www.bbc.com/news/business-13940431

BBC (2020) 'Coronavirus: EU Leaders Reach Recovery Deal after Marathon Summit', BBC News, 21 July, www.bbc.com/news/world-europe-53481542

Beeby, D. (2018) 'Liberal Government Writes Off $1.1B US Loan to Chrysler, Plus Interest, Docs Show', CBC News, 22 October, www.cbc.ca/news/politics/chrysler-auto-loan-canada-account-write-off-edc-bailout-taxpayer-wudrick-milke-1.4871648

Begin-Caouette, O. and Jones, G. (2014) 'Student Organizations in Canada and Quebec's Maple Spring', *Studies in Higher Education*, 39(3): 412–25.

Bélanger, E. and Falk Pedersen, E. (2014) 'The 2012 Provincial Election in Quebec', *Canadian Political Science Review*, 8(1): 141–9.

Belz, S., Cheng, J., Wessel, D., Gros, D. and Capolongo A. (2020) 'What's the ECB Doing in Response to the Covid-19 Crisis?', *Brookings: Hutchins Center*, 4 June, www.brookings.edu/research/whats-the-ecb-doing-in-response-to-the-covid-19-crisis/

Bengtsson, M., de la Porte, C. and Jacobsson, K. (2017) 'Labour Market Policy under Conditions of Permanent Austerity: Any Sign of Social Investment?', *Social Policy Administration*, 51(2): 367–88.

Benjaminsen, L. and Andrade, S.B. (2015) 'Testing a Typology of Homelessness across Welfare Regimes: Shelter Use in Denmark and the USA', *Housing Studies*, 30(6): 858–76.

Bentolila, S., García-Pérez, J.I. and Jansen, M. (2017) 'Are the Spanish Long-Term Unemployed Unemployable?', *SERIEs*, 8(1): 1–41.

Berger, S. (1996) 'Introduction', In S. Berger and R. Dore (eds) *National Diversity and Global Capitalism*, London/Ithaca, NJ: Cornell University Press, pp. 1–26.

Betzien, J. and Voss, M. (2012) 'Denmark: Red–Green Alliance Congress Grapples with Increased Influence', *Socialist Project: The Bullet*, 8 August, https://socialistproject.ca/2012/08/b674/

Bieling, H.J. and Lux J. (2014) 'Crisis-Induced Social Conflicts in the European Union – Trade Union Perspectives: The Emergence of "Crisis Corporatism" or the Failure of Corporatist Arrangements?', *Analysing Labour and the Crisis*, 5(2): 153–75.

Blanchard, O. (2012) 'Driving the Global Economy with the Brakes on', *IMF Direct*, 24 January, https://blogs.imf.org/2012/01/24/driving-the-global-economy-with-the-brakes-on/

Blanchard, O. and Leigh, D. (2013) *Growth Forecast Errors and Fiscal Multipliers*, IMF Working Paper WP/13/1, Washington: International Monetary Fund, www.imf.org/external/pubs/ft/wp/2013/wp1301.pdf

Blanco, I. and León, M. (2017) 'Social Innovation, Reciprocity and Contentious Politics: Facing the Socio-Urban Crisis in Ciutat Meridiana, Barcelona', *Urban Studies*, 53(9): 2172–88.

Blyth, M. (2001) 'The Transformation of the Swedish Model: Economic Ideas, Distributional Conflict, and Institutional Change', *World Politics*, 54(1): 1–26.

Blyth, M. (2013) *Austerity: The History of a Dangerous Idea*, Oxford: Oxford University Press.

Bone, J. (2014) 'Neoliberal Nomads: Housing Insecurity and Revival of Private Renting in the UK', *Sociological Research Online*, 19(4): 1–14.

Bonin, H. (2016) 'It's a Student Strike but a People's Struggle: Class in the 2012 Quebec's Maple Spring', *Journal of Labour and Society*, 19(3): 341–57.

Boyle, R. (1997) 'Civil Service Reform in the Republic of Ireland', *Public Money and Management*, 17(1): 49–53.

Boyle, R. and Mulreany, M. (2015) 'Managing Ireland's Budgets During the Rise and Fall of the "Celtic Tiger"', In J. Wanna, E.A. Lindquist and J. de Vries (eds) *The Global Financial Crisis and its Budget Impacts in OECD Nations: Fiscal Responses and Future Challenges*, Cheltenham: Edward Elgar, pp. 284–308.

Bray, J. and McCarthaigh, S. (2020) 'Fine Gael and Fianna Fáil Agree Historic Joint Framework Document for Coalition', *The Irish Times*, 15 April, www.irishtimes.com/news/politics/fine-gael-and-fianna-f%C3%A1il-agree-historic-joint-framework-document-for-coalition-1.4229027

Bredgaard, T., Larsen, F., Madsen, P.K. and Rasmussen, S. (2009) *Flexicurity and Atypical Employment in Denmark*, Aalborg: Centre of Labour Market Research, University of Aalborg.

Brennan, J. (2020) 'Central Bank Governor to Call for "Credible Path" to Cut State Debt Post-Covid-19', *The Irish Times*, 7 July, www.irishtimes.com/business/economy/central-bank-governor-to-call-for-credible-path-to-cut-state-debt-post-covid-19-1.4297730

Bubak, O. (2018) 'Flexicurity and the Dynamics of the Welfare State Adjustments', *Transfer: European Review of Labour and Research*, 24(4): 387–404.

Buendia, L. and Molero-Simarro, R. (eds) (2018) *The Political Economy of Contemporary Spain*, London: Routledge.

Burbach, R. and Robinson, W.I. (1999) 'The Fin de Siècle Debate: Globalization as Global Shift', *Science and Society* 63(1): 10–39.

Burroni, L., Gherardini, A. and Scalise, G. (2019) 'Policy Failure in the Triangle of Growth: Labour Market, Human Capital, and Innovation in Spain and Italy', *South European Society and Politics*, 24(1): 29–52.

Burtenshaw, R. (2020) 'There is Finally an Alternative in Ireland', *Jacobin*, 14 February, www.jacobinmag.com/2020/02/irish-election-sinn-fein-fianna-fail-fine-gael

Burton, J. (2016) Labour Market Reform: Why Skills Matter, *OECD Observer*, January.

Calviño, N. (2020) 'Respuestas Económicas en Tiempos de la COVID-19' ['Economic Responses in Times of COVID-19'], *El Norte de Castilla*, 3 May, www.elnortedecastilla.es/opinion/respuestas-economicas-tiempos-20200503195608-nt.html

Calvo, A. and Paúl, J. (2009) 'Efectos de la Crisis Financiera Internacional Sobre la Financiación de la Economía Española' ['Effects of the International Financial Crisis on the Financing of the Spanish Economy'], *CLM Economía*, 14: 55–80.

Cameron, B. (2014) 'Spain in Crisis: 15-M and the Culture of Indignation', *Journal of Spanish Cultural Studies*, 15(1–2): 1–11.

Campos Lima, M. and Artiles, M.A. (2011) 'Crisis and Trade Union Challenges in Portugal and Spain: Between General Strikes and Social Pacts', *Transfer: European Review of Labour and Research*, 17(3): 387–402.

Canadian Foundation for Labour Rights (2015a) Restrictive Labour Laws, www.labourrights.ca/restrictive-labour-laws?field_shared_province_value=gv&field_shared_legislation_tid=All

Canadian Foundation for Labour Rights (2015b) 'Submission to the Standing Committee on Finance Re: Bill C-377', www.labourrights.ca/research-publications/submission-standing-committee-finance-re-bill-c-377

Carroll, W., Graham, N., Lang, M. and Yunker, Z. (2018) 'The Corporate Elite and the Architecture of Climate Change Denial: A Network Analysis of Carbon Capital's Reach into Civil Society', *Canadian Review of Sociology*, 55(3): 425–51.

Carstensen, M.B. (2013) 'Projecting from a Fiction: The Case of Denmark and the Financial Crisis', *New Political Economy*, 18(4): 555–78.

Carswell, S. (2010) 'The Big Gamble: The Inside Story of the Bank Guarantee', *Irish Times*, 25 September, www.irishtimes.com/news/the-big-gamble-the-inside-story-of-the-bank-guarantee-1.655629

Casero-Ripolles, A. and Feenstra, R. (2012) 'The 15-M Movement and the New Media: A Case Study of How the New Themes Were Introduced into Spanish Political Discourse', *Media International Australia*, 144(1): 68–76.

CBC (2012) 'Ontario Budget Targets Public Sector Wages, Pensions', CBC News, 27 March, www.cbc.ca/news/canada/toronto/ontario-budget-targets-public-sector-wages-pensions-1.1136652

CBC (2015) 'Canada's Deficits and Surpluses, 1963 to 2015', CBC News, 21 April, www.cbc.ca/news/multimedia/canada-s-deficits-and-surpluses-1963-to-2015-1.3042571

CCC (Canadian Chamber of Commerce) (2020) 'Road Map to Recovery', Canadian Business Resilience Network, 7 August, www.canadianbusinessresiliencenetwork.ca/resources/recovery/

CCOO Economic Department (n.d.) High Temporary Employment, Wage Trends and Inequality, Presentation to Joint Conference of the Bank of Spain and the IMF, Madrid: CCOO.

CCPA (Canadian Centre for Policy Alternatives) (2020) 'Alternative Federal Budget Recovery Plan', *Canadian Centre for Policy Alternatives*, 21 July, www.policyalternatives.ca/publications/reports/alternative-federal-budget-recovery-plan

Cerny, P. (2000) 'Restructuring the Political Arena: Globalization and the Paradoxes of the Competition State', In R.D. Germain (ed.), *Globalization and its Critics: Perspectives from Political Economy*, London: Macmillan.

Chan, P.C.W., Morissette, R., Frenette, M. (2011) *Workers Laid-off During the Last Three Recessions: Who Were They, and How Did They Fare?*, Analytical Studies Research Paper series, Ottawa: Statistics Canada, www150.statcan.gc.ca/n1/en/pub/11f0019m/11f0019m2011337-eng.pdf?st=bUDWt0xh

Christensen, T. and Lægreid, P. (2007) 'Introduction: Theoretical Approach and Research Questions', In T. Christensen and P. Lægreid (eds), *Transcending New Public Management: The Transformation of Public Sector Reforms*, Burlington, VT: Ashgate, pp. 2–16.

Christoffersen, H. and Paldam, M. (2006) 'Privatization in Denmark, 1980–2002', In M. Kothenburger, H. W. Sinn and J. Whalley (eds), *Privatization Experiences in the European Union*, Cambridge, MA: MIT Press, pp. 117–40.

Cioffi, J.W. and Dubin, K.A. (2016) 'Commandeering Crisis', *Politics & Society*, 44(3): 423–53.

Clancy, E. (2020) 'Neasa Hourigan Warns Greens of "Most Fiscally Conservative" Government in a Generation', *Irish Broad Left*, 20 June, https://irishbroadleft.com/2020/06/20/neasa-hourigan-warns-greens-of-most-fiscally-conservative-government-in-a-generation/

Clarke, J. (2017) 'Articulating Austerity and Authoritarianism: Re-Imagining Moral Economies?' in B. Evans and S. McBride (eds) *Austerity: The Lived Experience*, Toronto: University of Toronto Press, pp. 20–39.

Clarke, S. (ed.) (1991) *The State Debate*, London: Palgrave Macmillan.

CLC (Canadian Labour Congress) (2020) 'Canada's Unions Urge Government to Stay on Fiscal Track', Canadian Labour Congress, 8 July, https://canadianlabour.ca/canadas-unions-urge-government-to-stay-on-fiscal-track/

Clendenning, A. (Jan 28, 2011) 'Spain Retirement Age Going to 67 in Austerity Push', *Deseret News* (AP), 28 January, www.deseretnews.com/article/700104907/Spain-retirement-age-going-to-67-in-austerity-push.html

Clift, B. (2014) *Comparative Political Economy: States, Markets and Global Capitalism.* London: Macmillan, Red Globe Press.

Coates, D. (ed.) (2005) *Varieties of Capitalism, Varieties of Approaches.* Basingstoke: Palgrave.

Collado, M.D., Iturbe-Ormaetxe, I. and Valera, G. (2004) 'Quantifying the Empact of Immigration on the Spanish Welfare State', *International Tax and Public Finance*, 11(3): 335–53.

Collett, E. (2011) *Immigrant Integration in Europe in a Time of Austerity*, Washington, DC: Migration Policy Institute.

Collombat, T. (2014) 'Labor and Austerity in Québec: Lessons from the Maple Spring', *Labor Studies Journal*, 39(2): 140–59.

Collins, N. and Cradden, T. (2007) 'Ireland's Bureaucratic Traditions', In N. Collins, T. Cradden and P. Butler (eds), *Modernising Irish Government*, Dublin: Gill and Macmillan, pp. 11–27.

Colomer, J.M. (1998) 'The Spanish 'State of Autonomies': Non-Institutional Federalism' *West European Politics*, 21(4): 40–52.

Commission on the Reform of Ontario's Public Services (2012) *Public Services for Ontarians: A Path to Sustainability and Excellence* [the 'Drummond Report'], Toronto: Ontario Ministry of Finance, www.fin.gov.on.ca/en/reformcommission/

Consejo Económico y Social (2015) *Economía, Trabajo y Sociedad: Memoria Sobre la Situación Socioeconómica y Laboral España 2014* [*Economy, Work and Society: Annual Report on the Socio-Economic and Employment Situation in Spain 2014*], Madrid: Consejo Económico y Social.

Conservative Party of Canada (2020) 'Scheer Responds to Economic and Fiscal 'Snapshot'', Conservative Party of Canada, 8 July, www.conservative.ca/scheer-responds-to-economic-and-fiscal-snapshot/

Constâncio, V. (2018) 'Past and Future of the ECB Monetary Policy', Speech presented by the Vice-President of the European Central Bank, Central Bank of Malta, 4 May, www.ecb.europa.eu/press/key/date/2018/html/ecb.sp180504.en.html

Cooper, V. and Paton, K. (2019) 'Accumulation by Repossession: The Political Economy of Evictions under Austerity', *Urban Geography*, doi: https://doi.org/10.1080/02723638.2019.1659695

COPE (2020) 'Unidas Podemos: Derogar la Reforma Laboral está "más Vigente que Nunca"' ['United We Can: Repeal the Labour Reform is "More in Force than Ever"'], COPE, 21 July, www.cope.es/actualidad/espana/noticias/unidas-podemos-derogar-reforma-laboral-esta-mas-vigente-que-nunca-20200721_824775

Council of Europe (2020) 'The Right to Affordable Housing: Europe's Neglected Duty', 23 January, Strasbourg: Council of Europe and the Commissioner for Human Rights, www.coe.int/en/web/commissioner/-/the-right-to-affordable-housing-europe-s-neglected-duty

Cox, R.H. (2013) 'Welfare States in North America: Social Citizenship in the United States, Canada and Mexico', In B. Greve (ed.), *The Routledge Handbook of the Welfare State*, London: Routledge, pp. 213–31.

Crafts, N. (2008) 'The Celtic Tiger in Historical and International Perspective', Warwick Economic Research Papers no. 867, Coventry: University of Warwick.

Crespy, A. and Vanheuverzwijn, P. (2017) 'What "Brussels" Means by Structural Reforms: Empty Signifier or Constructive Ambiguity?', *Comparative European Politics*, 17(1): 92–111.

Crouch, C. (2011) *The Strange Non-Death of Neoliberalism*, Cambridge: Polity.

CSI (Centre for Social Innovation) (2018) 'New Federal Fund Will Make Canada a Leader in Social Innovation', 22 November, https://socialinnovation.org/new-federal-fund-will-make-canada-a-leader-in-social-innovation/

Cullen, P. and Murphy, M. (2017) 'Gendered Mobilizations against Austerity in Ireland', *Gender, Work and Organisation*, 24(1): 83–97.

Curry, B. (2020) 'Bill Morneau Urged Trudeau to Stop Leaks from Senior PMO Staff to Media', *The Globe and Mail*, 20 August, www.theglobeandmail.com/politics/article-morneau-urged-trudeau-to-rein-in-senior-pmo-staff-prior-to-resignation/

Curry, B. and Carmichael K. (2010) 'Informal Setting Will Help G7 Reach Consensus, Flaherty Contends', *Global and Mail*, 5 February, www.theglobeandmail.com/news/politics/informal-setting-will-help-g7-reach-consensus-flaherty-contends/article1364802/

Curry, B. and McKenna, B. (2014) 'Stimulus Gamble: How Ottawa Saved the Economy – and Wasted Billions', *Globe and Mail*, 8 February, www.theglobeandmail.com/report-on-business/stimulus-gamble-how-ottawa-saved-the-economy-and-wasted-billions/article16760149/

Dahl, K.T. (2020) 'What Is Happening Right Here During the Corona Crisis: The Elderly Are Being Downgraded and Immigration Policy Is Being Relaxed', *Dansk Folkeparti*, 7 May, https://danskfolkeparti.dk/hvad-sker-der-lige-her-under-corona-krisen-de-aeldre-nedprioriteres-og-udlaendingepolitikken-lempes/

Damhuis, K. and Karremans, J. (2017) 'Responsive to Whom? A Comparison of the Mitterrand and Hollande Presidencies', *West European Politics*. 40(6): 1267–87.

Danforth, B. (2014) 'Worlds of Welfare in Time: A Historical Reassessment of the Three-World Typology', *Journal of European Social Policy*, 24(2): 164–82.

da Silva, S. (2009) 'Bank Bailouts and the 2009 Federal Budget: The Untold Story of Canada's $275-billion Financial bailout', In *Financial Meltdown: Canada, the Economic Crisis and Political Struggle*, Socialist Project, Socialist Interventions Pamphlet series. https://socialistproject.ca/content/uploads/2017/11/FinancialMeltdown.pdf

DCCA (Danish Competition and Consumer Authority) (2015) *Instant Cash Loan*, Copenhagen: DCCA.

DDCI (2016) *From Puerto Rico to the Dublin Docklands; Vulture Funds and Debt in Ireland and the Global South*, Dublin: Debt and Development Coalition Ireland. www.cadtm.org/From-Puerto-Rico-to-the-Dublin

Dean J. (2014) 'Tales of the Apolitical', *Political Studies*, 62(2): 452–67.

De Barron, I. (2016) 'The Payday Lenders Making a Killing in Spain', *El Pais* 19 January, https://english.elpais.com/elpais/2016/01/13/inenglish/1452690153_179436.html

Dellepiane, S. and Hardiman, N. (2013) 'The Politics of Fiscal Efforts in Spain and Ireland: Market Credibility Versus Political Legitimacy', UCD Geary Institute Discussion Paper series, November, www.ucd.ie/geary/static/publications/workingpapers/gearywp201321.pdf

Dellepiane-Avellaneda, S. and Hardiman, N. (2014) 'The Politics of Fiscal Efforts in Ireland and Spain: Market Credibility vs Political Legitimacy', In G. Karyotis and R. Gerodimos (eds) *The Politics of Extreme Austerity: Greece in the Eurozone Crisis*, London: Palgrave, pp. 198–221.

Department of Finance Canada (2009) *Canada's Economic Action Plan, Budget 2009*, Ottawa: DFC, www.budget.gc.ca/2009/pdf/budget-planbugetaire-eng.pdf

Department of Finance Canada (2020) 'Government Introduces Covid-19 Emergency Response Act, No. 2 to Help Businesses Keep Canadians in Their Jobs', 11 April, www.canada.ca/en/department-finance/news/2020/04/government-introduces-covid-19-emergency-response-act-no-2-to-help-businesses-keep-canadians-in-their-jobs.html

Desjardins, M. (2014) 'Les 50 Ans Du Code Du Travail. La Principale Pièce Législative Encadrant Les Relations de Travail Au Québec' ['Fifty Years of the Labor Code. The Main Legislative Piece Governing Labour Relations In Quebec'], Montréal: Bibliothèque Nationale du Québec.

Di Mascio, F. and Natalini, A. (2015) 'Fiscal Retrenchment in Southern Europe: Changing Patterns of Public Management in Greece, Italy, Portugal and Spain', *Public Management Review*, 17(1): 129–48.

DMF (Denmark Ministry of Finance) (2020a) *Denmark's Convergence Programme 2020*, Copenhagen: DMF, https://ec.europa.eu/info/sites/info/files/2020-european-semester-convergence-programme-denmark_en.pdf

DMF (2020b) *Denmark's National Reform Programme 2020*, Copenhagen: DMF, https://ec.europa.eu/info/sites/info/files/2020-european-semester-national-reform-programme-denmark_en.pdf

Doherty, M. (2011) 'It Must Have Been Love … but It's Over Now: The Crisis and Collapse of Social Partnership in Ireland', *Transfer*, 17(3): 371–85.

Doherty M. (2014) Can the Patient Survive the Cure? Irish Labour Law in the Austerity Era', *European Labour Law Journal*, 5(1): 81–94.

Dolan, M. (2020) 'Ireland: Regression or Revolution?', *Cherwell*, 16 February, https://cherwell.org/2020/02/16/ireland-regression-or-revolution/

Doménech, R., García, J.R. and Ulloa, C. (2018) 'The Effects of Wage Flexibility on Activity and Employment in Spain', *Journal of Policy Modeling*, 40(6): 1200–20.

Doorley, K., Eichhorst, W. and Kendzia, M.J. (2013) *The Social and Employment Situation in Ireland*, IZA Research Report no. 52, Brussels: European Parliament, http://ftp.iza.org/report_pdfs/iza_report_52.pdf

DPER (Department of Public Expenditure and Reform), Ireland (2011) 'Public Service Reform, 17 November 2011', Dublin: DPER. www.reformplan.per.gov.ie/2014/downloads/files/Reform%20Plan%202011.pdf

Due, J. Madsen, J.S., Jensen, C.S. and Petersen, L.K. (1994) *The Survival of the Danish Model: A Historical Sociological Analysis of the Danish System of Collective Bargaining*, Djøf Forlag, Cph.

Due, J. and Madsen, J.S. (2010) *Vedligeholdelsesforlig med Modelperspektiv* [*Maintenance Agreement with Modelperspektiv*], Copenhagen: Employment Relations Research Centre (FAOS), https://faos.ku.dk/pdf/forskningsnotater/forskningsnotater_2010/Fnotat_108.pdf

Duffy, K. and Walsh, F. (2011) *Report of Independent Review of Employment Regulation Orders and Registered Agreement Wage Setting Mechanisms*, Dublin: Department of Jobs, Enterprise and Innovation. www.djei.ie/publications/employment/2011/Report_ERO_REA.pdf

Dwan, R., Holman, M., Merrill, E. and Zhang, J. (2018) 'Protecting Danish Consumers from the Hazards of Payday Lending', *WPI*, 13 October, https://web.wpi.edu/Pubs/E-project/Available/E-project-101118-112828/unrestricted/Payday_Loan_Denmark_A18_Booklet.pdf

The Economist (2008) 'Zapatero's Bear Fight', 24 January, www.economist.com/europe/2008/01/24/zapateros-bear-fight

Edwards, S. (2017) 'Homelessness in Spain Is on the Rise, and Owners Are Getting Rough as They Try to Get Squatters Out', *NewsWeek*, 19 June, www.newsweek.com/homeless-spain-squatting-owners-getting-creative-627190

Eichhorst, W., Marx, P. and Wehner, C. (2017) 'Labour Market Reforms in Europe: Towards More Flexicure Labour Markets?', *Journal for Labour Market Research*, 51(3): 2–17.

Ejersbo, N. and Greve, C. (2014) *Moderniseringen af den Offentlige Sector* [*The Modernization of the Public Sector*], Copenhagen: Akademisk Forlag Business.

Elomaki, A. (2012) *The Price of Austerity: The Impact on Women's Rights and Gender Equality in Europe*, Brussels: Creative Commons European Women's Lobby. www.womenlobby.org/IMG/pdf/the_price_of_austerity_-_web_edition.pdf

Elvander, N. (2002) 'The Labour Market Regimes in the Nordic Countries: A Comparative Analysis', *Scandinavian Political Studies*, 25(2): 117–37.

EPSU (European Public Services Union) (2013) *Cuts in Public Sector Pay and Employment: The Impact on Women in the Public Sector*, Brussels: European Federation of Public Service Unions from Labour Research Department, www.epsu.org/sites/default/files/article/files/Impact_of_cuts_final_report.pdf

ESDC (Employment and Social Development Canada) (2018) *Inclusive Innovation: New Ideas and New Partnerships for Stronger Communities*, Ottawa: Government of Canada. www.canada.ca/en/employment-social-development/programs/social-innovation-social-finance/reports/recommendations-what-we-heard.html

España, Amnistía Internacional (2020) 'La Década Perdida. Austeridad en el Gasto Sanitario en España 2009–2018' ['The Lost Decade. Austerity in Health Spending in Spain 2009–2018'], *Amnistía Internacional*, www.es.amnesty.org/en-que-estamos/reportajes/decada-perdida-sanidad/

Esping-Andersen, G. (1990) *The Three Worlds of Welfare Capitalism*, Princeton, NJ: Princeton University Press.

Estrada, Á., Jimeno, J.F. and Malo de Molina, J.L. (2009) *The Spanish Economy in EMU: The First Ten Years*, Working Paper no. 0901, Banco de España.

Eurofound (European Foundation for the Improvement of Living and Working Conditions) (2013) *Denmark: Impact of the Crisis on Industrial Relations*, Dublin: Eurofound. www.eurofound.europa.eu/publications/report/2013/denmark-impact-of-the-crisis-on-industrial-relations

Eurofound (2015a) 'Spain: A First Assessment of the 2012 Labour Market Reform', www.eurofound.europa.eu/publications/article/2015/spain-a-first-assessment-of-the-2012-labour-market-reform

Eurofound (2015b) *Upgrading or Polarization? Long-Term and Global Shifts in the Employment Structure: European Jobs Monitor 2015*, Luxembourg: Publications Office of the European Union, www.eurofound.europa.eu/sites/default/files/ef_publication/field_ef_document/ef1516en_0.pdf

European Commission (2012) *Labour Market Developments in Europe 2012*, Brussels: European Commission.

European Commission (2020) *Youth Guarantee Country by Country: Denmark*, Brussels: Employment, Social Affairs and Inclusion, European Commission, https://ec.europa.eu/social/main.jsp?langId=en&catId=1161&intPageId=3330&

Eurostat (n.d.) General Government Gross Debt –Annual Data, https://ec.europa.eu/eurostat/web/products-datasets/product?code=teina225

Evans, B. (2017) 'Social Democracy and Social Pacts: Austerity Alliances and Their Consequences', In B. Evans and S. McBride, *Austerity: The Lived Experience*, Toronto: University of Toronto Press, pp. 293–317.

Fahy, G. (2018) 'Home Mortgage Debt Outstanding Legacy of Ireland's Financial Crisis', *Reuters*, 3 June, www.reuters.com/article/us-ireland-banks/home-mortgage-debt-outstanding-legacy-of-irelands-financial-crisis-idUSKCN1IZ06U

Fanelli, C. and Thomas, M.P. (2011) 'Austerity, Competitiveness and Neoliberalism Redux: Ontario Responds to the Great Recession', *Socialist Studies/Études Socialistes*, 7(1/2): 141–70.

Farnsworth, K. and Irving, Z. (2011) 'Varieties of Crisis' in K. Farnsworth and Z. Irving. (eds) *Social Policy in Challenging Times: Economic Crisis and Welfare Systems*, Bristol: Policy Press.

Faroohar, R. (2016) *Makers and Takers: The Rise of Finance and the Fall of American Business*, New York: Crown.

Fast, T.W. (2016) 'Varieties of Capitalism: A Critique', *Industrial Relations*, 71(1): 133–55.

FCAC (2016) *Payday Loans, Market Trends*, Ottawa: Financial Consumer Agency of Canada, Government of Canada, www.canada.ca/content/dam/fcac-acfc/documents/programs/research-surveys-studies-reports/payday-loans-market-trends.pdf

Felgueroso, F., García-Pérez, J.I., Jansen, M. and Troncoso-Ponce, D. (2018) 'The Surge in Short-Duration Contracts in Spain', *De Economist*, 166(4): 503–34.

Fernández, L. (2020) 'Gasto Sanitario Público Consolidado en España de 2010 a 2018', *Statista* ['Consolidated Public Health Expenditure in Spain from 2010 to 2018'], 5 August, https://es.statista.com/estadisticas/533955/gasto-publico-en-sanidad-espana/

Ferragina E. and Seeleib-Kaiser M. (2011) 'Thematic Review – Welfare Regime Debate: Past, Present, Future?', *Policy & Politics*, 39(4): 583–611.

Ferrera, M. (1996) 'The "Southern Model" of Welfare in Social Europe', *Journal of European Social Policy*, 6(1): 17–37.

Fianna Fáil and Fine Gael (2020) 'A Draft Document Between Fianna Fáil And Fine Gael to Facilitate Negotiations with Other Parties on a Plan to Recover, Rebuild and Renew Ireland After the COVID-19 Emergency', Fianna Fáil, 15 April, www.fiannafail.ie/framework-document-between-fianna-fail-and-fine-gael/

Fidler, R. (2012) 'Québec Solidaire: A Québécois Approach to Building a Broad Left Party', *Alternate Routes: A Journal of Critical Social Research* 23: 147–74.

Fine Gael (2011) Fine Gael Manifesto, web.archive.org/web/20111014163110/http:/www.finegael2011.com/pdf/Fine%20Gael%20Manifesto%20low-res.pdf

Finn, D. (2020) 'Ireland's Left Turn', *Jacobin*, 13 February, www.jacobinmag.com/2020/02/ireland-election-results-sinn-fein

Flaherty, J.M. (2012) 'Jobs, Growth and Long-Term Prosperity: Economic Action Plan 2012', Budget speech, 29 March, www.budget.gc.ca/2012/home-accueil-eng.html

Flaherty, J.M. (2013) 'Canada's Economic Action Plan 2013', Budget speech, 21 March, www.budget.gc.ca/2013/doc/speech-discours/index-eng.html

Flaherty, J.M. (2014) 'The Road to Balance: Creating Jobs and Opportunities. Economic Action Plan 2014', Budget speech, 11 February, www.budget.gc.ca/2014/docs/speech-discours/2014-02-11-eng.html

Fletcher, C., van Hellsum, A. and Roggeband, C. (2018) 'Water Privatization, Hegemony and Civil Society: What Motivates Individuals to Protest about Water Privatization?', *Journal of Civil Society*, 12(3): 241–56.

Fong, F. (2018) 'The Missing Ingredient Canada Needs to Address Precarity', *The Globe and Mail*, 4 January, www.theglobeandmail.com/report-on-business/rob-commentary/the-missing-ingredient-canada-needs-to-address-precarity/article37506560/

Food Banks Canada (2016) *Hunger Count 2016: A Comprehensive Report on Hunger and Food Bank Use in Canada, and Recommendations for Change*, Mississauga: Food Banks Canada, www.foodbankscanada.ca/getmedia/6173994f-8a25-40d9-acdf-660a28e40f37/HungerCount_2016_final_singlepage.pdf

Fondeville, N. and Ward, T. (2011) *Homelessness During the Crisis*, Research Note 8 Social Europe, London: European Commission and the Directorate-General for Employment, Social Affairs and Inclusion.

France, A. (2016) *Understanding Youth in the Global Economic Crisis*, Chicago: Policy Press.

Frank, H.A. (ed.) (2006) *Public Financial Management*, Boca Raton, FL: CRC Press.

Frayer, L. (2012) 'To Scrape By, the Poor in Spain go Dumpster Diving', NPR, 11 November, www.npr.org/2012/11/11/164803718/to-scrape-by-the-poor-in-spain-go-dumpster-diving

Fresmillo, I. (2013) 'We Don't Owe, We Don't Pay', *Red Pepper*, 10 March, www.redpepper.org.uk/spain-we-dont-owe-we-wont-pay/

Funcas (Fundación de las Cajas de Ahorros) (2020) 'Previsiones Económicas para España 2020–2021: Impacto del COVID-19' ['Economic Forecasts for Spain 2020–2021: Impact of COVID-19'], *Funcas*, 9 July, www.funcas.es/articulos/previsiones-para-la-economia-espanola-2020-2021-impacto-del-covid-19-abril-2020/

Gaál, N. (2017) *Nordic Heat Wave: Recent Housing Market Developments in Denmark and Sweden*, Economic Brief 031, Luxembourg: Publications Office of the European Union.

Gálvez, L. and Rodríguez-Modroño, P. (2016) 'A Gender Analysis of the Great Recession and "Austericide" in Spain', *Revista Crítica de Ciências Sociais*, 111: 133–52.

Gandesha, S. (2018) 'Understanding Right and Left Populism', *Open Democracy*, 23 May, www.opendemocracy.net/en/can-europe-make-it/understanding-right-and-left-populisms/

Gambarotto, F. and Solari, S. (2015) 'The Peripheralization of Southern European Capitalism within the EMU', *Review of International Political Economy*, 22(4): 788–812.

García Montalvo, J. (2006) 'Deconstruyendo la Burbuja: Expectativas de Revalorización y Precio de la Vivienda en España' ['Deconstructing the Bubble: Expectations of Revaluation and Housing Prices in Spain'], *Papeles de Economía Española*, (109): 44–75.

Geary, J. (2016) 'Economic Crisis, Austerity and Trade Union Responses: The Irish Case in Comparative Perspective', *European Journal of Industrial Relations*, 22(2): 131–47.

Gellatly, G. and Richards, E. (2019) *Economic Insights: Indebtedness and Wealth among Canadian Households*, Ottawa: Statistics Canada, www150.statcan.gc.ca/n1/pub/11-626-x/11-626-x2019003-eng.htm

GENC (2018) *Women's Equality in Canada: An Environmental Scan*, Toronto: Gender Equality Network Canada, www.canadianwomen.org/wp-content/uploads/2018/04/GENC-Environmental-Scan-Report-Final-EN.pdf

Gerbaudo, P. (2017) 'The Indignant Citizen: Anti-Austerity Movements in Southern Europe and the Anti-Oligarchic Reclaiming of Citizenship', *Social Movement Studies*, 16(1): 36–50.

Gialis, S. and Leontidou, L. (2016) 'Antinomies of Flexibilization and Atypical Employment in Mediterranean Europe: Greek, Italian and Spanish Regions during the Crisis', *European Urban and Regional Studies*, 23(4): 716–33.

Giles, C. and Bounds A. (2012) 'Brutal for Britain', *Financial Times*, 15 January, www.ft.com/intl/cms/s/0/5cc73ea0-3e04-11e1-91ba-00144feabdc0.html?siteedition=intl#axzz2eRZcSxXb

Gindin, S. (2020) 'The Coronavirus and the Crisis this Time', *Socialist Project: The Bullet*, 10 April, https://socialistproject.ca/2020/04/coronavirus-and-the-crisis-this-time/

Giroux, H. (2013) 'The Quebec Student Protest Movement in the Age of Neoliberal Terror', *Social Identities*, 19(5): 515–35.

The Globe and Mail (2020) 'Austerity Wasn't the Right Path before the Pandemic, and It Can't Be the Road Chosen after It', Editorial, 24 July, www.theglobeandmail.com/opinion/editorials/article-austerity-wasnt-the-right-path-before-the-pandemic-and-it-cant-be/

Glor, E. (2001) 'Has Canada Adopted the New Public Management?', *Public Management Review*, 3(1): 121–30.

González, S., Luque, D. and Guillén, A.M. (2013) *Las Organizaciones Sindicales ante las Políticas de Ajuste del Estado de Bienestar: Los Casos de España Y Portugal* [*Trade Union Organizations Faced with Welfare State Adjustment Policies: The Cases of Spain and Portugal*], Madrid: AECPA.

Good, D.A. and Lindquist, E.A. (2015) 'Canada's Reactive Budget Response to the Global Financial Crisis: From Resilience and Brinkmanship to Agility and Innovation', In J. Wanna, E.A. Lindquist and J. de Vries (eds), *The Global Financial Crisis and its Budget Impacts in OECD Nations: Fiscal Responses and Future Challenges*, Cheltenham: Edward Elgar, pp. 59–91.

Gough, I. (2011) 'From Financial Crisis to Fiscal Crisis', In K. Farnsworth and Z. Irving (eds), *Social Policy in Challenging Times: Economic Crisis*, Bristol: Policy Press.

Government of Canada (2009) *Canada's Economic Action Plan, Budget 2009*, Ottawa: Department of Finance Canada, www.budget.gc.ca/2009/pdf/budget-planbugetaire-eng.pdf

Government of Canada (2016) Population of the Federal Public Service. Human Resources Statistics, www.canada.ca/en/treasury-board-secretariat/services/innovation/human-resources-statistics/population-federal-public-service.html

Government of Canada (2019) *Social Innovation and Social Finance*, Ottawa: Government of Canada, www.canada.ca/en/employment-social-development/programs/social-innovation-social-finance.html

Government of Ireland (2010) *The National Recovery Plan 2011–2014*, Dublin: Stationery Office.

Graefe, P. (2012) 'Whither the Quebec Model? Boom, Bust and Quebec Labour', in J. Peters (ed.), *Boom, Bust and Crisis: Labour, Corporate Power and Politics in Canada*, Halifax: Fernwood.

Graefe, P. and Rioux X. (2017) 'Austerity of Imagination: Quebec's Struggles in Translating Resistance to Alternatives', In B. Evans and S. McBride (eds), *Austerity: The Lived Experience*, Toronto: University of Toronto Press, pp. 272–92.

Greene, T. and Gilmartin, E. (2020) 'Podemos can Change how Spain is Governed', *Jacobin*, 7 January, www.jacobinmag.com/2020/01/podemos-psoe-coalition-government-iglesias-sanchez

Greve, B. (ed.) (2013) *The Routledge Handbook of the Welfare State*, London: Routledge.

Greve, C. and Ejersbo, N. (2016) 'Denmark: Towards the Neo-Weberian State in the Digital Era', In G. Hemmerschmid, S. Van de Walle, R. Andrews and Philippe Bezes (eds), *Public Administration Reforms in Europe*, Cheltenham: Edward Elgar, pp. 119–28.

Gross, J. (2014) Migrant Integration and the Urban Crisis: A New Rhetoric for a New Reality, Paper presented at the City Futures Conference, 18–20 June, Paris.

Guajardo, J., Leigh, D. and Pescatori, A. (2011) 'Expansionary Austerity: New International Evidence', IMF Working Paper WP/11/158, www.imf.org/external/pubs/ft/wp/2011/wp11158.pdf

Guillén, A.M. and Gutiérrez, R. (2008) 'Treinta Años de Pactos Sociales en España: Un Balance' ['Thirty Years of Social Pacts in Spain: A Balance'], *Cuadernos de Información Económica*, 203: 173–80.

Guillén, A.M. and Pavolini, E. (2017) 'Spain and Italy: Regaining the Confidence and Legitimacy to Advance Social Policy', In P. Taylor-Gooby, B. Leruth and H. Chung (eds), *After Austerity: Welfare State Transformation in Europe after the Great Recession*, Oxford: Oxford University Press, pp. 136–54.

Gurría, A. (2016) *Sustaining Ireland's Recovery for All*, Paris: OECD Publishing.

Hall, P. (1993) 'Policy Paradigms, Social Learning and the State: The Case of Economic Policy-Making in Britain', *Comparative Politics*, 25(3): 275–96.

Hall, P. and Soskice, D. (eds) (2001) *Varieties of Capitalism: The Institutional Foundations of Comparative Advantage*, Oxford: Oxford University Press.

Hansen, N.W. and Mailand, M.M. (2013) 'Public Service Employment Relations in an Era of Austerity: The Case of Denmark', *European Journal of Industrial Relations*, 19(4): 375–89.

Hardiman, N. and MacCarthaigh, M. (2008) 'The Segmented State: Adaptation and Maladaptation in Ireland', Working Paper, Dublin, University College Dublin, Geary Institute, http://researchrepository.ucd.ie/handle/10197/1820

Hardiman, N. and MacCarthaigh, M. (2011) 'The Unpolitics of New Public Management in Ireland', In J. Eymeri-Douzans and J. Pierre (eds), *Administrative Reforms and Democratic Governance*, London: Routledge, pp. 55–67.

Hardiman, N. and MacCarthaigh, M. (2017) 'State Retrenchment and Administrative Reform in Ireland: Probing Comparative Policy Paradigm', *Journal of Comparative Analysis*, 19(2): 100–18.

Hardiman, N. and Regan, A. (2013) 'The Politics of Austerity in Ireland', *Intereconomics*, 48(1): 4–32.

Harvey, D. (2003) *The New Imperialism*, Oxford: Oxford University Press.

Harvey, D. (2005) *A Brief History of Neoliberalism*, New York: Oxford University Press.

Hastings, T. and Heyes, J. (2018) 'Farewell to Flexicurity? Austerity and Labour Policies in the European Union', *Economic and Industrial Democracy*, 39(3): 458–80.

Hastings, T., Sheehan, B. and Yeates, P. (2007) *Saving the Future: How Social Partnership Shaped Ireland's Economic Success*. Dublin: Blackhall.

Healy, A.E. (2019) 'Measuring Food Poverty in Ireland: The Importance of Including Exclusion', *Irish Journal of Sociology*, 27(2): 105–27.

Hedgecoe, G. (2020a) 'Spain Still Haunted by Spectre of Poverty Trap', BBC News, 10 March, www.bbc.com/news/world-europe-51737422

Hedgecoe, G. (2020b) 'In Spain, Austerity Legacy Cripples Coronavirus Fight', *Politico*, 30 March, www.politico.eu/article/in-spain-austerity-legacy-cripples-coronavirus-fight/

Helleiner, E., Pagliari, S. and Spagna, I. (2018) *Governing the World's Biggest Market*, Oxford: Oxford University Press.

Herndon, T., Ash, M. and Pollin, R. (2013) *Does High Public Debt Consistently Stifle Economic Growth: A Critique of Reinhart and Rogoff*, Working Paper 322, Political Economy Research Institute, University of Massachusetts at Amherst.

Heyes, J. (2013) 'Flexicurity in Crisis: European Labour Market Policies in a Time Austerity', *European Journal of Industrial Relations*, 19(3): 71–86.

Heyes, J. and Lewis, P. (2014) 'Employment Protection Under Fire: Labour Market Deregulation and Employment in the European Union', *Economic and Industrial Democracy*, 35(4): 587–607.

Hickland, E. and Dundon, T. (2016) 'The Shifting Contours of Collective Bargaining in the Manufacturing Sector in the Republic of Ireland: Government, Employer and Union Responses since the Economic Crisis', *European Journal of Industrial Relations*, 22(3): 235–49.

Hill, T. and Palacios, M. (2020) 'To Avoid Fiscal Crisis, Trudeau Government Must Learn from History' [blog], Fraser Institute, 5 August, www.fraserinstitute.org/blogs/to-avoid-fiscal-crisistrudeau-government-must-learn-from-history

Hinkley, S. (2017) 'Structurally Adjusting: Narratives of Fiscal Crisis in Four US Cities', *Urban Studies*, 54(9): 2123–38.

Hogan, J. (2010) 'Economic Crises and the Changing Influence of the Irish Congress of Trade Unions on Public Policy', In J. Hogan, P.F. Donnelly and B.K. O'Rourke (eds), *Irish Business & Society: Governing, Participating and Transforming in the 21st Century*, Dublin: Gill & Macmillan.

Holm, L., Nielsen, A.L. and Lund, T.B. (2018) 'Adapting to Financial Pressure on Household Food Budgets in Denmark: Associations with Life Satisfaction and Dietary Health', *Acta Sociologica*, 63(2): 191–208.

Holmes, M. and Shand, D. (1995) 'Management Reform: Some Practitioner Perspectives on the Past Ten Years', *Governance*, 8(5): 551–78.

Hood, C. (1991) 'A Public Management for all Seasons', *Public Administration*, 69: 3–19.

Hornbek-Copenhagen, M. (2018) 'Striking Number of Danish Households are Food Insecure', *Futurity*, 24 December, www.futurity.org/food-insecurity-mental-health-1939962-2/

Horvat, S. (2014) 'The Return of the Left in Europe?', Aljazeera, 31 May, www.aljazeera.com/indepth/opinion/2014/05/leftist-parties-eu-elections-201453115143690 7842.html

Hozic, A.A. and True, J. (eds) (2016) *Scandalous Economics: Gender and the Politics of Financial Crises*, Oxford: Oxford University Press.

HRSDC (Human Resources and Skills Development Canada) (2013) *Harnessing the Power of Social Finance*, Ottawa: Government of Canada. www.canada.ca/en/employment-social-development/programs/social-finance/consultations-report.html

HRW (Human Rights Watch) (2014) 'Shattered Dreams: Impact of Spain's Housing Crisis on Vulnerable Groups', 27 May, www.hrw.org/report/2014/05/27/shattered-dreams/impact-spains-housing-crisis-vulnerable-groups

HSC (Housing Services Corporation) (2014) *Canada's Social and Affordable Housing Landscape: A Province-to-Province Overview*, Toronto: HSC, www.homelesshub.ca/sites/default/files/attachments/531-Canada-Social-Housing-Landscape_2014.pdf

Huerta, J.P. (2019) 'FROB in the Restructuring of the Spanish Banking System: Where it Stands after a Decade of Activity (2009–2019) and Considerations for the Banking Union', *Banco de España Financial Stability Review*, 36: 25–43.

Hughes, N. (2011) 'Young People Took to the Streets and all of a Sudden all of the Political Parties Got Old': The 15M Movement in Spain', *Social Movement Studies*, 10(4): 407–13.

Hughes, O. (2003) *Public Management and Administration: An Introduction*, (3rd edn), Hampshire: Palgrave Macmillan.

Ibsen, C.L., Andersen, S.K., Due, J. and Madsen, J.S. (2011) 'Bargaining in the Crisis – a Comparison of the 2010 Collective Bargaining Round in the Danish and Swedish Manufacturing Sectors', *Transfer: European Review of Labour and Research*, 17(3): 323–39.

ICTU (Irish Congress of Trade Unions) (2019) Patricia King Address to Biennial Delegate Conference Trinity College Dublin, Biennial Delegate Conference, 3 July, Dublin, www.ictu.ie/bdc19/news/2019/07/03/patricia-king-address-to-biennial-delegate-confere/

ICTU (2020) 'No Going Back: A New Deal for a Safe and Secure Future for All', ICTU Publications, May, www.ictu.ie/publications/fulllist/no-going-back/

IFAC (Irish Fiscal Advisory Council) (2020) 'Long-Term Sustainability Report: Fiscal Challenges and Risks 2025–2050', July, www.fiscalcouncil.ie/long-term-sustainability-report/

IFRC (International Federation of the Red Cross and Red Crescent Societies) (2013) *Think Differently Humanitarian Impacts of the Economic Crisis*, Geneva: IRFC, https://media.ifrc.org/ifrc/wp-content/uploads/sites/5/2017/02/Report-02_Think-Differently-Report-2013_EN.pdf

Igan, D., Moussawi, H., Tieman, A.F. Zdzienicka, A., Dell'Ariccia, G. and Mauro, P. (2019) 'The Long Shadow of the Global Financial Crisis: Public Interventions in the Financial Sector', IMF Working Paper WP/19/164, International Monetary Fund.

ILO (International Labour Office) (2016) *Non-Standard Employment Around the World: Understanding Challenges, Shaping Prospects*, Geneva: ILO, www.ilo.org/wcmsp5/groups/public/---dgreports/---dcomm/---publ/documents/publication/wcms_534326.pdf

ILO (2019) *World Employment Social Outlook: Trends 2019*, Geneva: International Labour Office, www.ilo.org/wcmsp5/groups/public/---dgreports/---dcomm/---publ/documents/publication/wcms_670542.pdf

ILO (2020) Regional and Country Impact and Policies. www.ilo.org/global/topics/coronavirus/regional-country/lang--en/index.htm

IMF (International Monetary Fund) (2010) Ireland: Letter of Intent, Memorandum of Economic and Financial Policies, and Technical Memorandum of Understanding, 3 December, www.imf.org/external/np/loi/2010/irl/120310.pdf

IMF (2016) *World Economic and Financial Surveys: World Economic Outlook Database*, April 2016 Edition, International Monetary Fund, www.imf.org/external/pubs/ft/weo/2016/01/weodata/index.aspx

IMF (2020) 'Policy Responses to COVID-19', www.imf.org/en/Topics/imf-and-covid19/Policy-Responses-to-COVID-19

Infrastructure Canada (2014) 'The 2014 New Building Canada Fund: Focusing on Economic Growth, Job Creation and Productivity', Ottawa: Government of Canada, www.infrastructure.gc.ca/plan/nbcf-nfcc-eng.html

Inman, P. (2011) 'Irish Politicians likely to Demand Cuts in Debt Repayments', *The Guardian* 27 February, www.theguardian.com/business/2011/feb/27/ireland-government-bondholders-debt-repayments

Irimia-Dieguez, A. and Oliver-Alfonso, D. (2012) 'Models of Public-Private Partnerships in Megaprojects: The Spanish Case', *Organization, Technology and Management in Construction: An International Journal*, 4(3): 604–16.

Irwin, N. (2013) *The Alchemists: Three Central Bankers and a World on Fire*, New York: Penguin Press.

Isitt, B. and Moroz, M. (2007) 'The Hospital Employees' Union Strike and the Privatization of Medicare in British Columbia', *Canada's International Labor and Working-Class History*, 71(1): 91–111.

Iversen, T. and Soskice, D. (2015) 'Politics for Markets', *Journal of European Social Policy*, 25(1): 76–93.

Izquierdo Peinado, M., Jimeno Serrano, J.F. and Rojas Blaya, J.A. (2007) 'On the Aggregate Effects of Immigration in Spain', *Documentos de trabajo/Banco de España.*

Jackson, A. (2012) 'The Economics of EI Reform', *Behind the Numbers* 24 May, http://behindthenumbers.ca/2012/05/24/the-economics-of-ei-reform/

Jannessari, S. (2019) 'The Left Will Govern Spain, but the Far-Right Is the Real Winner', *Foreign Policy*, 16 November, https://foreignpolicy.com/2019/11/16/spain-election-vox-far-right-socialists-winner/

Jensen, L. and Davidsen, S. (2015) 'The Global Financial Crisis in Denmark and Sweden: a Case of Crisis Management "Lite"', In J. Wanna, E.A. Lindquist and J. de Vries (eds) *The Global Financial Crisis and its Budget Impacts in OECD Nations: Fiscal Responses and Future Challenges*, Cheltenham: Edward Elgar, pp. 174–204.

Jessop, B. (1993) 'Towards a Schumpeterian Workfare State? Preliminary Remarks on Post-Fordist Political Economy', *Studies in Political Economy*, 40(1): 7–39.

Jessop, B. (2003) *The Future of the Capitalist State*, Malden, MA: Polity.

Jessop, B. (2012) 'Narratives of Crisis and Crisis Response: Perspectives from North and South', In P. Utting, S. Razavi and R. Varghese Buchholz (eds) *The Global Crisis and Transformative Social Change*, Basingstoke: Palgrave, pp. 23–42.

Johansen, I. (2015) 'The Danish People's Party: A Journey to the Centre', *Transform! Europe*, 14 November, www.transform-network.net/es/publications/anuario/overview/article/yearbook-2015/the-danish-peoples-party-a-journey-to-the-centre-1/

Jones, B., Baumgartner, F.R., Breunig, C., Wlezien, C., Soroka, S., Foucault, M., Francois, A., Green-Pedersen, C., Koski, C., John, P., Mortensen, P.B., Varone, F. and Walgrave, S. (2009) 'A General Empirical Law of Public Budgets: A Comparative Analysis', *American Journal of Political Science*, 53(4): 855–73.

Jones, S. (2015) 'Spanish Election: Conservatives Win but Fall Short of Majority – as it Happened', *The Guardian*, 20 December, www.theguardian.com/world/live/2015/dec/20/spain-election-results-live-updates-podemos-ciudadanos

Jørgensen, H. and Schulze, M. (2011) 'Leaving the Nordic Path? The Changing Role of Danish Trade Unions in the Welfare Reform Process', *Social Policy & Administration*, 45(2): 206–19.

Jørgensen, M.B. and Thomsen, T.L. (2016) 'Deservingness in the Danish Context: Welfare Chauvinism in Times of Crisis', *Critical Social Policy*, 36(3): 330–51.

Jyllands-Posten (2020) 'The Liberal Party Will Focus on Aid To Corona-Affected Professions', 12 August, https://jyllands-posten.dk/politik/ECE12335556/venstre-vil-have-fokus-paa-hjaelp-til-coronaramte-erhverv/

Kappeler, A. and Nemoz, M. (2010) 'Public Private Partnerships in Europe – Before and During the Current Financial Crisis', Prepared for the Economic and Financial Report 2010/04, European Investment Bank, Luxembourg.

Katznelson, I. (2003) 'Periodization and Preferences: Reflections on Purposive Action in Comparative Historical Social Science', In J. Mahoney and D. Rueschmeyer (eds) *Comparative Historical Analysis in the Social Sciences*, New York: Cambridge University Press, pp. 270–302.

Keenan, G. (2015) 'Canadian Taxpayers lose $3.5-Billion on 2009 Bailout of Auto Firms', *Globe and Mail*, 7 April, www.theglobeandmail.com/report-on-business/canadian-taxpayers-lose-35-billion-on-2009-bailout-of-auto-firms/article23828543/

Kelly, E., McGuinness, S. and O'Connell, P. (2009) 'Benchmarking, Social Partnership and Higher Remuneration: Wage Setting Institutions and the Public-Private Wage Gap in Ireland', *Economic and Social Review*, 40(3): 339–70.

Kelly, F., Leahy, P., Bray, J., McGee, H. and O›Halloran, M. (2020) 'Programme for Government: What Are the Main Points in the Five-Year Plan?', *Irish Times*, 16 June, www.irishtimes.com/news/ireland/irish-news/programme-for-government-what-are-the-main-points-in-the-five-year-plan-1.4279046

Kernaghan, K. (2009) 'Putting Citizens First: Service Delivery and Integrated Public Governance', In O. Dwivedi, B. Sheldrick and T. Mau (eds), *The Evolving Physiology of Government: Canadian Public Administration in Transition*, Ottawa: University of Ottawa Press, pp. 249–71.

Kingdon, J. (1984) *Agendas, Alternatives and Public Policies*, Boston/Toronto: Little Brown and Company.

Kirby, P. (2002) *The Celtic Tiger in Distress: Growth with Inequality in Ireland*, Basingstoke: Palgrave.

Kirby, P. (2010) *Celtic Tiger in Collapse: Explaining the Weaknesses of the Irish Model* (2nd edn), New York: Springer.

Kluth, M. and Lynggaard, K. (2013) 'Explaining Policy Responses to Danish and Irish Banking Failures during the Financial Crisis', *West European Politics*, 36(4): 771–88.

Konzelmann, S.J. (2019) *Austerity*, Cambridge: Polity.

Korpi, W. (1983) *The Democratic Class Struggle*, Boston, MA: Routledge & Kegan Paul.

KPMG (2020) 'Denmark: Tax Developments in Response to COVID-19', KPMG Insights, 24 June, https://home.kpmg/xx/en/home/insights/2020/04/denmark-tax-developments-in-response-to-covid-19.html

Krasner, S.D. (1999) *Sovereignty: Organized Hypocrisy*, Princeton, NJ: Princeton University Press.

Kroeger, A. (1996) 'Changing Course: The Federal Government's Program Review of 1994–1995', In A. Armit and J. Bourgault (eds) *Hard Choices or No Choices: Assessing Program Review*, Toronto: Institute of Public Administration of Canada, pp. 8–21.

Krugman, P. (2013) 'Night of the Living Alesina, Continued', *New York Times*, 14 March, https://krugman.blogs.nytimes.com/2013/03/14/night-of-the-living-alesina-continued/

Lafraya, C. (2020) 'Hernández de Cos aboga por profundizar en la reforma laboral' ['Hernández de Cos advocates deepening the labour reform'], *La Vanguardia*, 23 July, www.lavanguardia.com/economia/20200723/482474710412/reforma-laboral-crisis-coronavirus-hernandez-de-cos-banco-de-espana.html

Lallement, M. (2011) 'Europe and the Economic Crisis: Forms of Labour Market Adjustment and Varieties of Capitalism', *Work, Employment & Society*, 25(4): 627–41.

Lancaster, T.D. (2017) 'The Spanish General Elections of 2015 and 2016: A New Stage in Democratic Politics?', *West European Politics*, 40(4): 919–37.

Lapavitsas, C. (2019) *The Left Case Against the EU*, Cambridge: Polity.

La Vanguardia (2020) 'La OMS Hace un llamamiento para "Evitar la Austeridad" y los Recortes en Sanidad tras la Crisis' ['The WHO Calls to "Avoid Austerity" and Health Cuts after the Crisis'], *La Vanguardia*, 28 May, www.lavanguardia.com/vida/20200528/481435711802/oms-llamamiento-evitar-austeridad-recortes-sanidad-coronavirus.html

Lawrence, F. and McSweeney, E. (2019) 'UN Experts Condemn Ireland's Migrant Fishing Workers Scheme', *The Guardian*, 19 February, www.theguardian.com/world/2019/feb/19/un-experts-condemn-irelands-migrant-fishing-workers-scheme

Leahy, P. (2020) 'Higgins Warns Against Austerity', *The Irish Times*, 22 May, www.irishtimes.com/news/ireland/irish-news/austerity-must-not-return-higginstells-communist-paper-1.4259339

Lecours, A. (2017) 'Dynamic De/Centralization in Canada, 1867–2010', *Publius: The Journal of Federalism*, 49(1): 57–83.

Lee, M. and Cohen M. (2005) *The Hidden Costs of Health Care Wage Cuts in BC*, Vancouver: Canadian Centre for Policy Alternatives.

Lee, S. (2017) 'Expansionary Fiscal Consolidation and the "Smarter State": An Evaluation of the Politics of Austerity in the United Kingdom, May 2010 to February 2016', In S. McBride and B. Evans (eds), *The Austerity State*, Toronto: University of Toronto Press, pp. 123–43.

Lenihan, B. (2009a) Financial Statement of the Minister for Finance, Government of Ireland, 7 April, www.budget.gov.ie/Budgets/2009Supp/FinancialStatement.aspx

Lenihan, B. (2009b) Financial Statement of the Minister for Finance, Government of Ireland, 9 December, www.budget.gov.ie/Budgets/2010/FinancialStatement.aspx

Lenihan, B. (2010) Financial Statement of the Minister for Finance, Government of Ireland, 7 December, www.budget.gov.ie/Budgets/2011/FinancialStatement.aspx

Lenihan, B. (2011) 'Financial Statement of the Minister for Finance', Government of Ireland, 6 December, www.budget.gov.ie/Budgets/2011/FinancialStatement.aspx

Lévesque, L. (2018) 'Normes du Travail: Québec Dévoile sa Réforme Attendue' ['Labour Standards: Quebec Unveils Its Expected Reform'], *La Presse*, 20 March, www.lapresse.ca/affaires/economie/quebec/201803/20/01-5158046-normes-du-travail-quebec-devoile-sa-reforme-attendue.php

Lin, C.Y.Y., Edvinsson, L., Chen, J. and Beding, T. (2013a) *National Intellectual Capital and the Financial Crisis in France, Germany, Ireland, and the United Kingdom* (Economics Book 13), New York: Springer.

Lin, C.Y.Y., Edvinsson, L., Chen, J. and Beding, T. (2013b) *National Intellectual Capital and the Financial Crisis in Greece, Italy, Portugal and Spain* (Economics Book 7), New York: Springer.

Lin, C.Y.Y., Edvinsson, L., Chen, J. and Beding, T. (2014) *National Intellectual Capital and the Financial Crisis in Australia, Canada, Japan, New Zealand, and the United States*, New York: Springer.

Lind, J. (2019) 'Denmark: The Sacred Cow of Collective Bargaining is Still Alive', In T. Müller, K. Vandaele and J. Waddington (eds), *Collective Bargaining in Europe: Towards an Endgame*, Brussel: ETUI, pp. 151–71.

Lind, J. and Knudsen, H. (2018) 'Denmark: The Long-Lasting Class Compromise', *Employee Relations*, (40)4: 580–99.

López Andreu, M. (2017) 'All Precarious? Institutional Change and Turning Points in Labour Market Trajectories in Spain', *Employee Relations*, 39(3): 406–22.

López-Andreu, M. (2019) 'Employment Institutions under Liberalization Pressures: Analysing the Effects of Regulatory Change on Collective Bargaining in Spain', *An International Journal of Employment Relations*, 57(2): 328–49.

López-Andreu, M. and Rubery, J. (2018) 'Austerity and Women's Employment Trajectories in Spain and the UK: A Comparison of Two Flexible Labour Markets', *Economic and Industrial Democracy*, March: 1–25.

Loxley, J. (2009) 'Financial Dimensions: Origins and State Responses', In J. Guard and W. Antony (eds), *Bankruptcies and Bailouts*, Halifax: Fernwood Press.

Lynn, L.E. Jr (2006) *Public Management: Old and New*, New York: Routledge.

MacCarthaigh, M. (2017) *Public Sector Reform in Ireland: Countering Crisis*, Belfast: Palgrave Macmillan.

Maccarrone, V., Erne, R. and Regan, A. (2019) 'Ireland: Life after Social Partnership', In T. Müller, K. Vandaele and J. Waddington (eds), *Collective Bargaining in Europe: Towards an Endgame*, Brussels: ETUI, pp. 315–35.

MacDonald, D. (2019) *Unaccommodating: Rental Housing Wage in Canada*, Ottawa: Canadian Centre for Policy Alternatives, www.policyalternatives.ca/unaccommodating

Madsen, P.K. (2006) 'How Can It Possibly Fly? The Paradox of a Dynamic Labour Market in a Scandinavian Welfare State', In J.L. Campbell, J.A. Hall and O.K. Pedersen (eds), *National Identity and the Varieties of Capitalism: The Danish Experience*, Montreal: McGill-Queens University Press, pp. 321–55.

Madsen, P.K. (2013) 'Shelter from the Storm?' Danish Flexicurity and the Crisis', *IZA Journal of European Labor Studies*, 2(6): 1–19.

Maestre, A. (2019) 'The Worrying Rise of Spain's Far Right,' *Jacobin*, 28 April, https://jacobinmag.com/2018/11/spain-vox-far-right-franco-partido-popular-podemos

Mailand, M. (2014) 'Austerity Measures and Municipalities: The Case of Denmark', *Transfer: European Review of Labour and Research*, 20(3): 417–30.

Mailand, M. and Larsen, T.P. (2018) *Hybrid Work: Social Protection of Atypical Employment in Denmark*, Study no. 11, Berlin: WSI Institute for Economic and Social Research, www.boeckler.de/pdf/p_wsi_studies_11_2018.pdf

Mailand, M. and Larsen, P.T. (2020) 'Danish Public Sector Industrial Relations and Welfare Services in Times of Trouble', In M. Keune, N.E.R. Martín and M. Mailand (eds), *Working Under Pressure: Employment, Job Quality and Labour Relations in Europe's Public Sector since the Crisis*, Brussels: ETUI, pp. 73–107.

Mair, P. (2013) *Ruling the Void*, London: Verso.

Malek, J. (2020) 'Seniors' Care Was in Crisis before COVID-19', *The Council of Canadians*, May, https://canadians.org/analysis/seniors-care-was-crisis-covid-19

Manchon, M. (2020) 'Raymond Torres: "España Tiene que Hacer un Esfuerzo Monumental de Inversión"' ['Raymond Torres: "Spain Has to Make a Monumental Investment Effort"'], *Crónica Global Media*, 21 June, https://cronicaglobal.elespanol.com/pensamiento/conversaciones-estado/raymond-torres-espana-esfuerzo-monumental-inversion_359679_102.html

Manow, P. (2015) 'Workers, Farmers and Catholicism: A History of Political Class Coalitions and the South-European Welfare State Regime', *Journal of European Social Policy*, 25(1): 32–49.

Martí, F. and Pérez, J.J. (2016) *Spanish Public Finances Through the Financial Crisis*, Documentos de Trabajo N. 1620, Madrid: Banco de España.

Mason, J.W. and Jayadev, R. (2019) 'The Crash of Austerity Economics', *The American Prospect*, 8 October, https://prospect.org/culture/books/the-crash-of-austerity-economics/

Mayores UDP (2017) *The Social State of the Nation 2017*, Madrid: Mayores UDP. www.mayoresudp.org/informe-estado-social-la-nacion-2017/

McBride, S. (1987) 'Hard Times and the "Rules of the Game": A Study of the Legislative Environment of Labour-Capital Conflict', In R. Argue, C. Gannage and D.W. Livingstone (eds), *Working People and Hard Times: Canadian Perspectives*, Toronto: Garamond Press, pp. 98–111.

McBride, S. (1992) *Not Working: State, Unemployment and Neo-Conservatism in Canada*, Toronto: University of Toronto Press.

McBride, S. (1995) 'Coercion and Consent: The Recurring Corporatist Temptation in Canadian Labour Relations', In J. Vorst, P.A. Phillips and C. Gonick (eds), *Labour Gains, Labour Pains: Fifty Years of PC 1003*, Winnipeg: Society for Socialist Studies, pp. 79–96.

McBride, S. (2001) *Paradigm Shift: Globalization and the Canadian State*, Halifax: Fernwood.

McBride, S. (2005) 'If You Don't Know Where You're Going, You'll End Up Somewhere Else: Ideological and Policy Failure in the Ontario NDP', In W.K. Carroll and R.S. Ratner (eds), *Challenges and Perils: Social Democracy in Neoliberal Times*, Halifax: Fernwood, pp. 25–45.

McBride, S. (2014) '"In Austerity We Trust": Elite Responses to Times of Crisis', In D. Baines and S. McBride (eds), *Orchestrating Austerity: Impacts and Resistance*, Halifax: Fernwood, pp. 10-20.

McBride, S. (2017) *Working: Employment Policy in Canada*, Oakville: Rock's Mills Press.

McBride, S. and Mitrea, S. (2017) 'Austerity and Constitutionalizing Structural Reform of Labour in the European Union', *Studies in Political Economy*, 98(1): 1–23.

McBride, S. and Whiteside, H. (2011) *Private Affluence, Public Austerity: Economic Crisis and Democratic Malaise in Canada,* Winnipeg and Halifax: Fernwood Publishing.

McBride, S. and Williams, R.A. (2001) 'Globalization, the Restructuring of Labour Markets and Policy Convergence', *Global Social Policy: An Interdisciplinary Journal of Public Policy and Social Development,* 1(3): 281–309.

McCarthy, C., McNally, D., McLaughlin, P., O'Connell, M., Slattery, W. and Walsh, M. (2009) *Report of the Special Group on Public Service Numbers and Expenditure Programmes. Vol. I* [the 'McCarthy Report'], Dublin: Department of Finance.

McGee, H. (2020) 'Q&A: What Are the Sticking Points in Government Formation Talks?', *The Irish Times,* 1 June, www.irishtimes.com/news/ireland/irish-news/q-a-what-are-the-sticking-points-in-government-formation-talks-1.4267925

McGee, H. and Bray, J. (2020) 'Greens Say Pandemic Makes Talks with Large Parties Inappropriate', *Irish Times,* 26 March, www.irishtimes.com/news/politics/greens-say-pandemic-makes-talks-with-large-parties-inappropriate-1.4212246

McGee, H. and Horgan-Jones, J. (2020) 'Government Formation Talks Hit Serious Pinchpoints', *The Irish Times,* 1 June, www.irishtimes.com/news/politics/government-formation-talks-hit-serious-pinchpoints-1.4267445

McVeigh, P. (2005) Embedding Neoliberalism in Spain: From Franquismo to Neoliberalism', In S. Soederberg, G. Menz and P.G. Cerny (eds) *Internalizing Globalization: The Rise of Neoliberalism and the Decline of National Varieties of Capitalism,* Basingstoke: Palgrave Macmillan, pp. 90–105.

Medina I. and Correa P. (2016) 'The 2015 Spanish Election: The Times They Are a' Changing', *Regional & Federal Studies,* 26(3): 1–11.

Meléndez, E.S. (2012) 'El Mercado de Trabajo Español en la Crisis Económica (2008–2012): Desempleo y Reforma Laboral' ['The Spanish Labour Market in the Economic Crisis (2008–2012): Unemployment and Labour Reform'], *Revista de Estudios Empresariales Segunda época,* (2): 29–57.

Mendez de Andes, A. (2014) 'Spain's Radical Tide', *Red Pepper,* 1 April, www.redpepper.org.uk/spains-radical-tide/

Mercille, J. (2014) 'The Role of the Media in Fiscal Consolidation Programmes: The Case of Ireland', *Cambridge Journal of Economics,* 38(2): 281–300.

Mercille, J. (2018) 'Privatization in the Irish Hospital Sector since 1980', *Journal of Public Health,* 40(4): 863–70.

Mercille, J. and Murphy, E. (2015) *Deepening Neoliberalism, Austerity and Crisis: Europe's Treasure Ireland*, New York: Palgrave Macmillan.

Merrion Street Irish Government News Service (2012) 'Update on Rationalisation of State Agencies', 31 October, https://merrionstreet.ie/en/News-Room/Releases/update-on-rationalisation-of-state-agencies.46984.shortcut.html

Miley, I. (2019) 'ICTU Critical of Low Pay in Hotel, Retail and Hospitalist Sectors', *Irish Congress of Trade Unions Press*, 13 May, www.ictu.ie/press/2019/05/13/ictu-critical-of-low-pay-in-hotel-retail-and-hospi/

Miley, T.J. (2017) 'Austerity Politics and Constitutional Crisis in Spain', *European Politics and Society*, 18(2): 263–83.

Minder, R. (2012) 'Despite Public Protests, Spain's 2013 Budget Plan Includes More Austerity', *New York Times*, 27 September, www.nytimes.com/2012/09/28/business/global/spain-unveils-sweeping-budget-cuts.html

Ministry of Finance, Denmark (1999) *Økonomistyring med Balance og Fokus* [*Financial Management with Balance and Focus*], Copenhagen: Schutlz.

Mitchell, J. (2020) 'Cornavirus Reveals the Cost of Austerity', *Tribune*, 10 April, https://tribunemag.co.uk/2020/04/coronavirus-reveals-the-cost-of-austerity

Mitchell, W. and Fazi, T. (2017) *Reclaiming the State: A Progressive Vision of Sovereignty for a Post-Neoliberal World*, London: Pluto Press.

Mitrea, S. (2017) 'Speaking Austerity: Policy Rhetoric and Design Beyond Fiscal Consolidation', In B. Evans and S. McBride (eds), *Austerity: The Lived Experience*, Toronto: University of Toronto Press, pp. 40–62.

Molina, O. (2014) 'Self-Regulation and the State in Industrial Relations in Southern Europe: Back to the Future?', *European Journal of Industrial Relations*, 20(1): 21–36.

Molina, O. and Godino A. (2020) 'Industrial Relations in Deep Water: The Spanish Public Sector During the Crisis', In M. Keune, N.E.R. Martín and M. Mailand (eds), *Working Under Pressure: Employment, Job Quality and Labour Relations in Europe's Public Sector since the Crisis*, Brussels: ETUI.

Montoro, C. (2012) 'Debate about the Passing of the Project of the Organic Law 2/2012 of Budget Stability and Financial Sustainability' ['Ley Orgánica de Estabilidad Presupuestaria y Sostenibilidad Financiera'], 29 March.

Murphy, M.P. (2016) 'Low Road or High Road? The Post-Crisis Trajectory of Irish Activation', *Critical Social Policy*, 36(3): 432–52.

Murphy, M.P. (2017) 'Irish Flex-Insecurity: The Post-Crisis Reality for Vulnerable Workers in Ireland', *Social Policy & Administration*, 51(2): 308–27.

Murphy, E. and Mercille, J. (2019) '(Re)Making Labour Markets and Economic Crises: The Case of Ireland', *The Economic and Labour Relations Review*, 30(1): 22–38.

Naidu-Ghelani, R. (2019) 'Number of Temporary Workers Jumped by 50% in last 20 Years, StatCan Says', CBC News, 14 May, www.cbc.ca/news/business/temporary-workers-employment-1.5135310

Natali, D. and Stamati, F. (2014) 'Reassessing South European Pensions after the Crisis: Evidence from Two Decades of Reforms', *South European Society and Politics*, 19(3): 309–30.

NDP (New Democratic Party of Canada) (2020) 'The Ultra-Rich Must Pay Their Share: NDP' [blog], 8 July, www.ndp.ca/news/ultra-rich-must-pay-their-share-ndp

Neal, L. and García-Iglesias, M.C. (2013) 'The Economy of Spain in the Euro-Zone before and after the Crisis of 2008', *The Quarterly Review of Economics and Finance*, 53(4): 336–44.

Nielsen, M., Dyreborg, J. and Lipscomb, H. (2019) 'Precarious Work among Young Danish Employees – a Permanent or Transitory Condition?', *Journal of Youth Studies*, 22(1): 7–28.

Noonan, M. (2012) 'Financial Statement of the Minister for Finance', Government of Ireland, 5 December, www.budget.gov.ie/Budgets/2013/FinancialStatement.aspx

Norris, M. and Byrne, M. (2017) 'A Tale of Two Busts (and a Boom): Irish Social Housing before and after the Global Financial Crisis', *Critical Housing Analysis*, 4(2): 19–28.

Nugent, C. (2017) *The Growth of Precarious Work in the Republic of Ireland*, Dublin: Nevin Economic Research Institute, www.nerinstitute.net/blog/growth-precarious-work-republic-ireland

Nugent, C. (2018) 'Wage Sufficiency in the Context of Irish Housing Emergency: Rents and Access to Homeownership', NERI Working Paper series, Dublin: Nevin Economic Research Institute, www.nerinstitute.net/sites/default/files/research/2019/20180105115417.pdf

O'Brien, M. and Kyprianou, P. (2017) *Just Managing? What it Means for the Families of Austerity Britain*, Cambridge: Open Book Publishers.

O'Connell, P.J. (2017) 'Unemployment and Labour Market Policy', In W.K. Roche, P.J O'Connell and A. Prothero (eds), *Austerity and Recovery in Ireland: Europe's Poster Child and the Great Recession*, Oxford: Oxford University Press, pp. 232–51.

O'Connor, F. (2017) 'The Presence and Absence of Protest in Austerity Ireland', In D. Della Porta, M. Andretta, T. Fernandes, F. O'Connor, E. Romanos and M. Vogiatzolglou, *Late Neoliberalism and Its Discontents in the Economic Crisis*, Cham: Palgrave Macmillan, pp. 65–98.

O'Connor, J. (1973) *The Fiscal Crisis of the State*, New York: St Martin's Press.

OECD (Organisation for Economic Co-operation and Development) (1994) *The Jobs Study: Facts, Analysis, Strategy*, Paris: OECD Publishing.

OECD (2009) *OECD Economic Surveys Ireland, Volume 2009/17*, Paris: OECD Publishing.

OECD (2011) *OECD Economic Surveys: Ireland 2011*, Paris: OECD Publishing.

OECD (2012) *Fiscal Consolidation: How Much, How Fast, and by What Means?*, OECD Economic Policy Papers no. 1, Paris: OECD Publishing.

OECD (2014) *The 2012 Labour Market Reform in Spain: A Preliminary Assessment*, OECD Publishing, Paris, https://doi.org/10.1787/9789264213586-en

OECD (2015a) *In It Together: Why Less Inequality Benefits All*, Paris: OECD Publishing.

OECD (2015b) *OECD Economic Surveys: Ireland 2015*, Paris: OECD Publishing.

OECD (2016) *OECD Economic Surveys Denmark: Getting the Incentives Right in an Ageing Society*, Paris: OECD Publishing.

OECD (2017) *Understanding the Socio-Economic Divide in Europe*, Paris: OECD Publishing.

OECD (2018a) Employment Rate (Indicator), OECD iLibrary, www.oecd-ilibrary.org/employment/employment-rate/indicator/english_1de68a9b-en

OECD (2018b) Unemployment Rate (indicator), OECD iLibrary, www.oecd-ilibrary.org/employment/unemployment-rate/indicator/english_997c8750-en

OECD (2018c) Long-Term Unemployment Rate (indicator), OECD iLibrary, www.oecd-ilibrary.org/employment/long-term-unemployment-rate/indicator/english_76471ad5-en

OECD (2018d) Part-Time Employment Rate (indicator), OECD iLibrary, www.oecd-ilibrary.org/employment/part-time-employment-rate/indicator/english_f2ad596c-en

OECD (2019a) *Government at a Glance 2019*, Paris: OECD Publishing, https://www.oecd.org/gov/government-at-a-glance-22214399.htm.

OECD (2019b) Unit Labour Costs (indicator), OECD iLibrary, www.oecd-ilibrary.org/economics/unit-labour-costs/indicator/english_37d9d925-en

OECD (2020a) General Government Debt (indicator), OECD Data, https://data.oecd.org/gga/general-government-debt.htm

OECD (2020b) General Government Deficit (indicator), OECD Data, https://data.oecd.org/gga/general-government-deficit.htm#indicator-chart

OECD (2020c) Finance – Monthly Monetary and Financial Statistics (MEI): Interest Rates, OECD Statistics, https://stats.oecd.org/

OECD (2020d) Unemployment Rate (indicator), OECD Data, https://data.oecd.org/unemp/unemployment-rate.htm

O'Hara, M. (2015) *Austerity Bites: A Journey to the Sharp End of Cuts in the UK*, Bristol: Policy Press.

O'Keeffe, B. (2010) Speech by the Minister of Enterprise, Trade and Innovation, 14 December, https://dbei.gov.ie/en/News-And-Events/

O'Kelly, K.P. (2010) 'The End of Social Partnership in Ireland?', *Transfer*, 16(3): 425–9.

O'Manique, S. (2015) 'Gender and Austerity in Post-Crisis Canada: How the Government Left Women Behind,' In T. Healy and S. Trew (eds), *The Harper Record 2008–2015*, Ottawa: Canadian Centre for Policy Alternatives,_www.policyalternatives.ca/sites/default/files/uploads/publications/National%20Office/2015/10/The_Harper_Record_2008-2015.pdf

Ontario (2007) *Ontario Budget: Investing in People, Expanding Opportunity: Ontario's New Economic Strength*, Toronto: Ministry of Finance, www.archives.gov.on.ca/en/historical_documents_project/7-11/2007SPEECH.pdf

Ontario (2009) *Ontario Budget: Confronting the Challenge, Building our Economic Future*, Toronto: Ministry of Finance, www.archives.gov.on.ca/en/historical_documents_project/7-11/2009SPEECH.pdf

Ontario (2013) *Ontario Budget: A Prosperous and Fair Ontario*, Toronto: Ministry of Finance, www.fin.gov.on.ca/en/budget/ontariobudgets/2013/statement.html

Ó Riain, S. (2014) *The Rise and Fall of Ireland›s Celtic Tiger: Liberalism, Boom and Bust*, Cambridge: Cambridge University Press.

Ordiz, E. (2020) 'España Recibirá 5.000 Millones Menos a Fondo Perdido que en la Propuesta Inicial y Tendrá que Abordar Reformas Laborales' ['Spain Will Receive 5,000 Million Less Non-Refundable Funds than in the Initial Proposal and Will Have to Address Labour Reforms'], *20 Minutos*, 21 July, www.20minutos.es/noticia/4330600/0/acuerdo-ue-fondos-papel-espana-cesiones/

Ortega Socorro, E. (2020) 'El Gobierno se Despide de su 'Contrareforma' Laboral y Tiene que Acelerar en Pensiones y Seguridad Social' ['The Government Says Goodbye to Its "Labour Counter-Reform" and Has To Accelerate in Pensions and Social Security'], *El Español*, 21 July, www.elespanol.com/invertia/economia/macroeconomia/20200721/gobierno-despide-contrarreforma-acelerar-pensiones-seguridad-social/506700382_0.html

Osberg, L. (2017) *Economic Inequality and Poverty: International Perspectives*, New York: Routledge.

Oxfam (2013) The True Cost of Austerity and Inequality. Oxfam Case Study, www-cdn.oxfam.org/s3fs-public/file_attachments/cs-true-cost-austerity-inequality-ireland-120913-en_0.pdf

Pakeman, K. (2015) *Canada Is Failing Those in Housing Need*, Homeless Hub, 3 February, www.homelesshub.ca/blog/canada-failing-those-housing-need

Palcic, D. and Reeves, E. (2011) *Privatisation in Ireland: Lessons from a European Economy*, Basingstoke: Palgrave Macmillan.

Panitch, L. (ed.) (1977) *The Canadian State*, Toronto: University of Toronto Press.

Panitch, L. and Gindin, S. (2013) *The Making of Global Capitalism: The Political Economy of American Empire*, London: Verso.

Panitch, L. and Swartz, D. (1988) *The Assault on Trade Union Freedoms: From Consent to Coercion Revisited*, Toronto: Garamond Press.

Papadopoulos, O. (2016) 'Economic Crisis and Youth Unemployment: Comparing Greece and Ireland', *European Journal of Industrial Relations*, 22(4): 409–26.

Parliamentary Budget Office (2020) 'National Debt – An Overview', Houses of the Oireachtas, April, https://data.oireachtas.ie/ie/oireachtas/parliamentaryBudgetOffice/2020/2020-04-21_national-debt-an-overview_en.pdf

Pavolini, E., León M., Guillén, A. and Ascoli, U. (2015) 'From Austerity to Permanent Strain? The EU and Welfare State Reform in Italy and Spain', *Comparative European Politics*, 13(1): 56–76.

Peck, J. (2014) 'Pushing Austerity: State Failure, Municipal Bankruptcy, and the Crises of Fiscal Federalism in the USA', *Cambridge Journal of Regions, Economy and Society*, 7(1): 17–44.

Peck, J. and Whiteside, H. (2016) 'Financializing Detroit', *Economic Geography*, 92(3): 235–68.

Pérez A.F. (2014) 'Concertación Social para el Empleo en España (2008–2014)' ['Social Agreement for Employment in Spain (2008–2014)'], *Anuario IET de Trabajo y Relaciones Laborales*, 2: 95–108.

Perez de Armino, K. (2014) 'Erosion of Rights, Uncritical Solidarity and Food Banks in Spain', In G. Riches and T. Silvasti (eds) *First World Hunger Revisited: Food Charity or the Right to Food?* (2nd edn), New York: Palgrave Macmillan.

Pérez-López, G., Prior, D. and Zafra-Gómez, J.L. (2015) 'Rethinking New Public Management Delivery Forms and Efficiency: Long-Term Effects in Spanish Local Government', *Journal of Public Administration Research and Theory*, 25(4): 1157–83.

Perl, A. and White D. (2002) 'The Changing Role of Consultants in Canadian Policy Analysis', *Policy, Organisation and Society*, 21(1): 49–73.

Peters, J. (2020) 'Inequality,' in H. Whiteside (ed.) *Canadian Political Economy*, Toronto: University of Toronto Press.

Petersen, O.H. (2010) 'Regulation of Public–Private Partnerships: the Danish Case', *Public Money and Management*, 30(3): 175–82.

Picot, G. and Tassinari, A. (2017) 'All of One Kind? Labour Market Reforms under Austerity in Italy and Spain', *Socio-Economic Review*, 15(2): 461–82.

Pierson, P. (1998) *Beyond the Welfare State? The New Political Economy of Welfare* (2nd edn), University Park, Penn: Pennsylvania State University Press.

Piketty, T. (2014) *Capital in the Twenty-First Century*, Cambridge, MA: Belknap Press.

Pineault, E. (2012) 'Quebec's Red Spring: An Essay on Ideology and Social Conflict at the End of Neoliberalism', *Studies in Political Economy*, 90(1): 29–56.

Pineault, E. (2014) 'Neoliberalism and Austerity as Class Struggle', In D. Baines and S. McBride (eds) *Orchestrating Austerity: Impacts and Resistance*, Halifax: Fernwood.

Point2 Homes (2018) 'Canadian vs. US Housing, 10 Years after the Global Financial Crisis', Zoocasa, 21 December, www.zoocasa.com/blog/canadian-vs-us-housing-10-years-after-the-global-financial-crisis/

Pollitt, C. (1990) *Managerialism and the Public Service: The Anglo American Experience*, Oxford: Blackwell.

Porter, A. (2015) 'Austerity, Social Program Restructuring, and the Erosion of Democracy: Examining the 2012 Employment Insurance Reforms', *Canadian Review of Social Policy*, 71: 21–52.

Poulantzas, N. (1978) *State, Power, Socialism*, London: New Left Books.

Power, M., Haynes, A. and Devereux, E. (2016) 'Reasonable People versus the Sinister Fringe: Interrogating the Framing of Ireland's Water Charge Protestors through Media Politics of Dissent', *Critical Discourse Studies*, 13(3): 261–77.

Press, J. (2016) 'Liberals to Repeal Controversial Tory Union Bills C-377, C-525', *HuffPost*, 28 January, www.huffingtonpost.ca/2016/01/28/liberals-tories-union-bills-c-377-c-525_n_9100578.html

Quaglia, L. and Royo, S. (2015) 'Banks and Political Economy of the Sovereign Debt Crisis in Italy and Spain', *Review of International Political Economy*, 22(3): 485–507.

Quiggin, J. (2010) *Zombie Economics: How Dead Ideas Still Walk Among Us*, Princeton, NJ: Princeton University Press.

Quinn, M., Lynn, T., Jollands, S. and Nair, B. (2016) 'Domestic Water Charges in Ireland – Issues and Challenges Conveyed through Social Media', *Water Resource Management*, (30): 3577–91.

Rajoy, M. (2013) 'Government Communication before the Congress on the Debate of the State of the Nation', 20 February, Parliament of Spain, Madrid.

Randstad (2017) 'Workforce 2025: The Future of the World of Work', Toronto: Randstad, http://content.randstad.ca/hubfs/workforce2025/Workforce-2025-Randstad-Part1.pdf

Rasmussen, L.L. (2009) Prime Minister Lars Lokke Rasmussen's Opening Address to the Folketing (The Danish Parliament), Tuesday 6 October, Copenhagen: Statsministeriet, www.stm.dk/soeg/?q=Prime+Minister+Lars+Lokke+Rasmussen%E2%80%99s+Opening+Address+to+the+Folketing

Rasmussen, L.L. (2010) Prime Minister Lars Lokke Rasmussen's Opening Address to the Folketing (The Danish Parliament) on 5 October, Copenhagen: Statsministeriet, www.stm.dk/soeg/?q=Prime+Minister+Lars+Lokke+Rasmussen%E2%80%99s+Opening+Address+to+the+Folketing

Rathgeb, P. (2017) 'No Flexicurity Without Trade Unions: The Danish Experience', *Comparative European Politics*, 17(1): 1–21.

Rathgeb, P. (2018) 'Labour Market Policy in Austria, Denmark and Sweden', In P. Rathgeb (ed.) *Strong Governments, Precarious Workers: Labour Market Policy in the Era of Liberalisation*, New York: Cornell University Press, pp. 35–53.

Reeves, E. (2011) 'The Only Game in Town: Public Private Partnerships in the Irish Water Services Sector', *The Economic and Social Review*, 42(1): 95–111.

Reeves, E. (2013) 'The Not So Good, the Bad, and the Ugly: Over Twelve Years of PPP in Ireland', *Local Government Studies*, 39(3), 375–95.

Reeves, E. (2014) 'Public Capital Investment and Public Private Partnerships in Ireland 2000–2014: A Review of the Issues and Performance', In E. Reeves (ed.) *Planning and Delivering a Fairer Future*, Dublin: Social Justice Ireland, pp. 67–88.

Reeves, E. (2015) A Review of the PPP Experience in Ireland: Lessons for Comparative Policy Analysis', *Journal of Comparative Policy Analysis*, 17(5), 467–80.

Regan, A. (2012) 'The Political Economy of Social Pacts in the EMU: Irish Liberal Market Corporatism in Crisis', *New Political Economy*, 17(4): 465–91.

Regan, A. (2017) 'Post-crisis social dialogue and economic governance in Ireland', In I. Guardiancich and O. Molina (eds) *Talking Through the Crisis: Social Dialogue and Industrial Relations Trends in Selected EU Countries*, Geneva: International Labour Organization, pp. 151–70.

Regeringen (2017) *Sammenhængsreform: Borgeren først – en mere Sammenhængende Offentlig Sektor* [*Coherence Reform: The Citizen First – A More Cohesive Public Sector*], Copenhagen: Danish Finance Ministry, https://fm.dk/media/14782/sammenhaengsreform_borgerenfoerst_enmeresammenhaengendeoffentligsektor.pdf

Reinhart, C.M. and Rogoff, K.S. (2010a) 'Growth in a Time of Debt', *American Economic Review: Papers & Proceedings*, 100(May): 573–78.

Reinhart, C.M. and Rogoff, K.S. (2010b) 'Growth in a Time of Debt', Working Paper no. 15639, Cambridge, MA: National Bureau of Economic Research, www.nber.org/papers/w15639

Reynolds, J. and Coulter, C. (2020) 'Ireland's New Government just Puts a Green Face on the Old Order', *Jacobin*, 1 July, www.jacobinmag.com/2020/07/fine-gael-ireland-green-sinn-fein-leo-varadkar-taoiseach

Roche, W.K. (2007) 'Social Partnership in Ireland and New Social Pacts', *Industrial Relations: A Journal of Economy and Society*, 46(3): 395–425.

Roche, W.K. (2017) 'Workplaces', In W.K. Roche, P.J. O'Connell and A. Prothero (eds) *Austerity and Recovery in Ireland: Europe's Poster Child and the Great Recession*, Oxford: Oxford University Press, pp. 194–213.

Roche, W.K. and Gormley, T. (2017a) 'The Advent of Pattern Bargaining in Irish Industrial Relations', *Industrial Relations Journal*, 48(5-6): 442–62.

Roche, W.K. and Gormley, T. (2017b) 'The Durability of Coordinated Bargaining: Crisis, Recovery and Pay Fixing in Ireland', *Economic and Industrial Democracy*, https://doi.org/10.1177%2F0143831X17718067

Rodríguez, C.J.F. and Lucio, M.M. (2012) 'Narratives, Myths and Prejudice in Understanding Employment Systems: The Case of Rigidities, Dismissals and Flexibility in Spain', *Economic and Industrial Democracy*, 34(2): 313–36.

Rodríguez, C.J.F., Rojo, R.I. and Lucio, M.M. (2016a) 'The Reform of Collective Bargaining in the Spanish Metals and Chemicals Sectors (2008–2015): The Ironies and Risks of Deregulating Employment Regulation', In A. Koukiadaki, I. Tavora and M. Martinez Lucio (eds) *Joint Regulation and Labour Market Policy in Europe During the Crisis*, Brussels: European Trade Union Institute, pp. 499–53.

Rodríguez, C.J.F., Rojo, R.I. and Lucio, M.M. (2016b) 'Austerity and Collective Bargaining in Spain: The Political and Dysfunctional Nature of Neoliberal Deregulation', *European Journal of Industrial Relations*, 22(3): 267–80.

Rodríguez-Modroño, P. (2019)' Youth Unemployment, NEETs and Structural Inequality in Spain', *International Journal of Manpower*, 40(3): 433–48.

Romanos, E. (2017) 'Late Neoliberalism and its Indignados: Contention in Austerity Spain', In D. Della Porta (ed.) *Late Neoliberalism and its Discontents in Economic Crisis*, Cham: Palgrave Macmillan, pp. 131–68.

Rose, J., Chaison, G. and de la Garza, E. (2000) 'A Comparative Analysis of Public Sector Restructuring in the US, Canada and Mexico and the Caribbean', *Journal of Labour Research*, 21(4): 601–25.

Rosenbach, E. (2019) 'The Rise of the Far Right in Spain', *Open Democracy*, 27 November, www.opendemocracy.net/en/can-europe-make-it/rise-far-right-spain/

Royall, F. (2017) 'Resisting Austerity? The Case of the Irish National Organisation of the Unemployed', *Journal of Contemporary European Studies*, 25(1): 73–87.

Royo, S. (2000) *From Social Democracy to Neoliberalism: The Consequences of Party Hegemony in Spain, 1982–1996*, London: Macmillan.

Royo, S. (2002) 'A New Century of Corporatism? Corporatism in Spain and Portugal', *West European Politics*, 25(3): 77–104.

Royo, S. (2009a) 'After the Fiesta: The Spanish Economy Meets the Global Financial Crisis', *South European Society and Politics*, 14(1): 19–34.

Royo, S. (2009b) 'Reforms Betrayed? Zapatero and Continuities in Economic Policy', *South European Society and Politics*, 14(4): 435–51.

Royo, S. (2013) 'How Did the Spanish Financial System Survive the First Stage of the Global Crisis?', *Governance*, 26(4): 631–56.

Russell, A. (2019) 'Debt and Deficits: Where the Parties Stand on Balancing the Books in Canada', *Global News*, 10 October, https://globalnews.ca/news/6006275/balanced-budget-canada/

Russell, E. (2017) 'Framing the Economic Case for Austerity' in B. Evans and S. McBride (eds) *Austerity: The Lived Experience*, Toronto: University of Toronto Press, pp. 97–118.

Russell, E. and Dufour, M. (2016) 'Why the Rising Tide Doesn't Lift all Boats: Wages and Bargaining Power in Neoliberal Canada', *Studies in Political Economy*, 97(1): 37–55.

Scharpf, F.W. (1991) *Crisis and Choice in European Social Democracy*, Ithaca, NY: Cornell University Press.

Schelkle, W. (2012) 'Collapsing Worlds and Varieties of Welfare Capitalism: In Search of New Political Economy of Welfare', Discussion Paper series, London: London School of Economics, http://eprints.lse.ac.uk/53194/1/LEQSPaper54.pdf

Scheuer, S., Ibsen, F. and Høgedahl, L. (2016) 'Strikes in the Public Sector in Denmark: Assessing the Economic Gains and Losses of Collective Action', *Transfer: European Review of Labour and Research*, 22(3): 367–82.

Schneider, M.P.A., Kinsella, P. and Godin, A. (2017) 'Redistribution in the Age of Austerity: Evidence from Europe 2006–2013', *Applied Economic Letters*, 24(10): 672–6.

Schwartz, H. (1994a) 'Public Choice Theory and Public Choices: Bureaucrats and State Reorganization in Australia, Denmark, New Zealand, and Sweden in the 1980s', *Administration & Society*, 26(1): 48–77.

Schwartz, H. (1994b) 'Small States in Big Trouble: State Reorganization in Australia, Denmark, New Zealand, and Sweden in the 1980s', *World Politics*, 46(4): 527–55.

Scoffield, H. (2019) 'Income-Gap Figures Don't Speak to Deepening Poverty', *The Star*, 22 August, www.thestar.com/politics/political-opinion/2019/08/22/income-gap-figures-dont-speak-to-deepening-poverty.html

Secretaria de Estado de Communicacion (2012) 'Reforms by the Government of Spain: Combating the Crisis with Determination', Madrid: Government of Spain.

Shefner, J. and Blad, C. (2020) *Why Austerity Persists*, Cambridge: Polity.

Sinn Féin (2010) 'The Road to Recovery: Sinn Féin Pre-Budget', www.sinnfein.ie/files/2009/Pre-Budget2010_small.pdf

Smith, C.W. (2018) 'Class, Power, and Neoliberal Employment Policy' in G. Albo and B.M. Evans (eds) *Divided Province: Ontario Politics in the Age of Neoliberalism*, Montreal: McGill-Queen's University Press.

Sola, J. and Rendueles, C. (2018) 'Podemos, the Upheaval of Spanish Politics and the Challenge of Populism', *Journal of Contemporary European Issues*, 26(1): 99–116.

Sørensen, P.B. (2010) 'Nedturen i dansk økonomi–Hvor meget var selvforskyldt' (The Downturn in the Danish Economy: How Much of It Was Self-Inflicted?), *Samfundsøkonomen*, 1: 29–35.

Spiegel, J. (2016) 'Performing in the Red: Transformations and Tensions in Repertoires of Contention during the 2012 Quebec Student Strike', *Social Movement Studies*, 15(5): 531–8.

Stanford, J. (2008) *Economics for Everyone*, Halifax: Fernwood.

Stanford, J. (2012) 'Ten Points on Recession, Deficits, and Austerity in Ontario', *Behind the Numbers*, 14 February, http://behindthenumbers.ca/2012/02/14/ten-points-on-recession-deficits-and-austerity-in-ontario/

Stanford, J. (2018) 'Staples Dependence Renewed and Betrayed: Canada's Twenty-First Century Boom and Bust', In M.P Thomas, L.F. Vosko, C. Fanelli and O. Lyubchencko (eds) *Change and Continuity: Canadian Political Economy in the New Millennium*, Montreal: McGill Queen's University Press.

Starke, P., Kaasch, A. and van Hooren, F. (2013) *The Welfare State as Crisis Manager: Explaining the Diversity of Policy Responses to Economic Crisis*, London: Palgrave Macmillan.

Steger, M.B. (2017) *Globalization: A Very Short Introduction*, Oxford: Oxford University Press.

Stiglitz, J.E. (2011) 'Rethinking Macroeconomics: What Went Wrong and How to Fix It', *Global Policy*, 2(2): 165–75.

Stiglitz, J.E. (2012) *The Price of Inequality*, London: Penguin.

Stoney, C. and Krawchenko, T. (2013) 'Crisis and Opportunism: Public Finance Trends from Stimulus to Austerity in Canada', *Alternate Routes*, 24: 32–58.

Streek, W. (2014) *Buying Time: The Delayed Crisis of Democratic Capitalism*, New York: Verso.

Strong, S. (2019) 'The Vital Politics of Foodbanking: Hunger, Austerity, Biopower', *Political Geography*, 75, https://doi.org/10.1016/j.polgeo.2019.102053

Sultana, R.G. (2013) 'Flexibility and Security? 'Flexicurity' and its Implications for Lifelong Guidance', *British Journal of Guidance & Counselling*, 41(2): 145–63.

Svarer, M. (2015) 'Labour Market Policies in Denmark', In T. Anderson, M. Bergman and S. H. Jensen (eds) *Reform Capacity and Macroeconomic Performance in the Nordic Countries*, New York: Oxford University Press, pp. 73–98.

Sweeney, B. and Hickey, R. (2017) '"Negotiate Your Way Back to Zero": Teacher Bargaining and Austerity in Ontario, Canada', In B. Evans and S. McBride (eds) *Austerity: The Lived Experience*, Toronto: University of Toronto Press, pp. 145–63.

Szabo, I. (2018) 'Trade Unions and the Sovereign Power of the State: A Comparative Analysis of Employer Offensives in the Danish and Irish Public Sectors', *Transfer*, 24(2): 163–78.

Tal, B. (2015) 'Employment Quality – Trending Down', Canadian Employment Quality Index, 5 March, CIBC Economics, www.ledevoir.com/documents/pdf/CIBC-eqi_20150305.pdf

Tarasuk, V., Mitchell A. and Dacher, N. (2011) *Household Food Insecurity in Canada*, Toronto: PROOF, https://proof.utoronto.ca/resources/proof-annual-reports/annual-report/

Taylor, C. (2020) 'The next Government Faces Tough Calls – But Do Not Call It Austerity', *The Irish Times*, 20 June, https://tinyurl.com/y3gvaweu

Thomas, C. (2018) 'Here's the Impact of Ireland's Economic Crisis on Housing in Graph Form', *The Journal*, 7 December, www.thejournal.ie/heres-the-impact-of-irelands-economic-crisis-on-housing-in-graph-form-2-4380759-Dec2018/

Thomas, M. and Tufts, S. (2016) 'Austerity, Right Populism and the Crisis of Labour in Canada. *Antipode*, 48(1): 212–30.

Thorning-Schmidt, H. (2011) Prime Minister Helle Thorning-Schmidt's Opening Address to the Folketing (The Danish Parliament) on Tuesday 4 October, Copenhagen: Statsministeriet, www.stm.dk/soeg/?q=Prime+Minister+Lars+Lokke+Rasmussen%E2%80%99s+Opening+Address+to+the+Folketing

Thorning-Schmidt, H. (2012) Prime Minister Helle Thorning-Schmidt's Opening Address to the Folketing (The Danish Parliament) on Tuesday 2 October, Copenhagen: Statsministeriet, www.stm.dk/soeg/?q=Prime+Minister+Lars+Lokke+Rasmussen%E2%80%99s+Opening+Address+to+the+Folketing

Togoh, I. (2020) '"Pivotal Moment": EU Agrees Landmark $860 Billion Coronavirus Rescue Package', *Forbes*, 21 July, www.forbes.com/sites/isabeltogoh/2020/07/21/pivotal-moment-eu-agrees-landmark-860-billion-coronavirus-rescue-package/#628549fe491d

Torres, R. (2020) 'La Recuperación, Amenazada por los Rebrotes' ['Recovery, Threatened by Outbreaks'], *FUNCASBlog*, 3 August, https://blog.funcas.es/la-recuperacion-amenazada-por-los-rebrotes/

Tremlett, G. and Moya, E. (2010) Spanish PM Makes Debt Crisis U-Turn with Emergency Cuts', *The Guardian*, 12 May, www.theguardian.com/business/2010/may/12/spanish-pm-debt-crisis-emergency-cuts

Trommer, S. (2019) 'Watering Down Austerity: Scalar Politics and Disruptive Resistance in Ireland', *New Political Economy*, 24(2): 218–34.

Tupper, A. (2000) 'The Contested Terrain of Canadian Public Administration in Canada's Third Century', *Canadian Studies*. 35(4): 142–60.

Utting, P., Razavi, S. and Varghese Buchholz, R. (2012) 'Overview: Social and Political Dimensions of the Global Crisis: Possible Futures', In P. Utting et al (eds), *The Global Crisis and Transformative Social Change*, Basingstoke: Palgrave, pp. 1–22.

Uxo, J., Febrero, E. and Bermejo, F. (2016) 'Crisis, Unemployment and Internal Devaluation in Spain', In M. Martin, S. Theodoropoulou and A. Piasna (eds) *Unemployment, Internal Devaluation and Labour Market Deregulation in Europe*, Brussels: ETUI.

Valdés, I. (2020a) 'De una Sociedad Enferma de Coronavirus a una Sanidad Enferma por Agotamiento' ['From a Society Sick with Coronavirus to Health Sick with Exhaustion'], *El Pais*, 29 June, https://elpais.com/espana/madrid/2020-06-29/de-una-sociedad-enferma-de-coronavirus-a-una-sanidad-enferma-por-agotamiento.html

Valdés, I. (2020b) 'La Precariedad de los 223 Nuevos Médicos de Familia en Madrid: "Las Condiciones son Indignantes"' ['The Precariousness of the 223 New Family Doctors in Madrid: "The Conditions Are Outrageous"'], *El Pais*, 5 June, https://elpais.com/espana/madrid/2020-06-04/la-precariedad-de-los-223-nuevos-medicos-de-familia-en-madrid-las-condiciones-son-indignantes.html

Valdivia, A.G. (2019) 'Rising Rents in Spain Threaten Low-Income Households', *Forbes*, 8 August, www.forbes.com/sites/anagarciavaldivia/2019/08/08/historic-highs-in-the-rental-market-in-spain-threaten-low-income-households/#7583e131c0cc

Venizelos, G. and Stavrakakis, Y. (2020) 'Left-Populism is Down but Not Out', *Jacobin*, 22 March, www.jacobinmag.com/2020/03/left-populism-political-strategy-class-power

Vila, S.T. and Peters, M. (2016) 'The Privatising Industry in Europe', Amsterdam: Transnational Institute, www.tni.org/files/publication-downloads/tni_privatising_industry_in_europe.pdf

Vilaseca, S.L. (2014) 'The 15-M Movement: Formed by and Formative of Counter-Mapping and Spatial Activism', *Journal of Spanish Cultural Studies*, 15(1–2): 119–39.

Vogt, R. (1999) *Whose Property? The Deepening Conflict between Private Property and Democracy in Canada*, Toronto: University of Toronto Press.

Walks, A. (2014) 'Canada's Housing Bubble Story: Mortgage Securitization, the State and the Global Financial Crisis', *International Journal of Urban and Regional Research*, 38(1): 256–84.

WEF (World Economic Forum) (2017) *The Global Gender Gap Report 2017*, www3.weforum.org/docs/WEF_GGGR_2017.pdf

Weir, E. (2012) 'Debunking Drummond', *Behind the Numbers*, 27 February, http://behindthenumbers.ca/2012/02/27/debunking-drummond/

Weiss, L. (1997) 'Globalization and the Myth of the Powerless State', *New Left Review*, 225: 3–27.

West, H. (2015) 'Scapegoating Canada's Public Sector: How the Government Used The Crisis to Attack Unions, Slash the Public Service and Increase Privatization', Canadian Centre for Policy Alternatives, www.policyalternatives.ca/Harper_Record_2008-2015/04-HarperRecord-West.pdf

Whelan, K. (2014) 'How the Economic Management Council Undermines Cabinet and Government', *Irish Times*, 7 November, www.irishtimes.com/news/politics/how-the-economic-management-council-undermines-cabinet-and-government-1.1991236

Wherry, A. (2019) 'Promising Back-to-Back Deficits isn't Political Suicide in Canada Anymore', CBC News, 30 September, www.cbc.ca/news/politics/trudeau-scheer-deficit-debt-2019-election-1.5302601

Whiteside, H. (2012) 'Crises of Capital and the Logic of Dispossession and Repossession', *Studies in Political Economy*, 89(1): 59–78.

Whiteside, H. (2015) *Purchase for Profit*, Toronto: University of Toronto Press.

Whiteside, H. (2016a) 'Neoliberalism as Austerity: The Theory, Practice, and Purpose of Fiscal Restraint since the 1970s', In S. Springer, K. Birch and J. MacLeavy (eds) *Handbook of Neoliberalism*, London: Routledge.

Whiteside, H. (2016b) *About Canada: Public-Private Partnerships*, Winnipeg and Halifax: Fernwood Publishing.

Whiteside, H. (2017a) 'The State's Estate: Devaluing and Revaluing "Surplus" Public Land in Canada', *Environment & Planning A*, 51(2): 505–26.

Whiteside, H. (2017b) 'The Canada Infrastructure Bank: Private Finance as Poor Alternative', *Studies in Political Economy*, 98(2): 223–37.

Whiteside, H. (2018) 'Foreign in a Domestic Sense: Puerto Rico's Debt Crisis and Paradoxes in Critical Urban Studies', *Urban Studies*, 56(1): 147–66.

Whiteside, H. (2019) 'Public-Private Partnerships: Market Development Through Management Reform', *Review of International Political Economy*, 27(4): 880–902, doi.org/10.1080/09692290.2019.1635514

Wickham, J. and Bobek, A. (2016) *Enforced Flexibility? Working in Ireland Today*, Dublin: The Think-tank for Action and Social Change, www.tasc.ie/download/pdf/enforcedflexibilityfinal.pdf?issuusl=ignore

Wilkinson, R.G. and Pickett, K. (2009) *The Spirit Level: Why More Equal Societies Almost Always Do Better*, London: Allen Lane.

Wolf, M. (2013) 'Austerity in the Eurozone and the UK: Kill or Cure?', *The Financial Times*, 23 May, http://blogs.ft.com/martin-wolf-exchange/2013/05/23/austerity-in-the-eurozone-and-the-uk-kill-or-cure/

Woll, C. (2014) 'Ireland and Denmark', In *The Power of Inaction: Bank Bailouts in Comparison*, Ithaca, NJ: Cornell University Press.

Wong, D. (2019) 'BC is Canada's Eviction Capital, Here's How Your Province Stacks Up', *Better Dwelling*, 27 November, https://betterdwelling.com/bc-is-canadas-eviction-capital-heres-how-your-province-stacks-up/#_

Wood, D.E. and Hayes, B. (2016) *The Labour Market Agreements: What Did They Really Do?*, Ottawa: Caledon Institute of Social Policy, https://maytree.com/wp-content/uploads/1094ENG.pdf

Wright, R. (2010) *Strengthening the Capacity of the Department of Finance: Report of the Independent Review Panel* [the 'Wright Report'], Dublin: Department of Finance.

Zapatero, J.L.R. (2010) 'Debate on the State of the Nation', speech by Prime Minister of the Spanish Government to the Congress of Deputies, 14 July.

Zapico-Goni, E. (2015) 'Spain facing the Global Financial Crisis: Cutting Public Spending and Struggling with Structural Reforms', In J. Wanna, E.A. Lindquist and J. de Vries (eds) *The Global Financial Crisis and its Budget Impacts in OECD Nations: Fiscal Responses and Future Challenges*, Cheltenham: Edward Elgar, pp. 205–30.

Index

Note: Page numbers for tables appear in *italics*

C

Q

R

S